# The Queen's Merchants

and the
Revolt of the Netherlands

The End of the Antwerp Mart, Part II

# The Queen's Merchants

### and the
### Revolt of the Netherlands

## G. D. Ramsay

Manchester University Press

Published by
Manchester University Press
Oxford Road, Manchester M13 9PL, UK
51 Washington Street, Dover, NH 03820, USA

*British Library cataloguing in publication data*
Ramsay, G. D.
    The Queen's merchants and the revolt of the Netherlands. – (The end of
    the Antwerp mart; pt. 2) 1. London   (England) –
    Commerce        2. London   (England) – History – 16th century
    I. Title        II. Series
    382'.09421'2              HF3510.L6

*Library of Congress cataloging in publication data*
Ramsay, G. D. (George Daniel)
    The queen's merchants and the revolt of the Netherlands.
    Continues: The City of London in international politics at the accession of
    Elizabeth Tudor. 1975.
    Includes index.
    1. Company of Merchant Adventurers of England –
    History.     2. Great Britain – Commerce – Netherlands –
    History.     3. Netherlands – Commerce – Great Britain –
    History.     4. Netherlands – History – Wars of Independence,
    1556–1648.   I. Ramsay, G. D. (George Daniel).      City of
    London in international politics at the accession of Elizabeth
    Tudor.   II. Title.    III. Title:  End of the Antwerp mart, part II.
    HF486.M17R36     1986       382'.0942'04920601          85–13789

ISBN 0 7190 1849 8 *cased only*

Printed in Great Britain by A. Wheaton & Co. Ltd., Exeter

# Contents

Preface     vi

Times and places     vii

Chapter I
*The ancient amity and the cloth trade*     1

Chapter II
*The interrupted colloquy, 1565–6*     17

Chapter III
*Antwerp, 1566: the outbreak that
scared the English*     34

Chapter IV
*The crumbling of the old order*     42

Chapter V
*The breaking of the storm*     85

Chapter VI
*Hamburg, the new rival*     116

Chapter VII
*Elizabeth, Alva and the merchants*     153

Chapter VIII
*The agony of the Antwerp mart*     174

Chapter IX
*Envoi*     195

Appendix
Royal instructions to the commissioners sent
to Bruges in 1565     206

A postscript on sources
and list of abbreviations used in notes     221

Index     225

# Preface

This study is complementary to *The City of London in international politics at the accession of Elizabeth Tudor*, published in 1975. Together the two volumes were planned as an enquiry into the end of the Antwerp mart in English history. They do not comprise an account of Elizabethan foreign policy (about which my views have been offered elsewhere) nor even a survey of Anglo-Netherlands relations; still less do they provide an account of business life in the City of London, though they contain information about all these topics. Readers will observe that the contents of this book are pivoted on the dramatic events of early 1569, before which the Company of Merchants Adventurers was in general a flourishing organization but subsequently embarked on its long decline. I hope to take a look at the Company over a much longer time-span, if Providence allows; but the marked personal and fortuitous element in its history can be illuminated only by close and limited surveys.

To ease the path of readers, I have indulged in a little recapitulation, mainly in the first chapter. But the note on times and places prefixed to the previous volume has not been reprinted in full, though it applies none the less to this one.

Since my researches for this volume were started, I have incurred many debts of gratitude, which will not here be enumerated; but my creditors in this heartening currency may rest assured that my recognition of the debts is no less real and sincere. A special obligation of a different hue is owed to the services of the Bodleian Library, where facilities are available for making use of a typewriter when consulting its treasures.

Above all, I am indebted to my wife, whose indispensable care in the checking of proofs is exceeded by her many other encouragements.

*Oxford, July 1985*                                              G.D.R.

# Times and places

Dates are given according to the Julian calendar, but the year is assumed to begin on the first day of January.

The word 'Netherlands' has always been used to designate the seventeen provinces of *Germania Inferior* acknowledging the rule of Charles V, and after him, of Philip II. To avoid confusion, the ambiguous word 'Dutch' has not been used, save to qualify the republican federation of the seven rebellious provinces from 1581.

# Chapter I

## The Ancient amity and the cloth trade

The fateful happenings discussed in the following pages were often an outcome of the traits of character that marked the most prominent actors – arising from their prejudices, misjudgments and lack of scruple as well as from their honest beliefs and loyalties. But while following the tale of events as distilled from clashes of personalities, the reader may find it helpful to bear in mind a couple of general processes that for a century and more had been providing a framework for the moulding of history in north-west Europe. While the movement of the stream of history was from time to time visibly deflected by the decision of an individual, the fullest significance of such decisions may best be understood within the context of certain current trends.

The basic process to recall was the traffic in woollen cloths shipped undyed and undressed from London to the nearby shores of the Low Countries, for use by well-to-do wearers chiefly in the interior of the continent. With only occasional setbacks or interruptions, this trade had long been thriving, whatever the political exchanges between the rulers of England and the Netherlands. As to its social and economic importance for the English people and its fiscal signficance for the English crown, some information has already been offered in the preceding volume, *The City of London in International Politics at the accession of Elizabeth Tudor*. In the high middle ages the major English export had been raw wool, but in the fifteenth and sixteenth centuries the Merchants of the Staple of Calais (Staplers), who held a chartered monopoly of the wool trade, found that there was less and less available in the countryside for them to buy for shipment: English wool was being increasingly woven at home into cloths. These also were in large measure being exported, but by the members of a different organization, the Merchants Adventurers, to be dyed and finished chiefly at Antwerp. However, despite or perhaps because of the dwindling of the shipments of English wool to the staple at Calais, eager buyers were still to be met there. English wool continued to be in demand by cloth manufacturers in certain Netherlands towns, even after the seizure of Calais by the French in 1558.

The second process to bear in mind was the gradual emergence of a power centre in the Netherlands that bade fair to develop and expand into a centralized state after the style of the neighbouring monarchies of France and England. This political authority began gradually to take shape under the Valois dukes of Burgundy in the fifteenth century, and was ultimately to reach both its climax and breaking-point during the viceroyalty of the Duke of Alva, 1567–73. Its growth was not effected in dynastic solitude but amid a complex network of family alliances. The last duke of the Valois line died in 1477, leaving a daughter who carried her inheritance by marriage into the Habsburg family, rulers of Austria and other territories in Germany, who – again by marriage – were soon also to acquire the kingdoms of Spain. Thus in the sixteenth century the Emperor Charles V and his son Philip II of Spain as rulers of the Netherlands personified for the English the House of Burgundy, with all the traditions and treaties that had formerly linked the kings of England to their predecessors and ancestors as dukes of Burgundy. In realistic and down-to-earth terms, these centred on the traffic in English woollen cloths and wool, and their contents went some way towards meeting the needs of merchants whose livelihood depended upon the freedom of the marketplace. But there was also a political and diplomatic side to the relationships established between successive kings of England and dukes of Burgundy. What in the sixteenth century came to be known, somewhat speciously perhaps, as 'the ancient amity' between the two rulers, may be traced back to the Hundred Years' War, and especially to the years 1419–35, when they were in active alliance against the French. In subsequent decades this 'ancient amity' was never forgotten, though it might at times seem to be in abeyance.

During the reign of Henry VII (1495–1509), Anglo-Netherlands animosity was provoked by the covert support given by the dowager Duchess of Burgundy, by birth a Yorkist princess, to rival pretenders to the English throne. Although Henry cherished trade, he did not scruple to use a commercial leverage to achieve his political aims and teach the House of Burgundy a lesson. On two occasions, in 1493 and again in 1505, he briefly diverted the English cloth export traffic from its usual market in the Netherlands, ordaining that the Merchants Adventurers should instead fix their mart at Calais, side-by-side in fact with the Staplers. The market arrangements he laid down in 1505 for the Merchants Adventurers at Calais followed closely those familiar to them at Antwerp, though how far Henry ever seriously meditated replacing the Fairs of Brabant by those of Calais is not known.[1] In any case, the friendship with the House of Burgundy was being reinforced by further accidents of dynastic planning. Henry had turned to Spain for an ally, arranging for the marriage of his son and heir to the younger daughter of the Catholic Kings, known in English history as Katherine of Aragon; but her elder sister, the ultimate heiress of the Catholic Kings, married the son of the heiress of the last Valois Duke of Burgundy. Thus was achieved not only the political union of the Burgundian and Spanish dominions but also the forging of a new dynastic link to join the Tudors with the House of Burgundy. Henry, despite his occasional brusque handling of Anglo-Netherlands relations and his spirited defence of English mercantile interests, had new grounds for not jettisoning 'the ancient amity'.

The old grounds for Henry's cautious but generally friendly attitude towards the House of Burgundy however remained strong, in that the cloth trade continued to flourish and even the traffic in wool was more or less holding its own, at least as far as London and the Calais staple were concerned.[2] A clear and simple but comprehensive Anglo-Netherlands commercial treaty, known later as the *Magnus Intercursus* – or to the English more briefly as the Intercourse – was concluded in February 1496.[3] Among its clauses was an undertaking by the contracting princes that the merchants should continue to enjoy the liberties and privileges they had possessed during the preceding fifty years, which was generally taken to mean that no additional taxes would be exacted from them. The importance of the Intercourse was long term rather than immediate. It was violated almost at once by the Duke of Burgundy; but it was resuscitated by agreement between the parties in 1507 and provided a useful starting-point for many a conference and consultation throughout the sixteenth century and even later, particularly when the merchants were threatened by novel financial demands. The Intercourse rather than the trade embargoes typified the outlook of Henry VII, who in general restrained the growth of Anglo-Netherlands friction and fostered the traditions of 'the ancient amity' as a conventional description of relations between the English crown and the House of Burgundy.

The 'ancient amity' gathered weight in the first half of the sixteenth century, when England was ruled by Henry VIII and the House of Burgundy was represented by Charles of Habsburg, who was also ruler of Spain and as Holy Roman Emperor the titular sovereign of Germany, remembered today as the Emperor Charles V. He was by birth a French-speaking prince, always mindful of his Burgundian inheritance; the Netherlands were the political centre of his far-flung dominions and the source from which he drew most of his finance. With Henry he was for long on cordial terms, until he took the King of France prisoner in battle in 1525. Charles now seemed to have achieved a dangerous mastery of the continent, and the English momentarily turned against him. Cardinal Wolsey thought to revive the policy of Henry VII a generation earlier by withdrawing the Merchants Adventurers and all other dealers in commodities from the Netherlands to Calais: the proclamation announcing this, dated 13 July 1527, seemed positively to envisage Calais as a trading metropolis to replace Antwerp.[4] It was not a move welcome to the mercantile community at London and it fell flat, though not with speed sufficient to avert political repercussions as soon as its implications spread abroad, doubtless magnified by rumour. Something like a boycott of English cloths was set afoot in Netherlands towns.[5] On either side of the sea trade was halted and merchants detained; but as Wolsey had to face discontent in clothmaking counties, the Emperor had enough on his hands and nobody sought war, the episode in time blew over. By April 1528 the Regent of the Netherlands had released her hostages and restored freedom of movement.[6] But the trade that summer remained in the doldrums, with 'very slack and hurtful markets'.[7] Prosperity returned with the conclusion of general European peace in 1529.

Wolsey's abortive experiment was the more important than those of his predecessor Henry VII because of the quantitative change that was in process of transforming the cloth export business from a brisk local movement of goods into a major European commercial current. At the beginning of the century, in the five years 1501–5 inclusive, an annual average of 46,029 'short cloths' (or statutory broadcloths) had been shipped from London and registered at the custom house at Billingsgate. Twenty years later, for the years 1521–5 the figure had risen to 61,854, an increase of not quite 33 per cent. Nearly twenty years later still, for the years 1539–44, it had climbed to 99,580: an increase of over 100 per cent over forty years, and was still rising.[8] Most of the shipments were for the Netherlands, though the precise proportions cannot be determined, whether the exporting merchants were English or foreign. The repercussions of this expansion of trade were visible in England – in the increased wealth of the merchants who dominated the City of London and in the more intensive industrialization of the major clothmaking districts. The parties to lose were the exporters of wool, whose shipments declined especially in the second quarter of the century, and above all the King himself, whose revenues fell as the customs on heavily-taxed wool were replaced by a more slender yield from the comparatively lightly-taxed cloths. Abroad, the buoyant trade in English cloths stimulated the activity of the international entrepôt at Antwerp, where there had accumulated an industrial population skilled in the finishing processes applied to textiles, and where merchants of many nations gathered to buy and re-distribute goods of all sorts. Antwerp was also the seat of an international money market that now in the reign of Charles V entered its most brilliant phase, before various state bankruptcies undermined its stability.

The reign of the Emperor Charles V as prince of the Netherlands (1515–55) marked the high noon of the state that had gradually taken shape under the rule of his forbears the Burgundian dukes in the previous century. For a few glamorous decades, Brussels became the diplomatic and Antwerp the commercial capital of Europe. In political terms, Charles completed the assembly of the seventeen contiguous provinces of Lower Germany (hence 'the Low Countries' or 'Netherlands') that were now gathered into his hand, by the removal of the ancient French suzerainty over Flanders, the annexation of Gelderland and the reduction of the bishopric of Utrecht to dependent status. He sought, with some success, to carry the progress of administrative centralization a few steps further. But Charles was often absent, sometimes for years at a time, in his other dominions, and the task of running the government of the seventeen provinces he committed to a Regent permanently in residence: his aunt Margaret of Austria until her death in 1530, then his sister Mary, former Queen of Hungary, who continued in office until her death in 1555. Local business arising from, for example, the commodity traffic at Antwerp, fell within the responsibilities of the Regent. From time to time, the Governor of the Merchants Adventurers called upon these ladies and their officials to seek their favour in matters affecting the cloth trade and its merchants. Governor John Hackett claimed to have spent an expensive twelve months in attendance at the court of the Lady Margaret during the season of Wolsey's ill-fated experiment in 1527–8.[9]

At the topmost international level, Henry VIII and the Emperor Charles V were well acquainted with each other. On various occasions, there were carefully-staged meetings and consultations between them. In addition, the Emperor usually maintained a resident envoy at the court of the King of England: for many years, it was the wily Eustace Chapuys. Reciprocally, it was the habit of Henry to accredit an envoy to accompany Charles on his restless travels through his scattered dominions in western and central Europe. Whatever the jealousies of their underlings, it suited them to appear good friends, and in matters of commerce the only major breach to separate them was that provoked by Wolsey in 1527–8. There was, of course, no lack of minor incidents to ruffle the surface of Anglo-Netherlands relations: these were handled through the regular channels of diplomacy, supplemented if necessary by the assembly of a special conference between English and Netherlands representatives. There had been such a colloquy at Bruges in 1515–6, a fairly thoroughgoing affair. Then, following the election of Charles as Emperor a couple of years later, a solemn agreement, including a renewed Intercourse, was concluded between the two potentates in April 1520.[10] There was also some discussion of the Intercourse at the international peace negotiations of 1529, when it was re-affirmed as part of the final treaty.[11] As English and Netherlands discontents were still not quenched, a further meeting was arranged at Bourbourg, east of Calais but inside the Netherlands frontier, in 1532.[11] Into the squabbles, embargoes and conferences of the next dozen years it is not necessary to enter, save to mention that at a moment of disharmony in the summer of 1534 the watchful Chapuys reported that Henry might be meditating the transfer of the English cloth mart from Antwerp to one of the Hanse cities on the German coast. The apprehension however proved no more than a prophetic vision of an event that transpired a generation later.[12]

Below the level of princely contacts and diplomatic negotiations, relations between the municipal authorities of London and Antwerp were usually amicable. For either side, the commodity traffic was too valuable to be disturbed; and the greater its volume, the tighter their interdependence. If the Merchants Adventurers took offence at some fancied breach of the Inter- course or some other piece of administrative high-handedness at Antwerp, they could, as in 1547, move their mart to Barrow, without invoking political attention and without even altering the arrangements for financial settlements;[13] the lords of Antwerp were always too well aware of the prosperity brought by the cloth mart to their city to wish to frighten away the merchants who served it. What attracted the attention of the delegates at the periodic Anglo-Netherlands colloquies and con- ferences was not so much any grumbles about the cloth traffic in the Scheldt as the outcries of the seafarers and wool-buyers of the nearby maritime provinces of Holland and Zeeland. These small traders lived in a world different from that graced by the patricians of Antwerp.[14] They resented the inefficient or dis- honest packing of the sacks, cloves and pockets of wool they bought at Calais, and the rapacious demands for miscellaneous fees and harbour dues at London and also the English outports – balliage, anchorage, scavage, head money, the personal fees claimed by customs officers in addition to the royal levies; en- forcement of the Statutes of Employment – employment i.e. of the sterling money in which foreigners were paid for their wares; and also alleged piracies and admiralty sloth or partiality in giving verdicts when a case was brought.[15] These topics pro- vided much of the meat for diplomatic gatherings to chew.

International conflicts were always liable to cast a shadow over the market at Antwerp, even when the King of England and the Emperor were in alliance. They needed each other's help in the 1540s in their war against the King of France: there was there- fore a measure of political display in the solemn renewal of the Intercourse in 1543.[16] But money was required for waging war, and Charles had to raise more from his Netherlands. His method of doing this included the levy of an export tax of one per cent on all goods leaving the country, a proportion of them owned by English merchants.[17] Throughout the year 1544 they protested with vigour and obstinacy, appealing to the terms of the Intercourse, but securing no more than a grudging and conditional exemption.[18] On the other side, ill-will was pro- voked by English seizures of little ships, often belonging to fishermen in the provinces of Holland and Zeeland, which were requisitioned for military purposes or alleged to be carrying contraband cargoes to the enemy.[19] So high did resentment rise

that in January 1545 the Emperor had with reluctance to consent to lay an embargo on the English merchants and their
goods, to the dismay of the mercantile world of Antwerp and its
outport Barrow. This 'arrest' meant little more than holding
back the departure of the ships and was politely effected; it does
not appear to have greatly harmed the busy cloth traffic and it
was lifted in April.[20] But there was further unpleasantness a
little later when Charles tried to exact another levy from the
Netherlands, this time in the shape of a five per cent property
tax, from which the English also claimed exemption. Another
conference at Bourbourg in the summer of 1545 was needed to
assuage tempers.[21]

With the death of Henry VIII in 1547 the absence of a re-
solute direction of government in England gradually became
evident. Many years earlier, Chapuys had ominously deemed it
his duty to remind his master how dependent the Londoners
were upon their trade with the Netherlands;[22] now, while the
King was almost on his death-bed, he characteristically pointed
out to the Regent of the Netherlands how the English might be
put in their place after his demise by the re-imposition of
an embargo such as had been enforced in early 1545.[23]
Rumours of such an action percolated in time down to the cloth
market, where in the summer of 1548 trouble was feared;[24] but
the severe crisis that actually overtook it in 1550 was due to
complex causes that do not include any politically-motivated
intervention.[25] Then in 1551, with the renewal of international
warfare, some venerable problems re-appeared. English shipping, being neutral, lay open to charges of conveying contraband goods to the enemy; and English merchandise in continental harbours was a tempting object for emergency taxes. In
August, news reached the Privy Council at London that English
ships had twice been held up at Antwerp, and the English
envoys in the Netherlands were instructed to lodge a protest
with the Emperor.[36]

It was not a timely move, as events were to show. The trade
depression of 1550 was now long past, and at the autumn mart
of 1551 business was brisk. The English ambassador at Brussels,
Sir Thomas Chamberlain, reported home in mid November
how the Governor of the Merchants Adventurers had confided
in him that the members of his Company had never had so
much to bring back as a result of their sales of cloths. Their
goods were on some fifteen or twenty ships at anchor in the

Scheldt, awaiting departure for England. Such wealth was the talk of the town, and the hard-pressed Regent and her councillors could hardly be expected to ignore it. It was resolved at Brussels that the English, like everyone else, should pay an emergency impost of ten shillings in each hundred pounds' worth of exports. The Governor and some of his merchants in alarm again made their way to Brussels, and on 1 December saw the ambassador, asking him to protest to the Regent, and to appeal to the terms of the *Intercursus*. Chamberlain's advice was to give caution for payment and slip away as soon as possible; his private opinion was that the merchants were to be blamed for 'their own insatiable greediness, wilfulness and disorder' in allowing so much to pile up aboard their ships. He did not think that in the circumstances any appeal to the letter of the Intercourse would cut much ice with the Regent. Unfortunately, he delivered his advice too late, and the merchants were not at once given clearance to sail by the quayside officials. The situation was worsened by a false rumour that Netherlands ships were being detained in English ports; time passed before this could be dispelled. Chamberlain was dismayed to find the Regent evasive and reluctant to overrule her subordinates, and although after a week or so the ships were ultimately allowed to sail on giving security for the payment of the impost, the Governor remained dangling at Brussels for some time longer.[27] The episode dimly foreshadowed the grimmer interruptions of Anglo-Netherlands trade a dozen or more years later.

Yet more difficulties were being raised by the accelerated pace of ecclesiastical change in England. The Emperor was the defender of the old religion in his dominions and entering into sharper struggles with the protestants of Germany. As early as July 1550, the Privy Council with this in mind was pointing out to the Merchants Adventurers that it might be dangerous to leave their stocks of goods in the Emperor's jurisdiction.[28] In August 1551, it was feared that since his first cousin the Princess Mary had been forbidden to hear Mass there might be retaliation;[29] and in fact services according to the new English liturgy were forbidden to the English ambassador at Brussels the next year.[30] The importance of the Emperor's dynastic interests became evident when in July 1553 the Princess Mary succeeded her brother and became Queen of England, not without opposition. There was some 'wild talk' among the protestant young Englishmen at Antwerp, in the face of which he politely but speedily made known to the merchants there his support for her claim.[31] A few months later, there occurred a rebellion in Kent against her authority: it had been provoked by her proposed marriage to his son Philip. Charles again acted swiftly, issuing an order of 'arrest' against the English merchants and their property at Antwerp. The embargo was lifted after a few days, as soon as it was known that London had declared for the Queen and that the revolt had collapsed.[32] But a renewed warning of English dependence upon the will of the ruler of the Netherlands had been served. Fifteen years later, it was still remembered.

The marriage of Philip and Mary, celebrated in July 1554, placed England and the Burgundian dominions under the same rulers for over four years. During this period, there could be no overt disagreement to threaten their common trade links, while the resolution of humbler administrative problems was made more smooth. Thus when in the summer of 1555 the English merchants in the Netherlands were voicing their ancient intermittent grievance that customs officers there were exacting the 'double tax', i.e., enforcing the payment of duties on goods passing through the waters of Zeeland and Brabant in both provinces – Mary instructed her envoy to raise their complaint with the Emperor and with the Regent at Brussels.[33] Less than three weeks later, the Emperor's Council gave its verdict that the Englishmen need pay only in one or other province, and that the sums paid in the second should be refunded.[34] No doubt many a merchant at London was pleased at this, whatever the misgivings of religious zealots. But in retrospect the brief Anglo-Netherlands union was seen to bear a less rosy colour, for Philip while maintaining peace between his Netherlands and Scotland – with which England was at war – insisted that the English should participate in his war with France. The fruits of this co-operation proved bitter, for the bridgehead of Calais, quondam rival to Antwerp and long the headquarters of the Staplers' Company, was in January 1558 seized by the French and so forever lost.

But as far as the advantage of the crown was concerned, this was more than offset by a drastic reform of the English customs administration, the central feature of which was the imposition of a new Book of Rates four months later, in May. By this measure the sums payable by merchants at English ports were substantially raised: in particular, the duty levied upon a standard broadcloth on shipment abroad by any Englishman was increased nearly six-fold, from fourteen pence to six shillings and eight pence. As the annual shipments of cloth exports were now running into six figures, the crown suddenly acquired a durable income of respectable size. The effects of this were both long-term and far-reaching. The architect of this coup was the Lord Treasurer Winchester, an astute old man who in all likelihood would have liked to effect it in the period immediately following his appointment in 1550, but had perhaps been dissuaded by a petition from the merchants. They had pointed out that an increase in English taxation – in 1551, as we have seen, international war was again being resumed – would be used as an excuse for a parallel rise in the levies exacted by the Netherlands government.[35] But now, seven years later, the political circumstances had changed and were propitious. Not least, Philip as King of England had given his consent to the measure without seeking to burden the English merchants any further in his Netherlands. The lucrative privilege of collecting heavier taxes on English woollen cloth shipments had fallen to the English crown.

While the political union of England and the Netherlands lapsed with the death of Mary in November 1558, a great deal remained to link the two countries closely. They were both at war with the King of France, and the traffic in cloths and wool remained a bond to unite their economies. The strategic position of England made it an essential ally for the monarchy which ruled in Spain and the Netherlands, so that it is not in the least surprising that Philip on the decease of his wife offered his hand to her successor Elizabeth Tudor. Already while the Staplers were looking round for a mart town to replace Calais as their headquarters, he was at once seeking to attract them to the Netherlands – in fact, they settled at Bruges.[36] Elizabeth, though she declined the offer of marriage, was well aware that in the face of French enmity Philip was an essential ally and friend. She fully comprehended the importance of the cloth trade to Antwerp. She effected a bargain with the London merchants; and so with the usual parliamentary life grant of tonnage and poundage she was able to continue to exact the sums due by the customs tariff published in May 1558.[37] Thus she was able to count on a larger assured revenue than any of her predecessors before that date, from the cloth export levy alone. The elementary facts of politics and finance dictated to both sides a continuance of the close Tudor-Habsburg alliance.

There was however an almost imperceptible erosion of the personal trust that at the outset had firmly linked Philip and Elizabeth. From one point of view, the basic trouble lay in the withdrawal of Philip from northern Europe to central Castile in August 1559. He had to delegate much power to others: to exchange messages with him from England or the Netherlands was a business of months rather than weeks, so that high responsibility devolved on envoys and other agents who were all too often not equal to their tasks. In the course of time, misunderstandings arose and took root in the memory of international diplomacy. However, for the vitally important position of Regent of the Netherlands during his absence, Philip made a prudent selection in the person of his half-sister Margaret, Duchess of Parma. As Governor of the Provinces of Lower Germany[38] she fitted into the vacant niche as successor to her aunt and great aunt without any breaking of tradition. She counted as a member of the House of Burgundy – born indeed on the wrong side of the blanket, but this was a matter of small moment. She knew how to cultivate the loyalty of the Netherlanders. But her attitude to the English and their Queen was not quite the same as that of Philip.

Into the succession of incidents that marked some evaporation of faith and ultimately of friendship between Philip and Elizabeth in the early 1560s it is unnecessary to delve.[39] Philip strongly disapproved of the restoration of a heretical church in England, but as a matter of politics he could not query Elizabeth's right to break with the Pope. Her military interventions in Scotland and France likewise were not at all to his taste, though again for political reasons he could but remain aloof. He did not like even to offer encouragement to the papist Irish leaders.[40] Meanwhile, his Regent in the Netherlands was further provoked by the movement of many of her subjects to England, where they were enabled to follow heretical religious practices, and by the news of their relative freedom, which contributed to the instability of the ecclesiastical regime in her viceroyalty. English piracies in the Channel were always a source of indignation. But perhaps most of all she was galled by the success of the Queen of England in collecting the greatly increased cloth export tax – met ultimately, as she felt, by the higher prices paid by purchasers in the Antwerp mart. She would have preferred the money to be used in ways other than the financing of heretical policies. In the spring of 1563 she sent to London the lawyer

Christophe d'Assonleville, a member of her Privy Council, to expostulate and spy out the purposes of the English. In August, she forwarded his 'long and prolix' report, with a commentary, to the distant King in Castile.[41] In October he dispatched an answer empowering her to take action.[42] The stage was thus set for a delicate and risky project.

The course now followed by the Duchess of Parma had in all likelihood been originally indicated by her closest adviser the Cardinal Granvelle, whom Philip had placed at her side; but it was refined and encouraged by the report of Assonleville, newly back from England. As a diplomat, Assonleville stood in the tradition of Chapuys: he believed that the English, dependent as they were upon the Netherlands market, could be brought to heel by firm handling. In the minds of the Regent and her councillors, there lingered the memory of Wolsey's disastrous experiment of 1527–8, when the English after imposing an embargo on their exports had had to climb down, and again of the effectiveness of the 'arrest' imposed by the Emperor Charles in the early months of 1545. She reminded her brother in Spain how on both occasions the English had learnt their lesson, received their chastisement, and gladly reverted to the old amity, even closer than before.[43] The prevalence of plague suddenly seemed to offer a special opportunity for implementing the scheme of the Cardinal: before the end of November, she directed the provincial authorities not to permit the landing of cloths or wool from England, on the ground that they brought infection.[44] It was in fact an interdiction of trade, masked by an ingenious though threadbare excuse that made possible the continuance of peaceful diplomatic contacts. The expectation was that the English would not long be able to endure the stoppage.

During the course of the year 1564 the whole scheme misfired. Against all expectation, the English found a substitute market of sorts for their cloths at Emden, beyond the frontier of the Netherlands. The embargo was found to hurt Antwerp and other centres in the Netherlands appreciably more than the textile interests in England. Then in the spring the Cardinal, leading promoter of the action, was removed from the Netherlands for irrelevant political reasons by the distant King. Too late, the Duchess, with the Prince of Orange and other newly-returned advisers at her side, resolved to offer an olive branch, only to discover that the Queen and her merchants had hardened in their resolution to transfer trade to Emden and were not prepared to go into reverse. The balance of advantage had shifted and now lay with the English and not with the Netherlanders. Only with the arrival of Don Guzman de Silva, Canon of Toledo, at the court of Elizabeth Tudor as ambassador of Philip II in June, did a faint hope of the restoration of Anglo-Netherlands trade begin to appear.

Silva deserves a place in history as one of the most accomplished diplomats of his time. He soon discovered that the Queen, though she extended to him every courtesy, was not eager to proceed to the renewal of Anglo-Netherlands trade. But by September her attitude was softening. She disliked the diminution of her revenue owing to the smaller size of the cloth market at Emden, and she did not wish to stir up unrest in the English clothmaking regions. Soon it became evident that the will to compromise was shared on either side. Silva went into conference with Secretary Cecil and other negotiators named by the Queen, and progress was rapid. As to Philip II himself, he was content to leave responsibility in the hands of his sister the Regent.[45] Behind the scenes, possible topics of friction were on each side discreetly smoothed over. Silva at first thought of raising the major question of the English customs tariff of 1558, only to be told by the Regent that the abatement of these duties was not to be treated as an essential point for the preliminary agreement.[46] She also dealt smartly with even the new Bishop of Bruges when he made difficulties about allowing English merchants, as heretics, Christian burial.[47] On the English side, an informer who in the exchequer at Westminster tried to exploit the statute of 1563 forbidding the import of smallwares was stopped by the Lord Treasurer at the behest of Cecil.[48] But since the Regent, pressed by the lords of Antwerp and by the great seigneurs of her Council of State for a re-opening of traffic at virtually any price, was in a weaker position than the Queen, whose subjects were seen to be capable at a pinch of trading to Emden or Hamburg, it fell to her to make the wider preliminary concessions at the outset.

Before the end of November, a formula acceptable to the rulers of both England and the Netherlands had been devised. An instrument embodying it was duly subscribed by each.[49] The differences between their two states were to be laid before a commission of six persons sitting at Bruges, where similar meetings had taken place so often in the past. The three commissioners from each country were to comprise a nobleman, i.e.

a Knight of the Golden Fleece and a Knight of the Garter, a privy councillor, and a trained lawyer. Any regulations issued since 21 January 1559 to the detriment of trade were to be suspended: the date had been so fixed probably because of the insistence of the Queen that the yield of her customs should not be affected. The Intercourse and the freedom of traffic that went with it was to be restored for the duration of the colloquy and for three weeks subsequently – which in the event of a failure to come to an agreement left the future in doubt. But the arrangements for the conference to assemble were concise and unambiguous.

## NOTES TO CHAPTER I

[1] The trade embargo of 1493 had been effected directly by a brief proclamation, HL, No. 31. That of 1505 was implemented by a long and detailed order addressed to the Mayor and Sheriffs of London, dated 15 January: calendared in *CPR 1494–1509*, 404–6 and by Smit, *Bronnen*, No. 180. The City was to pass the royal instructions on to the merchants, both native and foreign. The second embargo was a much more closely calculated stroke of policy than the first. For the political background see Smit, *ib.*, pp. 127–8n. For the Fairs of Brabant, see *ante* 23 &c.

[2] See discussion by P. H. Ramsey, 'Overseas trade in the reign of Henry VII: the evidence of the customs accounts', *EcHR*, sec. ser., VI (1953–4), 173–82.

[3] The text is in Rymer, V (4), 82–7; it is also conveniently calendared in TP, II, 11–15, as well as by Smit, *Bronnen*, No. 96. See also *ante*, 22 &c.

[4] HL, No. 115.

[5] Dymock to Henry VIII, 15 September 1527, *LPH*, IV, No. 3432; *State Papers*, VII, 4.

[6] Hackett to Wolsey, 6 April 1528, Rogers, No. 59.

[7] John Stile to Wolsey, 28 August 1528, Smit, *Bronnen*, No. 487.

[8] The figures are drawn from *England's Export Trade 1275–1547*, ed. E. M. Carus-Wilson and O. Coleman (Oxford, 1963), 112–18. Customs returns for 1544–5 have not survived.

[9] Memorandum of John Hackett, November 1529, *LPH*, IV, No. 6070.

[10] Rymer, VI (1), 183–5. Conveniently calendared by Smit, *Bronnen*, No. 363.

[11] Tunstall, More and Hackett to Henry VIII, 2 and 5 August 1529, *LPH*, IV, Nos. 5822, 5824 and 5830. The instructions to the Netherlands delegates to the Bourbourg conference, which included a full list of the grievances they were to present to the English, were printed by Schanz, No. 32. See also Knight and Tregonwell to Hackett, June 1532, Rogers, No. 147.

[12] Chapuys to Charles V, 23 June 1534, *LPH*, VII, No. 871.

[13] Smit, *Bronnen*, No. 810; printed also by W. P. M. Kennedy, 'A General Court of the Merchant Adventurers in 1547', *EHR*, XXXVII (1922), 105–7.

[14] For the lords of Antwerp and the government of their city see *ante*, 11–13.

[15] The grievances as they were felt *c.* February 1532 are to be found in the documents printed by Schanz, II, No. 32, and Smit, *Bronnen*, Nos. 536 and 537.

[16] Text of renewal, 11 February 1543, *LPH*, XVIII, No. 144. See also Queen Regent to Chapuys, 22 February, *ib.*, No. 196.

[17] Chapuys to Queen Regent, 12 May 1543, *ib.*, No. 531.

[18] Many documents in *LPH*, XVIII, are concerned with this.

[19] *Querelae generales subditorum Caesariae Maiestatis*, undated *c.* May 1545, Schanz, II, No. 40, from Cotton Galba B x.

[20] Articles signed 6 April 1545, *LPH*, xx, i, No. 494.

[21] The final dispatch of Chapuys to Charles V, dated 15 July 1545, is at *LPH*, xx, i, No. 1197. For English grievances at this time see Smit, *Bronnen*, No. 756, and for Netherlanders', 785.

[22] Dispatches of Chapuys, 24 October 1531 and 11 January 1532, *LPH*, v, Nos 488 and 707; also 24 November, 6 and 16 December 1533, *ib.*, VI, Nos. 1460, 1501 and 1528.

[23] Chapuys to Regent, 29 January 1547, *LPH*, xxi, ii, 756.

[24] Smith to Paget, 19 July 1548, SP 68/2/103.

[25] See discussion by J. D. Gould, *The Great Debasement* (Oxford, 1970), 140 *et seq.* and, from the currency angle, C. E. Challis, *The Tudor Coinage* (Manchester, 1978), 183 *et seq.* The topic was first broached by F. J. Fisher, 'Commercial Trends and Policy in sixteenth-century England', *EcHR*, x, (1940), 95–117.

[26] Draft letter of Council to Wotton and Morison, 15 August 1551, SP 68/8/429.

[27] The information in this paragraph is drawn from Chamberlain's dispatches home, 14 November 1551, SP 68/9/482, and 4, 5, 7 and 17 December, Cotton Galba B xii, ff. 67 *et seq.*

[28] *APC 1550–2*, 88.

[29] Draft letter of Council to Wotton and Morison, 15 August 1551, SP 68/8/429.

[30] Minute of Council, 13 January 1552, SP 68/10/526.

[31] Mason to Council, 28 November 1553, *CSPF 1553–6*, No. 84;

[32] Renard to Charles V, 17 February 1554, *CSPSp. 1554*, 106.

[33] Leters to Charles V and to the Regent, 23 July 1555, *CSPSp. 1554–8*, 235.

[34] Mem. by Emperor's Privy Council, 15 August 1555, *ib.*, 421–2. Calendared by Smit, *Bronnen*, No. 915.

[35] Merchants to Privy Council, undated *c.* 1551–2, SP 10/13/82.

[36] Philip II to Feria, 3 March 1558, *CSPSp. 1554–8*, 365.

[37] *Ante*, 150–2.

[38] *Gubernatrix provinciarum Germaniae inferioris* was a title she used.

[39] They have been discussed *ante*, 85 *et seq.*

[40] Philip II to Silva, 6 August 1564, *CSPSp. 1558–67*, 370.

[41] Regent to Philip II, 12 August 1563, Gachard, *MP*, III, 67 *et seq.* See also *ante*, 171.

[42] Philip II to Regent, 13 October 1563, *ib.*, 121.

[43] Regent to Philip II, 12 August 1563, *ut supra*.

[44] Her directive to the city of Antwerp, 28 November 1563, was printed by Smit, *Bronnen*, No. 1024.

[45] Philip II to Silva, 7 October 1564, *CSPSp. 1558–67*, 383–4.

[46] Regent to Philip II, 8 October 1564, Gachard, *MP*, III, 450–1.

[47] Regent to Bishop of Bruges, 28 December 1564, Gachard, *Correspondance de Philippe II*, I, 520–1.

[48] Cecil to Winchester, 24 November 1564, SP 46/27, f. 234.

[49] The document, dated 30 November 1564, was printed by Weiss, VIII, 514–15. See also Smit, *Bronnen*, No. 1050; *CSPF 1564–5*, No. 830; and *HMC Salisbury*, XIII, 66. Also Regent to Philip II, 30 November 1564, Gachard, *MP*, III, 492–6 and 502–3.

# Chapter II
## *The interrupted colloquy, 1565–6*

During the early months of 1565, preparations were afoot both in England and the Netherlands for the conference – 'colloquy' – at Bruges that was to enquire into international grievances and strengthen the Intercourse between England and the Low Countries. The team of three commissioners on either side was to be led by a nobleman sufficiently exalted in station to be a worthy representative of his sovereign. The Count of Egmont, Governor of Flanders, was the first choice of the Regent for this post, but as he shortly departed on a mission to Spain his place was filled by the Sieur de Montigny, brother of the Count of Hoorn. This led to a corresponding alteration in the composition of the English team, the Earl of Sussex, whom Elizabeth had at first nominated to lead her commissioners, being replaced by Viscount Montague, whose lesser rank was more appropriate. The other English commissioners were Nicholas Wotton, Dean of both Canterbury and York and privy councillor; and Walter Haddon, a civil lawyer of varied experience and an accomplished writer of Latin prose – important since the official language of the conference was to be Latin and communication was to be through the written rather than the spoken word. Wotton was a man of lengthy experience in diplomacy and had been employed at Cateau-Cambresis in 1558–9. He had at various times evaded promotion to the episcopal bench, even to the see of Canterbury, and was now an elderly man of unsure health; but he remained a penner of clear, terse and shrewd dispatches and was probably the most resourceful negotiator at the disposal of the Queen. Among the three English commissioners, he shouldered the heaviest burden.[1] The assembly of the conference was long delayed, partly because of the illness of Wotton and partly owing to the replacement of Egmont and Sussex.[2] Only in April did the delegates meet. They remained in session, somewhat intermittently, until October, when they adjourned until the following March. The second session of the colloquy was much briefer, lasting only for a few weeks in May and June 1566.[3]

On either side, the commissioners were bound by the direc-
tives that their respective governments had issued to them; even
so, it was frequently necessary to interrupt proceedings in order
to ascertain the attitude of Queen or Regent on particular issues.
The instructions for the Netherlands delegation carried the date
28 February. They were in two parts, the first laying down
principles and tactics, the second enumerating specific regulations and actions to which objection was taken.[4] The commissioners were told to greet their English colleagues politely and
scrutinize their credentials with care, and on the second day to
express on behalf of the Regent and her brother the wish to
restore the old amity and trade relations, after which the English
might be invited to raise their complaints and the Netherlanders
in turn might state theirs. The standard for legal reference was
set by the Intercourse as stated in the treaty of 1496 and confirmed at various subsequent dates. In discussion, the Netherlanders were to deny responsibility for the trade stoppage of
1563–4, but if pressed by the English were to point to the drastic
customs rises imposed in May 1558, and to the protests lodged
by Assonleville when he had been in England in 1563.[5] This
looks like a disingenuous method of drawing attention to the
very topic that the Queen had insisted upon leaving outside the
discussion when the agenda for the colloquy had been indicated
in the autumn of 1564.

The second part of the Netherlanders' instructions covered in
some detail the alleged violations of the Intercourse by parliamentary enactments and English actions at sea, at the ports,
and in the High Court of Admiralty. The fisheries, the wool
trade and naturally the cloth traffic all had a place in the cata-
logue of denunciations. The instructions in fact contained a
thoroughgoing attack on the whole English commercial system
as it had developed since the fourteenth century, though especially during the preceding half-dozen years. Resentment was
directed at the differential rates of taxation levied on goods at
English ports, where foreigners habitually had to pay more,
sometimes substantially more, than native Englishmen, and
where goods carried on non-English ships attracted heavier tax.
Rises in the various harbour dues and in customs officers' fees
were criticised, as were the increasingly vexatious practices said
to be adopted by the officers. The manipulation of the wool
staple in favour of the Company of Merchants of the Staple was
exposed, not for the first time. But above all, the English were

denounced for their long-term intention of achieving for themselves and their shipping a monopoloy of the international trade between their island and the continent: so far had they already succeeded that the Company of Merchants Adventurers, it was alleged, now numbered three or four hundred merchants (which was probably true) while a mere score of Netherlanders traded in cloths to England. The regulations drawn up by the Governor of the Company at Antwerp, it was said, together with the recent legislation of Parliament, revealed English ambitions. And, of course, since 1558 the crown had been charging much higher customs. It was a formidable indictment, doubtless framed by Assonleville with the aid of his friends in business.

The instructions issued to the English commissioners were defensive in tone and sometimes descended to great detail, particularly with regard to the incidence of port charges in England.[6] They bore signs of the personal concern of the Queen in their drafting; she signed the master copy with her own hand both at the top of the first page and the bottom of the last, and there can be little doubt that she followed the progress of the negotiations throughout. She expected doubtful issues of any importance to be referred back to her. Her commissioners were ordered as their first responsibility to make it clear that her overriding purpose was 'to keep firm and inviolable the ancient amity' with Philip II. Next, they were reminded that the cloth export tax-rate was 'of great weight and consequence to Her Majesty and the crown of this realm', and instructed that the recent rise of the tariff was to be defended on the ground that it did not bring her so much revenue 'as her progenitors have had by the quantity of wool which is therein contained' and that the King of Spain, ruler of the Netherlands, would readily understand how, in view of the increasing costs of maintaining government, 'all other princes in all countries ... devise to set new taxes upon their subjects and people'. They were to add that because of 'the expectation that the Queen's Majesty maketh of the sincere friendship of the said King towards her' it was not expected that his commissioners would 'press this particular matter of the custom of the cloth'. Particular laws might each be measured against the accepted rules of the Intercourse, modifications being practicable in certain instances while not in others: thus the increased charges for buoyage were justified by the placing of further aids to navigation in the Thames. The commissioners were to take with them a copy of the 1558 Book of Rates and 'a collection of ancient statutes and laws' for ready reference, and to remind their Netherlands colleagues that laws in England might be amended only with the consent of Parliament.

An impressive entry into Bruges was provided for the English commissioners at the outset of the colloquy by the Constable of the Staplers and thirty mounted men of his Company: Bruges was now the seat of the wool Staple.[7] But more significant than the members of this procession were the four official agents nominated by the City of London, assuredly upon the invitation of the Queen, to attend and counsel her commissioners, who were expected to accept their guidance 'in cases concerning themselves'.[8] First and foremost among them was Governor Marsh of the Merchants Adventurers, who in January 1565 had methodically been collecting the grievances of all English merchants trading to Antwerp, including those from the outports.[9] But as he was no more than an occasional visitor to the Netherlands, the chief purveyor of detailed information on commercial points must have been the well-versed John Fitzwilliams, for many years a resident at Antwerp, and now likewise named among the agents of the City. Fitzwilliams by the terms of the charter issued in July 1564 had been 'disfranchised from the fellowship' of the Merchants Adventurers because of his foreign marriage and domicile; but he was now – as he believed, on the solicitation of Cecil – once more admitted to his place in the counsels of the Company, much to his pleasure, and he also returned to his office of Deputy Governor at Antwerp.[10] Of the two other agents named by the City, one was a lawyer and the other a goldsmith, who thus completed a comprehensive spread of interests.[11] The English commissioners at Bruges could never have lacked prompt and professional advice on trade affairs.

On the Netherlands side, the unanimity among the commissioners was less marked than on the English. Antwerp did not hold so dominant a position in the Netherlands as London enjoyed in England. There is no reason to doubt that the Regent genuinely sought a restoration of normal trade relations. But unlike the Queen, she was not the ruler of a unitary state, and she thus had a more devious and difficult course to steer. Her commissioners reflected the tangle of conflicting interests in which she was now caught. They comprised, besides Montigny, the inevitable Assonleville and Joachim Gillis, who held the office of *advocat fiscal* in Brabant. Since Montigny had some links

with Flanders, where the manufacturing interest was hostile to
the trade of the Merchants Adventurers, it seemed a good omen
that Gillis, an Antwerper by birth, should be a member of
the Netherlands delegation. The lords of Antwerp, who had
pressed the Regent to have someone from their own province
included, were accordingly gratified – as Fitzwilliams pointed
out to Cecil, the councillors of the Regent tended each to favour
the interests of his native province. As to Assonleville, he was by
birth a 'Burgundian', i.e. a French-speaker – he came from
Artois – but he was feared 'the rather to lean unto Flanders'.[12]
During the regime of the Cardinal, events had shown how little
he was a friend of the English.[13] He had survived the downfall
of his patron, and remained in some sort the specialist in English
affairs at the court of the Regent. Fitzwilliams reported of him:
'the said Monsieur d'Assonleville is counted to be of more
courage than good knowledge, and seeketh to do somewhat
whereby he might have some preferment, thinking that and if
he can use himself stoutly in this matter, he may be thought
meet to be an ambassador hereafter'.[14] The presence of this
plausible but shallow careerist at the conference table was not a
good omen.

From the point of view of the lords of Antwerp, and of the
English merchants trading to their city, it was also unfortunate
that the great seigneurs whose influence was now preponderant
at Brussels – Orange, Egmont, Hoorn and the rest – chose in
their lofty way to interest themselves in the cause of the Flemish
woollen cloth industry, stimulated as it had been by the recent
stoppage of trade with England. There is little reason to suppose
that even in the case of Orange, the shrewdest by far among
them, they were fully alive to the material issues at stake here. It
was learnt at Antwerp with great alarm that Orange and his
friends were bent on a scheme for reviving Netherlands clothmaking by prohibiting the sale by retail or the wearing of English
cloth thoughout the seventeen provinces, and were investigating
the benefits alleged to be conferred on the country by the presence of the Merchants Adventurers at Antwerp.[15] The lords of
the city quickly got out a memorandum explaining the importance of the Englishmen to their merchants and workfolk and the
disasters that would ensue if they took their trade elsewhere.[16] It
looks as if the arguments of this paper were sufficiently weighty
to end the advocacy of any such scheme in the Council of State,
though it may be that the dependence of clothmaking in Holland

and Flanders upon English wool was an even more effective deterrent. The English government was fully aware of the power that its control over the supply of what was still a necessary raw material for sectors of Netherlands industry gave it, and in 1566 it exploited this weapon by holding up a shipment of wool as a reminder of what any interference with the cloth trade would entail.[17] No doubt someone reminded the great seigneurs of this too. But the episode of their flirtation with the clothmaking interest illustrated the perilous situation of Antwerp, in that it was not like Venice or Hamburg a city-state but depended for its well-being upon the sympathy of its masters at Brussels. For no sooner had the international traffic on which its prosperity rested been rescued from the disaster overhanging it by reason of the clerical and absolutist policy of the Cardinal, than it had to set about the practical education of his enemies and successors.

If the debates in the Council of State at Brussels had simply mirrored a tussle between the lords of Antwerp and the cloth-making interests of Flanders and Holland, the issue could hardly have been in doubt – indeed, it had been resolved near the end of the previous century, at the conclusion of the *Magnus Intercursus*. But an ominous and fatally unsettling element was now to emerge, in the form of the small but vociferous group of Antwerp merchants with a stake in the English trade. The leader of this faction was Gillis Hooftman, an ingenious and lively entrepreneur born at Trier, a patron of Ortelius and other cartographers, a friend of Orange and of Gresham, and a creditor of the English crown.[18] Hooftman's business interests were represented at London by a couple of partners. On the evidence of the English tax assessments, his was by far the wealthiest foreign firm in the City, richer even than that represented by Jacob de la Faille.[19] We may safely imagine it as a large elaborate organization on the Italian pattern of administration. The spread of Hooftman's trading ventures, which with a basis on the London-Antwerp axis extended from Morocco to northern Russia, recalls that of Garrard, Chester and other prominent London contemporaries and rivals of his. When opportunity later seemed to offer, he momentarily professed himself a Calvinist.[20] He assuredly shared the English resentment at the policy of the Cardinal for reasons commercial and ecclesiastical if not political. With the re-opening of the London-Antwerp traffic in January he and some smaller men at Antwerp doubtless hoped to share too in the profits of the renewed and vigorous cloth trade.

In this, they were to be disappointed. They had no doubt reckoned with the differential cloth tax at the enhanced rate exacted since 1558. But there was also the problem of licences, all the more intractable because their issue lay in the hands of the Company of Merchants Adventurers, not only for the 30,000 cloths granted directly to them by the crown, but also for the very large numbers leased by the Queen to Leicester – who in the previous summer had sold to the Company the right to issue them.[21] Hooftman and his friends were thus in the humiliating position of having to pay their rivals the Merchants Adventurers for permission to ship unfinished English cloths, at what price per cloth is not known – nor indeed whether the Company was willing to sell licences to foreigners at all, at a moment when its own members must have been eager to snap them up. Their anger may easily be understood. They promptly complained to the Regent at Brussels of the unfair advantages exploited by the Merchants Adventurers, and put forward the plausible argument that they were entitled to parity of treatment, i.e. privileges at London comparable to those enjoyed by the Company at Antwerp.[22] They also went into the question of founding a company of their own, corresponding to that of the Merchants Adventurers and able to look it in the face.[23] At London, they presented a petition to the Privy Council against the exaction of licence money and other indignities, only to be dismissed as trouble-makers; Cecil especially incurred their indignation for his remark that they were 'worthy not only to be banished out of England but also out of their own countries for their doings'.[24] These men now proceeded to hire the services of a lawyer named Nikolaas van Emeren, who had practised in the Admiralty Court at Westminster and also in the fifties had acted as counsel for the Merchants Adventurers against the Hansards, for which the Company had rewarded him with a pension of £10. By mid February it was known that he was putting the case for Hooftman and his allies before the Council of State at Brussels. It was also said that he was very free in his derogatory remarks about England.[25]

The lords of Antwerp were, not surprisingly, horrified at the activities of Hooftman and his friends, who flouted their authority by carrying their complaints direct to the Court at Brussels.[26] This was bad enough. But the issue went deeper than this. The lords of Antwerp were fully aware that the wealth of their city depended on the free access of all merchants to its markets, without any awkward stipulations about reciprocal privileges for its citizens in other countries. In particular, they disliked any prospect of further trouble with the Merchants Adventurers, which would inevitably jeopardise the security of the newly re-established trade in English cloths. So they treated Hooftman and his allies as simply a group of 'particular men, which seek but their particular commodity', and refused them any support by either counsel or money. Behind the scenes, they did their best to discredit them in the eyes of the Netherlands government.[27] Unhappily, they soon learnt that Assonleville was 'addicted to these particular suitors', so that it was in vain that they plied him with arguments to prove that 'their suit is but for the commodity of a few and would be prejudicial to their commonwealth'.[28] During the conference recess in the winter of 1565–6, Hooftman and his business associate Radermacher continued with some persistence to furnish Assonleville with other arguments of quite a different colour, drawing attention to the needs of Hollanders and Zeelanders, urging that merchants from Lille as well as Antwerp who had a stake in the trade with England should be invited to give evidence, dissipate 'misunderstanding' and thus by inference demonstrate the one-sided nature of the submissions of the lords of Antwerp.[29]

Assonleville made the most of this dissident minority interest. It afforded him leverage to press for an equalization of cloth duties as between Englishmen and Netherlanders by the imposition of an extra levy on the imports of the Merchants Adventurers at Antwerp: this would both make English cloths more expensive, to the advantage of the Netherlands textile industry, and put the Merchants Adventurers on an equal footing, as far as customs payments were concerned, with Hooftman and his friends. Assonleville converted Montigny to this plausible but dangerous expedient, and the Regent actually summoned them from Bruges to put the case for it before the Council of State. There it was turned down because of the fear that it might provoke the English to break off negotiations altogether.[30] But the rebuff did not lead Assonleville to alter his attitude to the English trade. In November 1565, during the winter recess, he was writing to his exiled patron the Cardinal, to lament how the Queen of England by her export taxes was drawing more wealth from the Low Countries than the King of Spain ever could. For long, he commented, these Netherlands have been the Indies of England.[31]

Since these were the lines on which the mind of the most active negotiator of the Netherlands delegation was running, it is scarcely to be wondered that the conference proved long drawn-out and ultimately abortive. Into the day-to-day progress of discussion it is unnecessary here to enter.[32] After some difference of opinion about procedure had been smoothed, each side settled down to examine the grievances of the other, communication being partly in writing and partly – perhaps increasingly – by word of mouth. The English heard frequently from home and were clearly instructed as to the assurances they might offer and the bargaining points they might exploit. In the background, the government at London was demonstrating its will to suppress piracy by having numerous malefactors actually executed, and on one occasion by summoning to the Star Chamber a Cornish jury that upon sufficient evidence had failed to convict.[33] The Spanish ambassador at London was convinced that the Queen was indeed in earnest in her intention to make an end of the pirates.[34] There were English offers to rationalize the export licencing system and to mitigate the operation of the Statutes of Employment.[35] As to the cloth export tax, although the English would not impose the same rates indifferently on their own and foreign merchants, they were prepared to reduce the sum payable by the latter per cloth from 14s. 6d. to 10s. 3d., so that the differential should be no greater than it had been before 1558. With regard to the alleged shortcomings in the supply of English wool to the Netherlands, it was difficult to contest the argument that this had always been a private concern of the merchants and had better be left so.[36] If the Netherlanders were not satisfied on this point, they had the remedy in their own hands: they could arrange for wool to be shipped from Spain to make good the English deficiencies.[37] There was thus a political element in the replacement of English by Spanish wool in the Netherlands textile industry during the 1560s.

The first hopes of a speedy agreement soon withered as the delegates settled down to a wrangle about customs and other charges at the English ports – always the crucial topic of the conference. The English assertion that the import levy known as poundage had always been as high as a shilling in the pound was rashly queried. Proofs were requested. So for some weeks in June and July, discussions were virtually suspended while a

Netherlands delegation, headed by the inquisitive lawyer
Emeren, crossed to London to verify the truth of English statements by rummaging in the public records.[38] Meanwhile, the
outer world was apprised that the negotiations, in the words of
the Florentine agent at Antwerp, were proceeding slowly, very
slowly, *adagissimo*.[39] It was reported soon to the English government that Emeren had indiscreetly let it be known that he expected to win his point by bribery, whatever the records might
indicate.[40] This was not to be the case. The Netherlands investi-
gators 'had divers searches in divers books touching customs,
scavage and other duties paid by their countrymen as well in
books of the exchequer as in the Guildhall in London', only to
discover that the established rate of poundage was of great
antiquity.[41] The Queen had at first received these visitors very
coolly, but – perhaps after she had learnt that they were going to
be disappointed – she subsequently mollified her attitude.[42] The
Netherlanders did not cease to cite poundage as a grievance, but
henceforth they agreed that it was an ancient and not a recent
one.[43] However, this check diminished the tension, and during
the latter part of August 1565 it looked as if there might be
sufficient agreement for a new Anglo-Netherlands treaty. The
Regent reported to her brother that the conference was either at
breaking-point or on the verge of success.[44] On the English side,
Cecil too was not without hope: as he put it, apart from the cloth
tax, 'our Intercourse standeth upon narrow points'.[45]

But it was not to be. The ultimate and irremovable obstacle to
agreement remained – the greatly enhanced English cloth export tax first levied in May 1558. However, much as the Regent,
with Assonleville at her ear, might profess to resent this, neither
she nor the Council of State were willing to provoke another
rupture of commercial relations with England. The lords of
Antwerp and their allies had sufficient influence to prevent this.
Thus the Brussels government would neither accept the English
tax, which as the English liked to remind them, had originally
been imposed when Philip II was King of England, and had
now been in operation for half-a-dozen years, nor would they
break off the colloquy because of it. In her exasperation, the
Regent actually voiced a suspicion that the English were craftily
prolonging the conference so that another cloth fleet could
discharge its freight at the next mart without fear.[46] The discussions at Bruges became more and more pointless. At quite an
early stage Montigny had grown so irregular in his attendance

that Elizabeth gave leave to Montague to return home and leave the conduct of affairs to Wotton and Haddon.[47] At the brief second session in 1566, Montigny did not appear at all, his place being filled by another member of his family, the Sieur d'Assincourt. This marked a further deterioration in the situation. As Wotton explained to Cecil, Assincourt was 'a good plain gentleman whom Assonleville ruleth even at his pleasure, which he could not do with Monsieur de Montigny. And therefore are we now in so much the worse case, for that Montigny now and then when he perceived Assonleville to sing out of tune would make him hold his peace, whether he would or not. Whom now no man can rule'.[48] When Assonleville was thus allowed to get the bit between his teeth, the weakness of the Regent's position became evident: unlike the Queen of England, she was not the head of a well-knit centralized administration and needed more sedulously to conciliate the various interests that predominated in the seventeen provinces, some of them with a disproportionate weight in the politics of the central government at Brussels.

An incidental victim of the abortive negotiations was supplied by the Company of Merchants of the Staple, whose headquarters had in 1558 been moved to Bruges.[49] Their intrinsic weakness lay in their dependence upon the Netherlands as the consumer as well as the market for English wool, so that they were a tied sacrifice. By the deliberate policy of the Queen, they had been made to share the trials of the embargo throughout 1564 without the reward of a sudden onrush of business the following year.[50] Instead, they were faced by a series of complaints from their chief customers the wool-dealers of Holland, who alleged a decline in the quality and packing of English wool as well as irregularities in delivery. These they answered as best they could.[51] Before long, there was further evidence that they might expect only second-class treatment at the hands of the government. When in June 1566 the international discussions at Bruges were evidently running into sand, the Staplers' ships all laden with wool were waiting in English ports to sail. But they were 'suddenly stayed' by command of the Queen, as a means of putting pressure on the Netherlands delegates: the Staplers were being used as a diplomatic weapon on behalf of interests not their own.[52] Their best remaining hope they understandably conceived to be their absorption into the ranks of the Merchants Adventurers, by acquiring the right to deal in cloth as well as wool. This had long since been sought in vain, and in 1566 was again refused.[53]

As the Queen meanwhile followed the course of the negotiations, her dismay increased, if only because the discussions bore
more and more upon her customs duties and especially that
mainstay of her revenue the cloth export levy. Surely her 'good
brother' Philip could not wish thus to impoverish her crown!
During the winter recess, she seized the opportunity offered by
the dispatch of a new ambassador to Spain to make a personal
approach to the King, as from one monarch to another. The
envoy, Dr John Man, was instructed when admitted to audience
with Philip to try tactfully to persuade him 'to think that the
controversy is more fit to be judged of by himself as a king, than
of councillors or ministers, whose office properly is to regard
only how to make discourse or argument to maintain one part of
the controversy'. Man was then to remind the King how 'we that
be princes at this day have for ourselves and our persons the use
of nothing more for our own persons than our progenitors have
had and yet, as the time requireth, none of us is able to rule our
countries and people either in peace or war with the like small
charges as our progenitors did', and that 'all that which is now
misliked by his subjects was devised and established in the very
names of the King and our dear sister Queen Mary'. Further,
although the volume of foreign trade was 'double to that it was
in ancient time', yet the customs yield was 'scant the half ... as
our progenitors have continually had'. In a general survey of the
dealings at Bruges, Man was instructed to mention how the
Netherlands commissioners had been so unreasonable as to
impugn the validity of poundage, 'without interruption paid to
the crown of England above three hundred years'. As to the
demand for fiscal reciprocity, it was without precedent: 'neither
can the policy of this realm bear it'. It would simply provoke the
Queen to permit her merchants to bring their trade to other
parts of the world where they would be made more welcome.
Man was not to press his case unreasonably upon the King or his
council, but to try to elicit a speedy answer.[54] This, alas, was not
forthcoming.

The King was absent when the letter reached Madrid, so that
not until 25 April did the ambassador have an opportunity to
broach the matter to him.[55] By the time the Queen learnt that
her message had been favourably received, it must have been
near midsummer, when she could still fortify herself with the
delusion that Philip was likely to return before long to north-
western Europe. Meanwhile, such slow-moving diplomacy could

not affect the actual course of events. During the winter recess, both parties to the conference were taking counsel on their future policy at its resumption. The English Privy Council sought yet again to examine and clarify the points on which the crown should stand firm and those on which it might be prepared to bargain.[56] At Brussels, the Regent near the end of February 1566 put the issues once more before her Council of State. This body now committed itself to the fateful resolution to advise rejection of the compromise suggested by the English with regard to the cloth export tax, i.e., to restore merely the differential rate to its pre-1558 level.[57] Its reasons for this were that it did not wish to make English cloths too cheap, and that in any case the ancient differential, like the ancient rate of poundage, was not acceptable. The King in a brief marginal comment on the report of the Regent accepted this advice.[58] Did he, one wonders, recollect this when he later received the personal message of the Queen? When the commissioners once more were gathered together at Bruges, it was accordingly not long before it became clear that the deadlock of the previous autumn was not going to be resolved. In addition, with the passage of time various external events were making their significance felt. The Regent had become nervous because of the revolutionary situation developing within the Netherlands. She suspected that the English were seeking to take advantage of it; their deliberate withholding of the Staplers' wool seemed to lend substance to this fear.[59] She therefore became anxious for a further adjournment of the conference.

This, as it happened, was now a wish shared by the Queen of England. She had begun to count upon an early return of Philip II to the Netherlands, when they as princes could amicably settle matters between themselves. As she saw it, there were too many interested parties with a finger in the negotiations. It thus became readily possible for the commissioners at Bruges to reach an entirely amicable agreement to postpone discussions to an unspecified date – the one firm point of unanimity that they reached.[60] As to the reasons to be offered to the world for this new prorogation, Elizabeth was very definite. She had indeed refused to consent to any practical uniformity in taxation as between the English and the foreign merchants shipping cloth from her kingdom: had not the Merchants Adventurers often enough protested that fiscal equality would be their 'utter undoing'?[61] But the basic reason for the lack of any positive

agreement remained the Netherlands refusal to acquiesce in the
rates of the English customs charges – including poundage and
other ancient dues, but above all the cloth export tax as fixed in
1558.[62] Or, to put the same facts in a different way, in the last
resort the conference at Bruges had come to nothing because
the Queen of England would not sacrifice her customs revenue.
But her commissioners were ordered to connive at a little piece
of deceit. She explained to them that 'for the manner of your
breach, it hath been thought meet that our Merchants Adventurers and the mayor and citizens of London should understand that you do persist in the articles which concern them, as
indeed that of impost of cloths toucheth our merchants indirectly; and that if the treaty shall break, it shall be for their
interest. Wherfore, you shall do well also so to order your
speeches to our merchants there and their counsellors as they
may understand the like'.[63] The Queen well knew the public
image of herself that she wished to foster.

As to the immediate international significance of the adjournment, a few loose ends hardly seemed for the moment to
matter. Within a few months, the King was expected back in the
Netherlands, when both parties looked forward to resuming
discussions under more favourable circumstances. But if the
impasse were not resolved, and the long-standing commercial
connection between London and Antwerp were to be weakened,
and the trade agreements on which it rested no longer recognized, might this not in time affect the traditional Anglo-
Burgundian alliance? When the Regent first raised this point
with Philip II, she met with a confident answer. Changes
in matters of trade, he assured her in September 1565, had
nothing to do with the ancient close amity and alliance, which in
the event of the Intercourse not being renewed need not lose
any of its customary vigour – a remarkable revelation of how the
mind of the King worked.[64] The following summer the Regent,
one suspects at the prompting of Assonleville, was able to improve on this statement by urging that the lack of any trade
agreement would bring home to the Queen of England the
insecurity of the great profit she drew from the cloth trade, and
thus help to ensure her docility.[65] On the English side, the
attitude to this vital question was directly to the contrary. The
English commissioners in June 1565 were instructed to explain
how essential to the maintenance of the political amity was an
agreement with regard to trade.[66] Wotton, from the beginning

to the end of the negotiations a pessimist, at an early stage warned Montigny in private conversation of this,[67] mentioning that the Queen might interpret a failure to agree as a rupture of the political alliance.[68] At the final assembly of the colloquy in June 1566, the English commissioners once again made it clear that the Queen considered the trade agreement to be an essential part of the political alliance, and that the one could not be abrogated without damage to the other. If the interests of the merchants were hurt, then the relations of the princes would suffer. 'And so it might come to pass, that the affection and amity which now was perfect and sound betwixt the princes, might partly be diminished and decayed'.[69] The issue was shortly to be put to the test.

## NOTES TO CHAPTER II

[1] All three are noticed in the DNB, where the account of Wotton is a characteristic contribution from the pen of A. F. Pollard. For the pre-eminence of Wotton, see Montague to Leicester, 29 May 1565, *HMC Pepys*, 59; also *ante*, 120–1.

[2] Queen to Regent, 28 January 1565, KL, IV, 1623; Regent to Philip II, 29 February 1565, Theissen, *MP*, I, 2.

[3] See royal proclamation to continue trade with the Netherlands, 16 October 1565, HL, II, No. 537, also *HMC Salisbury*, I, No. 1062.

[4] Calendared by Smit, *Bronnen*, Nos. 1059 and 1060.

[5] For the trade stoppage of 1563–4 see *ante*, 194–7.

[6] For the text of the instructions see Appendix, *infra.*, 206–19.

[7] Sheres to Cecil, 25 March 1565, KL, IV, 193.

[8] Queen to English commissioners, 3 August 1565, SP 70/79/1097.

[9] Marsh to merchants of York, 19 January 1565, Sellers, *York Mercers*, 174–8. Presumably identical or similar letters went to other outports. For Governor Marsh, see *ante, passim*.

[10] *Ante*, 25; Fitzwilliams to Cecil, 18 January 1565, KL, IV, 159–61. The letters patent for the restoration of Fitzwilliams to the Company were dated 6 April 1565, C 66/1010, m. 26. Richard Saltonstall was similarly restored on 24 August, *ib.*, m. 29.

[11] William Arroberry, doctor of laws, and Thomas Nicholles, goldsmith. There is a copy of the commission of the City of London to these four agents, dated 3 March 1565, at Add. 48,007, f. 84. They were appointed *nostros veros et legitimos atturnatos factores et procuratores conjunctim et divisim*, which makes it evident that they were not all expected to be at the elbow of the commissioners at the same time. There can be little doubt that Fitzwilliams was the most often there.

[12] Fitzwilliams to Cecil, 23 February 1565, KL, IV, 183–5 offered a survey of the Netherlands delegation.

[13] *Ante, passim.* Assonleville is noticed by Baelde, 227–8, and in both the *Dictionnaire de Biographie française* and the *Biographie nationale de Belgique*. His forbears were citizens of Arras.

[14] Fitzwilliams to Cecil, 7 February 1565, KL, IV, 173.

[15] Fitzwilliams to Cecil, 9 and 23 June 1565, KL, IV, 211–13.

[16] What looks like an English summary of this document is preserved in Cotton, Galba C II, No. 54.

[17] English commissioners to Privy Council, 17 June 1566, SP 70/84/408; *infra.*, 27.

[18] For some account of Hooftman, see J. Denucé, *Anvers et l'Afrique* (Antwerp, 1937), 13–15. In 1557, he was importing Toulouse woad in quantity from Bordeaux, which might suggest that he was interested in the cloth-finishing business – C. Wyffels, 'Een Antwerpse Zeeverzekeringspolis uit het Jaar 1557', *Bulletin de la Commission Royale d'Histoire*, CXIII (1948), 95–103.

[19] Certificate of assessment of foreigners in London, undated *c.* 1566, SP 12/ 41/ 60. 'Gyles Hoftman' with his partners 'Peter Panhewes' and Francis Wynter were jointly rated at £300 – the next highest rating being 'Jacob de la Follia & his Company' at £200. Most were rated at £10 or thereabouts.

[20] *Infra.*, 39.

[21] *Ante*, 56.

[22] Fitzwilliams to Cecil, 18 January 1565, KL, IV, 159–61.

[23] Smedt, *EN*, I, 297.

[24] Fitzwilliams to Cecil, 18 January 1565, KL, IV, 159–61.

[25] *Ib.* to *ib.*, 17 February 1565, KL, IV, 178–80. There is also information in Emeren's chancery bill, C3/1/31.

[26] Fitzwilliams to Cecil, 18 January 1565, KL, IV, 159–61.

[27] *Ib.* to *ib.*, 7 February 1565, *ib.*, 172–3. In fact, the number of Antwerp merchants trading to England was only a score or so, some of them being small men of negligible importance: Smit, *EN*, I, 324, note 56.

[28] *Ib. ib.*, 17 February 1565, KL, IV, 178–80.

[29] The letters of Hooftman and Radermacher are at *AGR*, 401, ff. 82, 84, 89, 142.

[30] Regent to Philip II, 19 August 1565, Theissen, *MP*, I, 78–83.

[31] Assonleville to Granvelle, 20 November 1565, Gachard, *Correspondance de Philippe II*, I, 382.

[32] Materials exist for a detailed history of the colloquy of Bruges, mostly unprinted, at London, Brussels and elsewhere. There is much valuable material in the volume Cotton Galba C II. A summary of the Regent's instructions to the Netherlands commissioners, 28 February 1565, was printed by Smit, *Bronnen*, Nos. 1059 and 1060, *ut supra*.

[33] Silva to Philip II, 22 October 1565, *CSPSp. 1558–67*, 496; *APC 1558–70*, 206–7, 210.

[34] Silva to Philip II, 25 June 1565, *CSPSp. 1558–67*, 440–1.

[35] *Supra*.

[36] Instructions to English commissioners, 12 June 1565, Add. 48,011, f. 50; and 3 August 1565, SP 70/79/1097.

[37] Regent to Philip II, 21 June 1566, Gelder, *MP*, II, 221; also 17 November 1566, *ib.*, III, 38.

[38] Regent to Queen, 1 June 1565, KL, IV, 205–6; Cecil to Smith, 3 June 1565, Wright, I, 108–9.

[39] G.-B. Guicciardini to prince Francesco de' Medici, 13 May 1565, Battistini, 251.

[40] Fitzwilliams to Cecil, 4 June 1565, KL, IV, 209–10.

[41] Gras, *EECS*, 526 *et seq.*, prints an account showing poundage at 12*d.* in the pound for 1382–3. The Netherlanders were duly supplied with certified copies of the documents they sought – 'Extract from an old book in the Exchequer', undated, SP 12/41/61.

[42] Regent to Philip II, 22 July 1565, Theissen, *MP*, I, 60–1.

[43] Regent to Council of State, 2 February 1566, Gelder, *MP*, II, 143.

[44] Regent to Philip II, 19 August 1565, Theissen, *MP*, I, 78–83.

[45] Cecil to Smith, 30 August 1565, Wright, I, 208.

[46] Regent to Philip II, 19 August 1565, Theissen, *MP*, I, 78–83.

[47] Queen to English commissioners, 3 August 1565, SP 70/79/1097.

[48] Wotton to Cecil, 26 May 1566, SP 70/84/350. Montague had reported a little earlier to Leicester in similar terms, 8 May 1566, *HMC Pepys*, 86.

[49] See discussion by Rich, *Ordinance Book*, 21–35.

[50] *Ante*, 273–5.

[51] Complaints of the merchants of Holland, February 1565, SP 70/76/838; Staplers' answer, 839.

[52] English commissioners to Queen, 17 June 1566, SP 70/84/408. However, by way of compensation they were permitted to dispose of their stocks of wool to clothiers at home: licence dated 19 June 1566, enrolled at C 66/1026, m. 2.

[53] Merchants Adventurers to Privy Council, undated *c.* 1566, SP 12/75/102.

[54] Instructions to Man, 20 February 1566, SP 70/82/94; another copy at Cotton, Vespasian C VII, No. 83, with marginal notes by Cecil. The whole document reads like a personal effusion of the Queen. For the diplomatic mission of Man, see *ante*, 101–4.

[55] Man to Queen, 18 May 1566, Cotton, Vespasian C VIII, No. 85.

[56] 'The opinion of the counsell for a full answer...', 21 March 1566, Cecil Papers, 154/144.

[57] Explained, *ante*, 151–2.

[58] Discourse of the Regent to the Council of State, with marginal comments by Philip II, 28 February 1566, Gelder, *MP*, II, 143–7.

[59] Regent to Silva, 13 July 1566, KL, IV, 317–18.

[60] Queen to English commissioners, 1 June 1566, SP 70/84/361; English commissioners to Council and to Cecil, 17 June 1565, SP 70/48/408 and 409; Regent to Philip II, 17 June 1566, KL, IV, 304–5n.

[61] Merchants Adventurers to Council, 6 June 1566, Cecil Papers, 3/74, was their most recent statement.

[62] As stated in the declaration of adjournment by the Netherlands Commissioners, 21 June 1566, Smit, *Bronnen*, No. 1109: *videlicet de pondagio ratis pannorum et lanarum vectigali.*

[63] Queen to English commissioners, draft in the hand of Cecil, 22 June 1566, SP 70/84/422.

[64] Regent to Philip II, 19 August 1565, Theissen, *MP*, I, 78–83; Philip II to Regent, 17 September 1565, *ib.*, 92.

[65] Regent to Philip II, 17 June and 4 July 1566, KL, IV, 304–5n and Gelder, *MP*, II, 242.

[66] Instructions to English commissioners, 12 June 1565, Add. 48,011, f. 50.

[67] Wotton to Leicester, 11 May 1565, Pepys Papers, I, 383; *ib.* to Cecil, 24 June 1566, SP 70/84/424.

[68] Regent to Philip II, 19 August 1565, Theissen, *MP*, I, 78–83.

[69] English commissioners to Council, 17 June 1566, SP 70/84/408.

# Chapter III

## Antwerp, 1566: the outbreak that scared the English

The year 1566 afforded dramatic illustration that the maintenance of the traffic of the Merchants Adventurers at Antwerp was not merely the affair of the Company and the English crown on one side and the lords and merchants of Antwerp and the government of the Netherlands on the other. Parties hitherto silent raised their voices. Antwerp was a great and unruly city, and the Netherlands themselves were seething with discontents that were social, ecclesiastical and political in their origins. In particular, this was the moment at which the new heresy of Calvinism had struck root there. Its authoritarian system of elders and consistories was well suited not only to the maintenance of a tight ecclesiastical discipline but also to the preparation of organized protests and even revolts. Calvinism introduced into popular movements an element of forethought and conspiracy that the relatively simple-minded anabaptist and other heretics had hithero lacked. The English merchants at Antwerp were now to be the startled spectators of some extraordinary events, and the English government was to be forced to ponder some unexpected problems. What was to happen to commercial life in Antwerp if the discontents of an urban proletariat were harnessed to the ambitions of able and ruthless Calvinist leaders? What security might remain for the well-to-do? Was it to be expected that the traffic of the Merchants Adventurers should remain unaffacted? This is not the place for any general investigation of the phenomena of violence and revolution that now made their appearance at Antwerp, but a small digression is necessary to survey the situation that could give rise to some new apprehensions in the minds of the Englishmen.[1]

The political commotions that were shaking the Netherlands government during the first half of the year 1566 caused widespread uneasiness among the business community at Antwerp. The Bourse grew very quiet, and some nervous merchants were said to be removing their capital out of the country.[2] However,

Netherlands politics were not the direct concern of the Merchants Adventurers. They were most of them transient visitors,
whose attention was focussed on the sale of their cloths and
on the commodity market, which remained comparatively
unaffected. The Sinksen mart passed with nothing unusual to
report.[3] The Englishmen were no doubt accustomed to the
dilapidated state of the parish churches and to the ill observance
of fast and feast days, and the offhand way in which the Antwerpians strolled about their collegiate church without any show of
reverence even while divine service was being celebrated, just
like St Paul's at home.[4] Some of them may have been aware of
the restlessness of the four cities of Brabant under the remaining ecclesiastical constraints to which they were subject, and of
the protests they were making to secure some further relaxa-
tions.[5] But by midsummer the little colony of Englishmen
remaining at Antwerp could not but take notice that something
unusual was afoot. The storm-clouds that for several months
had been hanging over the Netherlands were about to burst
over their mart town.

The first rumblings of thunder were noted by John Fitzwilliams, resident Deputy Governor of the Merchants Adventurers.
He thought it worth writing to inform Secretary Cecil how
on Saturday and Sunday, June 29 and 30, there began open
preaching of sermons by avowed heretics in the fields outside
the city. Heretical sermons were of course no novelty at
Antwerp, but hitherto they had been clandestine exhortations to
a handful of the faithful. Now, the veil of secrecy was dropped.
The sermons were delivered some in French but more in the
Teutonic speech of the people. The two days passed, Fitzwilliams commented, somewhat quietly, though the lords of
Antwerp, alarmed by a phenomenon likely to get them into hot
water with the Regent at Brussels, not to mention the King in
Spain, posted men at the city gate and used other means to
dissuade the inhabitants from attending – with scant success.
Tuesday July 2 was a feast day of the collegiate church and
therefore a holiday, so that there was an opportunity for more
sermons; those attending were alarmed by the appearance of
some mounted men on chargers prancing dangerously nearby.
By now, the lords of Antwerp were sufficiently scared to invoke
the authority of the Regent and to post at the Town Hall and
elsewhere her proclamation forbidding attendance at the
sermons, commanding all who had no business at Antwerp to

depart, and warning strangers that they incited Netherlanders to break the laws at their peril. Nevertheless, on the next Sunday, July 7, according to the information reaching Fitz-williams, attendance at the sermons reached the extraordinary total of twelve thousand – surely an exaggeration – and the congregations were protected against any threats by an armed force of horsemen, improvized and paid for by well-to-do sup-porters of the cause. Inside the city, the church of the Grey Friars was the scene of an uproar when the papist preacher attempted a counterblast.

At this point, the tension snapped, and the possibility of some serious upheaval drew suddenly much closer. A rumour spread that the Regent was preparing to introduce troops to put down the preaching. There must have been many Antwerpians who could well remember how in 1555 the Emperor had quelled the city by the stealthy introduction of his soldiers.[6] So on the evening of the next day, Monday July 8, the alarm sounded and there was 'a marvellous stir'. The trained bands of the city, consisting of 'good substantial men', forced the lords of Ant-werp, by now thoroughly frightened, to surrender to them the keys of the city gates, with control over their opening and shut-ting. Henceforth, Antwerp was 'well guarded both by day and night like a town of war, both at the gates and every corner of the town'. It is tempting to see in the events of the day some likeness to those that in the France of 1789 accompanied the phenomenon known as 'la grande peur'. They were certainly the first steps of an incipient revolution.[7]

Such were the events that passed before the astonished gaze of the English residents. Behind the preachings stood two allied forces. There was the noisy group of small nobles – nicknamed *Gueux* or Beggars – who in previous months had been making trouble for the Regent on the pretext that the King was planning to introduce the full-scale Spanish-style Inquisition into the Netherlands. They were in league with some big merchants of Calvinist sympathies, the pillars of the Antwerp consistory. Between them, these allies had arranged for the supply of sermons, French-speaking preachers being secured by arrange-ment with the Calvinist headquarters at Geneva, Flemish or Low German-speaking preachers through the Elector Palatine or some other neighbouring sympathizers.[8] Before long, the interest of the *Gueux* was openly manifested. After the first sermons had indicated the danger of the situation, the Governor

of Gelderland and another nobleman in the confidence of the
Regent, presumably at her request, moved on July 2 into
Antwerp to hearten the forces of law. Two days later, they were
followed by Count Brederode and three other leaders of the
*Gueux*, who entered with an escort of 200 horsemen. They too
established themselves within the city, with popular acclaim.
Brederode put up at the sign of the *Lion Rouge*, where he
dispensed a lavish hospitality and was readily to be seen by all.[9]
The *Gueux* were fully alive to the central significance of Antwerp
in Netherlands politics, 'accounting that side to which Antwerp
leaneth, to be the stronger side'.[10]

The lords of Antwerp were now confronted by a situation of
some delicacy. They had earned the disapproval of the Regent
and the Council of State for bungling the suppression of open
heresy, while they had failed to conjure away the popular anger
and the widespread suspicion of their actions. Altogether,
they were short of friends. They could not dare to arrest the
preacher and so put an end to the source of the trouble: they
lacked any reliable forces. What were they to do? In their
embarrassment they turned perforce to the Regent and began
more and more urgently to plead with her to move in person to
Antwerp with her Court – but without any military escort that
might frighten away the foreign merchants or provoke an insurrection on the part of the people. Whether Stralen, the most
influential personage among the lords of Antwerp, lately burgomaster and still an alderman, really believed that she would
– or could – accept such an invitation may be wondered. Not
unnaturally, she was reluctant to move into a situation where her
personal safety could not be guaranteed. In any case, she
probably lacked the troops to overawe the city. With her
prudent refusal to commit herself in person, any faint possibility
of stifling the infant movement in its cradle came to an end.[11] As
we have seen, the attendance at the sermons on Sunday July 7
established a new record. On top of this came the loss of control
over the town gates by the lords of Antwerp. After this, the
Governor of Gelderland and his companion abandoned their
attempt to stem the tide and departed with undignified haste
amid the jeers of the populace.[12] Brederode and his colleagues
remained.

The Regent now played her last card by dispatching to
Antwerp its hereditary High Steward or *Burggraf*, the Prince of
Orange. He was a dignitary of vast possessions and reputation,

the greatest of the seigneurs of the Netherlands, and well versed in politics. As he entered the city gate on the evening of Friday July 13, he was greeted by crowds shouting *Viva le Gues*.[13] This he deprecated. He was still a catholic and a regular attendant at Mass. But he was also a realist. He was in close touch with the leaders of the *Gueux*; one observer thought it significant that some of his retainers wore their badge.[14] He was also a friend of Stralen, and believed to be one of his major debtors.[15] At the instigation of Orange, the lords of Antwerp now tried to elicit the views of the good people of their town, not only by summoning a Great Council, embodying representatives of the gilds and the wards, but also by consulting other recognized organizations, from the chambers of rhetoric to 'the company of the masters of the poor'. All declared themselves hostile to any attempt to arrest the preachers, and in favour of awaiting a decision from the Estates of Brabant. So the sermons continued, with congregations variously estimated from twelve to thirty thousand, all protected by the organized guard of men both mounted and on foot, armed by well-off supporters of the movement. On Sunday July 21, 'after the sermon was done and the psalms sung', there was a peal of guns, thunderous and defiant.[16] Three weeks later, on August 11, there was the special attraction of a local man convicted of heresy a year earlier, who had returned from exile by special invitation to join boldly in the preaching, as if to spite the authorities. Excitement grew as sermons were delivered not only on Sundays and holidays but also on ordinary weekdays, and 'the common people' were more and more 'bent against the papists'.[17] Ecclesiastics were threatened in the streets – it was said that at the point of the dagger the dean of the collegiate church had been made to shout *Vive les Gueux*.[18] Although similar scenes were being enacted all over the industrial districts of the Netherlands, nowhere was the likelihood of a murderous explosion more to be feared than in the greatest city of the land. All the tact and dexterity of Orange was needed to avert it.

The Prince could not linger indefinitely at Antwerp. He remained over the week-end of Sunday August 18, when services in the churches were sung without hindrance; there was the usual annual procession from the collegiate church with a specially honoured statue of the Virgin Mary, which met with nothing worse than an occasional jeer or a bespattering of earth. Next day, Orange departed to attend a chapter meeting of the

Order of the Golden Fleece at Brussels. The explosion then occurred. Trouble, evidently well planned, broke out on Tuesday August 20 during the service of compline at the collegiate church, when 'a company of knaves' began to sing psalms. The Margrave arrived in person with half-a-dozen of his men but failed to restore order. The intruders increased in number and invaded the choir, breaking and destroying as they went. The image so recently carried around the town was 'utterly defaced' and the furniture of the church systematically taken down, carried off or destroyed. When the commotion had subsided, Gresham's manager Clough in the late evening was moved by curiosity to enter the building. In his words, 'it looked like a hell, where were above 10,000 torches burning, and such a noise as if heaven and earth had gone together, with falling of images and beating down of costly works'. He estimated that 'the garnishing of Our Lady church had cost above two hundred thousand marks' – i.e. £133,000 sterling – but that it was now 'in fine all spoilt'.[19] The same treatment was then meted out to the other churches of Antwerp. When the organized iconoclasts had done their work, there was no lack of others to loot and pilfer what they could of the gold and jewellery lying around. Respectable citizens were appalled by such thefts, as well as by the indiscriminate destruction of tombs, memorials and works of art. There was widespread fear of a social uprising that might put in jeopardy the lives as well as the property of the rich. As Clough saw it, Antwerp was 'in danger to be spoiled for that all the vagabonds of the country draw to this town: God send us quietness'.[20]

Such fears were not without ground, for while the outward form of these convulsions at Antwerp and elsewhere in the Netherlands was ecclesiastical, their substance was political and still more social. Brederode and the other landed gentry who led the *Gueux* were not intellectual or disinterested converts to Calvinism; they had their own fish to fry. At Antwerp, the well-off merchants prominent in the Calvinist consistory were Marcus Perez, who belonged to a celebrated Jewish family and had as a child been brought there by his parents from his birthplace at Saragossa in Spain, and Giles Hooftman, who had risen by his own efforts from obscurity to wealth and was discontented with the commercial policy of the lords of the town. There is no reason to doubt the sincerity of their religious beliefs – in particular, there is no evidence that Perez wavered in his acceptance of Christianity.[21] But neither belonged by origin to the established order, and thus each was *prima facie* likely to be all the more uninhibited in his aspirations. A disapproval of temporal regulations and a dislike of the ecclesiastical order were easy to conflate in an age when church and state were so intertwined in their jurisdictions. As far as the government at Brussels was concerned, the really ominous fact was the *entente* that made some of the money of the Antwerp capitalists available to the landed gentry, and conversely lent much greater power of political expression to the dissident Antwerpians: conjoined, the allies counted for much more than the sum of their parts. In addition, their acceptance of Calvinist discipline with the consistory system put at their disposal a remarkable technique of social and political organization. The sympathies and energies of many ordinary people might now be galvanized and directed into whatever channels the Calvinist leaders thought fit. A conflagration much more serious than the destruction of images was not impossible. For kindling it, there was much social tinder.[22]

Heresy had a long history in the Netherlands, and Antwerp was understandably notorious as its centre. Many of the skilled artisans who comprised so large a proportion of the population of the city may well have been acquainted and even in sympathy with either the anabaptism indigenous to their country or the heresies affected by the various foreign communities in their midst. But in the summer of 1566 there were some broad-based psychological reasons for the popular discharge of some resentment against the established church. There was a lack of alternative targets, and there was much pent-up emotion. The workfolk of the city had until recently known good times. Their real wages had tended to rise from c. 1542, at first gradually and then from 1557 very sharply. There was a shortage of labour to meet the demands both of the building industry and of foreign trade, and in the early sixties there were middle-class outcries at excessive wages and the spendthrift ease of the artisans. This otherwise happy epoch was abruptly cut short by the cessation of the English cloth traffic in 1563–4. The skilled craftsmen who finished the English cloths lost their livelihood and descended the social scale, whether to find work in building or simply to become part of the general labour pool. Wages fell. The violent scene at the execution of Fabricius in the autumn afforded an indication of the extent of popular resentment.[23]

Although the English traffic was resumed with ebullience in

January 1565, the hardships of the previous year did not end.
There had been a poor harvest in the autumn, so that a scarcity
of corn soon made itself felt. Poor people were affected by the
exceptionally severe weather – so cold as to freeze both Thames
and Scheldt. Worst of all, the Sound, through which imports of
Baltic corn had to pass, was closed by order of the King of
Denmark. His purpose in doing this was merely to deprive his
enemy the King of Sweden of his contacts with western
armament-makers, but the action incidentally cut the Netherlands off from their marginal source of food. The revival of the
English cloth trade was therefore offset by the rocketing price of
corn, which nearly doubled in the first five months of 1565.
When the Sound momentarily passed under Swedish control,
the Regent in vain dispatched an envoy to Stockholm to secure
passage for Netherlands shipping. The King of Sweden did in
the end agree to re-open the waterway, but on the demand, not
of the Netherlands government but of the King of Poland. Even
this freeing of the corn trade did little to improve the situation.
The corn merchants, speculating upon the yield of the forthcoming harvest, preferred to hoard their purchases, or to divert
shipments to France, where even better prices might be expected. When the government at Brussels tried to clip the activities of speculators by forbidding the export of corn, shipments
from the Baltic were landed at Emden, beyond its reach. The
Regent arranged for some emergency imports from Spain, but
these do not seem to have affected prices significantly. Only at
the end of May 1566 was the corn dealers' ring broken. The
price of corn then fell towards its pre-crisis level.[24]

As far as the Antwerp working-class was concerned, there had
thus been a multiple three-year crisis, 1563–6, during which its
way of living had been seriously threatened, even if few had
actually starved. The social pattern underlying the sequence of
events that reached a climax in the sacking of the churches at
Antwerp on August 20 was therefore not dominated by a
famished proletariat but, more dangerously, by an artisan class
that for three years had been facing an unpleasant descent of its
standard of life. We may suspect that its feelings had been
sharpened by observations – that its difficulties were not shared
by the rich merchants who hoarded corn, nor by the rulers of
the Netherlands at Brussels – where during the autumn of 1565
the marriage of the son of the Regent to a Portuguese princess
was celebrated amid scenes of tactless pomp and splendour.

With the dispersal of the clouds towards the end of May 1566, the prevailing attitude of mind may be explained. There was a feeling of release, a general euphoria, a readiness to accept a new message, even a new gospel, characteristic of mass psychology on the lifting of danger.[25] This is not to deny that there were plenty of very poor people in Antwerp – there certainly were. The city teemed with youths who had come hopefully or desperately to seek a living there, or others who simply wanted to hide and lose their identity. There were obscure splinter groups of heretics that ranged from a few individuals meeting together to pray, to secret societies, some with a criminal tinge, and to organized bands of desperadoes. There were all too many ready to loot. But these were not the folk who almost made a revolution in the summer and autumn of 1566. This was the handiwork of honest artisans who were thankful at the return to tolerable conditions and responded to the newly-organized sermons with their rousing appeals to cast out idolatry from their hearts and their worship.

Meanwhile, the events of July and August at Antwerp thoroughly frightened the business community there, especially the many foreign merchants. As soon as open heretical preaching began, the Italians and Spaniards were quick to protest to the lords of the town, confessing that they feared for their own personal safety and that they would have to depart if the sermons were not stopped.[26] Their perturbation was all the more intense when it became evident that the lords of the town were quite incapable of achieving this. Orange on his arrival lost no time in reporting to the Regent how the merchants, citizens and inhabitants of Antwerp were nonplussed by the disobedient gatherings outside the walls, whose effect was to cut down business and bring their usual traffic to an end.[27] Already, so many of the southern merchants had gone that the postmaster reckoned that the mail collected for Italy had fallen to less than half of its usual weight.[28] A little later, it was being reported how the Italians and Spaniards had sent away most of their wares, and that the further removal of goods had been forbidden, presumably by the lords of Antwerp, save to England or France. The southerners had mostly not gone very far; many had got no further than Mechelen, though some were considering a move to Bruges and some to Middelburg. But business was disrupted and the city 'marvellously desolated'.[29] Ready money disappeared from the Bourse; the Regent was led to be believe that the merchants had dispatched out of the country what they could by exchange or other means.[30] Early in August, Orange himself addressed the foreign communities, requesting them to continue in their traffic as usual, lest by their absence the common folk be roused to commit some disorder; with one voice, he assured the Regent, they promised him that they would do this.[31] But he was too late: it was just at this time that the Florentine agent wrote home to report that trade was virtually at a standstill.[32]

The evidence thus strongly suggests that many merchants, including most of the southerners, had fled from Antwerp before the sacking of the churches on August 20. The outbreak of that day, though organized by a small minority, stunned the city. For a number of weeks to come, the remaining well-to-do were 'in great fear of some commotion'.[33] An attempt to enter and loot the mansion of the mercantile Lucchese family of Affaitadi was actually made on 19 September and foiled only by the stout defence put up by the inmates.[34] The Bourse was dead, and bills of exchange signed by Antwerp merchants were not accepted elsewhere.[35] Ecclesiastics doffed their distinctive attire while the jingling phrase ran current, *Papen bloet, Papisten goet*, i.e. 'we will have the blood of the priests and the property of the papists'.[36] For the moment, the city seemed to lie in the grip of the Calvinists. On Sunday August 25, the pulpits of the ruined churches were occupied by Calvinist ministers, though their sermons were not delivered without some opposition.[37] Two days previously, the Regent in her weakness had published – by agreement with the leaders of the *Gueux* – a compromise order that none should be molested in the practice of his religion. This proclamation cut both ways. It certainly gave the congregations attending Calvinist preaching some security, but it also entitled the catholics to worship in their churches. The use of the churches now became the immediate practical issue around which political negotiations converged.

The progress of revolution was halted by the actions of Orange, who before the end of the month had returned to Antwerp. The forces of law and order gradually recovered heart. Among the first actions of the Prince was the public hanging of three convicted malefactors in the marketplace before the Town Hall, for pillaging churches and committing sacrilege.[38] He also made sure that on the next Sunday, September 1, Mass was being sung once more in some of the churches.

But as a step towards a general pacification he now entered into an agreement with the Calvinist leaders of Antwerp by which in return for the use of three churches within the walls they undertook that their followers would not be armed, nor seditious or insulting in their bearing, and that the catholics would not be disturbed in their use of the other churches. His diagnosis of the situation that drove him to this step was clear and probably accurate. Despite the close watch at the gates, all sorts of people were filtering into the city. As a result of the general cessation of business throughout the Netherlands, the countryside was full of vagabonds and workless, who if the sermons continued to be preached outside the walls might easily slip into Antwerp with the returning congregations. There, they would reinforce the great number of workfolk in the city who 'as a consequence of these troubles and the stoppage of merchandise' lacked the wherewithal to maintain themselves, their wives and their children. Together, they might rise and sack the city, 'the most opulent in the whole country and the place where there is most to loot'. Orange believed that many were hoping just for this.[39] His alarm was fortified by the knowledge that within Antwerp lurked many anabaptists and libertines.[40] On merely ecclesiastical issues he was prepared to bargain, but as a champion of the social order he was unflinching.

Orange's working agreement with the Antwerp Calvinists went further than the Regent could be expected to accept. She could not approve the handling of churches over to heretics; in all the other towns of the Netherlands, 'which have their eyes glued to Antwerp', she feared that corresponding concessions would be expected.[41] The upshot of this was that the agreement was revised. The heretics ceased to have the use of any church, but were permitted to build within the walls at their own expense five *temples*, three for Calvinists and two for Lutherans – the latter doubtless at the insistence of the German element and perhaps with the sympathy of Orange, though he tactfully avoided being drawn in to lay any foundation-stone.[42] These buildings, erected with speed and enthusiasm, had a short life, co-terminous with the six months' freedom of worship that the heretics were to enjoy. Their spirits began to flag with the realization that they were after all not a majority and that the government was gradually accumulating the forces to put them down. On September 4, Orange again assembled representatives of the foreign merchant communities, and this time with greater

plausibility assured them that they might now put fear aside as
the troubles were over. He asked them to bring back their
colleagues to trade freely as before, adding that if they wanted
anything for their further assurance he would do his best to
supply it.[43] This appeal evidently met with some response, since
a month later he was able to report to the Regent how despite
the harrassing of catholic services in the churches the city gilds
were beginning to function and trade was again flowing.[44] Before departing to his governorship in Holland on October 12, he
called before him once again representatives of the foreign
traders, more of whom had returned, thanking them for the
continuance of their traffic. He added that he would soon be
back and that they might meanwhile go about their business
without fear.[45] This encouragement was underlined a few days
later when six men who attempted to raise a riot in the collegiate
church were speedily caught and hanged. As Fitzwilliams told
Cecil, 'this execution hath somewhat stayed their humours', and
the city was now quieter.[46]

Before long, Calvinists and Lutherans began to bicker among
themselves, and in the new year the catholic reaction gathered
strength.[47] The final loss of power by the protestants occurred
very suddenly, as a result of a menacing confrontation of forces
within the city during March 1567. This was the moment at
which count Louis of Nassau, younger brother of Orange, tried
too late to lead a general insurrection in the Netherlands. Inside
Antwerp, business again drew to a standstill and there was
another exodus of nervous merchants, as a force under *Gueux*
leadership appeared and camped only a mile or so outside the
walls. The alarm was great. As Gresham, who happened then to
be at Antwerp, reported to Secretary Cecil, 'this town is in very
hard case, and happy is the man that is out of it'.[48] The critical
hour struck on the morning of March 13, when within sight of
the citizens the *Gueux* were put to flight by some troops dispatched from Brussels by the Regent. The Calvinists inside the
walls had also armed, but they emerged too late to save the day.
They then withdrew and fortfied themselves in and around the
broad street still called the Meir, and challenged the lords of
Antwerp to surrender the keys of the city. The answer of the
lords of Antwerp was to barricade themselves in the Town Hall,
where they were protected by a much smaller mixed force,
marshalled in the marketplace and in the yard of the collegiate
church now known as the Groenplaats. For three days, the

opposing camps faced each other and peace hung by a thread. Once more, cool and skilful mediation on the part of Orange averted bloodshed, pillage and destruction. The confidence of the Calvinists ebbed. By 5 o'clock on the afternoon of March 15 the armed men had vanished and the artillery had been 'carried away into the store-houses as though there had been nothing done in the town'.[49] The revolution had evaporated.

Before the end of April, the Regent in person moved with her court to Antwerp, there to reside for several weeks and complete the pacification. With her came a body of troops, who were installed as a garrison. In her eyes, Antwerp had been the mainspring of all the troubles, the headquarters to which all the heretics in the Netherlands looked for guidance, the place that had recently been threatening to inflate itself into 'another Geneva or Münster'.[50] Even after the suppression of the iconoclasts, weeks had elapsed before masses might be sung in its churches without fear of interruption, and before the clergy could put aside their secular garb and resume their ecclesiastical habit.[51] But now the great city, always recalcitrant and recently rebellious, lay at her feet. The events of the preceding months had left visible scars: the collegiate church was much damaged, its altars dismantled and its pictures torn, and the other churches and abbeys, especially that of the Cordeliers, had also suffered. There was striking evidence of depopulation.[53] The advent of the Regent marked a stage in the return to normality. The heretical sermons were brought to an end, the *temples* were handed over to the soldiers for demolition, and to all outward appearance the conformity of the *ancien régime* was restored.[53] The lords of Antwerp set a contingent of men to work at the repairing of the collegiate church, and in the name of the city they were quick to offer the Regent a gift of 50,000 ducats – about £16,000 sterling – to obtain her pardon for all misdeeds.[54] There were not lacking in her entourage men to urge upon her that this was the opportunity to curb the liberties of the city and symbolically to erase the cheeky SPQA displayed everywhere on its public buildings as if, to quote one such, 'they were a free republic and the prince could order them to nothing without their free consent'.[55]

Characteristically, the Regent hesitated. She took no extreme course. On her orders, a site was selected and the first steps taken towards the erection of a citadel within the walls that for the future should keep the unruly element in order. This was

not an action that necessarily damaged the commercial prospects of Antwerp. Indeed, it was plausibly argued that it restored confidence to the well-off merchants, foreign and native, by
ensuring their 'defence from popular tumults'.[57] So timorous an
attitude was characteristic especially of the Italians and Spaniards, more fearful of heretical outbreaks than the
northerners.[58] As a further precaution, when the customary
invitation to merchants to attend the Sinksen Mart at Whit and
to enjoy the privileges customarily attaching to it was issued,
there were certain categories of person specifically excluded
from the usual safe-conduct: members of the Calvinist consistory, those who had taken up arms against the King, or had
practised treason or had broken images.[59] Although it was said
that this 'much astonished the common people', it was probably
inevitable under the circumstances. Those who had opposed the
will of the King in politics or religion and then admitted their
guilt by taking to flight could hardly expect to return with
impunity to the city for the duration of the fairs. In any case, the
moderate Stralen appeared to be high in the favour of the
Regent, and he was known to be pressing the opinion still prevalent among the lords of Antwerp, that any great severity in
matters of religion would scare away the foreign merchants and
thus endanger the life of the city.[60]

For the lords of Antwerp, this was indeed the capital question
that stared them in the face. How far, if at all, might it be taken
for granted in an age of religious cleavages that the enforcement
of uniformity of ecclesiastical observance was compatible with
the prosperity of a commercial metropolis where traders from
all lands were encouraged to come and bring their traffic? The
timorous Mediterranean merchants who had fled from Antwerp
in the summer of 1566 had made their way back when the
Calvinists were silenced.[61] But now, there was another emigration of a different religious hue and far greater in size. For the
thousands who had committed themselves in word or deed to
the new religion, the restoration of royal authority was fraught
with threats.[61] Already in April 1567 the Regent was lamenting
to the King how the guilty ones, of whom, as she reminded him,
there was a great multitude at Antwerp, were seeking refuge in
flight, some to France, others to England, Scotland, Cleves,
Emden and elsewhere in Germany.[63] Over a month later, she
was reporting that these departures were not ceasing, in numbers that could serve to populate whole towns, so that business

was being paralyzed. Practical arts, with manufacturing and business skills of all sorts, were being transported away, to the benefit of adjacent countries. She argued that since the guilty persons were so numerous, it would be impossible to punish them all without depopulating and ruining not merely Antwerp but the whole Netherlands, and that the only solution was to issue a general pardon – with, of course, certain necessary qualifications. This she was bold enough to authorize on May 24, without waiting for authority from the King.[64]

Philip learnt of her action with indignation, and with a promptitude unusual for him instructed her at once to revoke it.[65] It was duly annulled by a special letter to the Margrave of Antwerp dated July 23.[66] A large number of citizens of all classes, if they chose to remain at Antwerp, therefore stood liable to severe punishment whenever thoroughgoing investigations into the events of 1566–7 might be started. In the face of the continuing exodus of inhabitants, the lords of Antwerp were thrown into great trepidation. They implored the Regent to revisit their city to witness for herself the general alarm, to intercede with the King for at least a period of grace during which incriminated persons might arrange in orderly fashion for their departure, and for some assurances to be given to the foreign merchants.[67] No doubt the lords of Antwerp were only too well aware that time was running short, since Spanish troops under the command of the Duke of Alva had already crossed the southern frontier into the Netherlands and were expected before long at Brussels. But the most revealing commentary on the outlook at Antwerp was a fall in house rents, reversing a trend of long duration. The city had passed its population peak.[68]

Throughout the months of tumult during 1566 and 1567, the English at Antwerp preserved their detachment. At the beginning, there had been a suspicion at the court of the Regent that the Governor and other important members of the Company of Merchants Adventurers were in active league with the heretics of Antwerp, but no practical evidence of this could be unearthed.[69] Gresham's manager Clough was disgusted to learn that among those pillaging the Antwerp churches after the outbreak on August 20 were criminals who had escaped from England; and one of the three men executed by order of Orange just a week later for theft and sacrilege was English.[70] A couple of English merchants, very exceptionally, had got involved in the Calvinist movement at Bergen-op-Zoom.[71] But by and large, the English had little or no connection with the disturbances. The cloth fleet in the spring of 1566 had come and gone before the open preaching of heretical sermons began, so that there must have been relatively few Englishmen in Antwerp during the hectic months of July and August. Then, before the next cloth fleet arrived, for the Cold Mart at the end of October, the sharpest paroxysms were over. After all, the Londoners came to Antwerp strictly on business, departing as soon as it was concluded; their minds were on the disposal of their wares, on the exactions of the customs officials, or on the legal uncertainties of their position.[72] On the decisive occasion of 15 March 1567, when a pitched battle between the Calvinists and the papists in the streets of Antwerp seemed imminent, Orange bade the English remain indoors – armed – to protect their property. They had therefore no share in the dramatic events of the day at the end of which Orange, happening to pass the English House, took the opportunity to halt and offer his 'thanks unto the Company for that they used themselves so quietly'.[73]

We may be sure that this aloof attitude was in accordance with the views of the Queen – perhaps she had passed on her wishes through Secretary Cecil to Governor Marsh. She was never in doubt as to the duty of subjects to obey their prince, and from the first she thoroughly disapproved of the agitations of Brederode and the *Gueux*.[74] To the Spanish ambassador she protested in all sincerity that the heretical preachings in the Netherlands were 'a great insolence and evil', and she repeatedly professed to rejoice in the forthcoming arrival of the King to chastise the rebels.[75] In addition, the general loss of confidence incommoded the dealings of the English crown on the Bourse at Antwerp, where even during the early months of 1566 money was tight. By August, Clough was reporting in alarm that he could find nobody willing to lend for the repayment of bonds that were about to mature, 'all men here being clean out of money.'[76] Unfortunately, it was just at this time that the Queen was seeking not merely to re-borrow 32,000 Flemish pounds now due, but also to raise a further 20,000, for expenses in Ireland.[77] Clough in his next letter lamented how the financiers Christopher Pruin and Giles Hooftman were badgering him daily for repayment, and all he could do was 'to give fair words'. Money there was, he believed, but its owners 'are in doubt to whom to deliver it because of this troublesome time', and he added that if Gresham himself came, 'your presence would help

in the matter'.[78] Evidently the troubles in the Netherlands had a
more incisive impact upon the royal finances than upon the
cloth traffic of the Merchants Adventurers.

Gresham left London on August 23. In the course of his
journey he learnt of the iconoclastic outbreak at Antwerp, and
he was appalled by what he found on reaching his destination six
days later. His factor Clough had warned him beforehand that
'all kind of merchandise' was 'at a stay and most men of reputation fled abroad' and that Antwerp was 'in danger to be spoiled
for that all the vagabonds of the country draw to this town'.[79] He
himself was invited on arrival to dinner with Orange, who
warned him that Philip II was unlikely to rest content with the
existing state of affairs and enquired if the English were
'minded to depart this town or not'. Gresham reported to Secretary Cecil in alarm that he 'liked none of their proceedings' but
apprehended 'great mischief', and urged that the English government should 'do very well in time to consider some other
realm and place' for marketing English products.[80] It was a
message that helped to shape the course of events.[81] Gresham
meanwhile explored the financial world, reporting home how he
had 'gone through all the money men by one practice or other'
only to learn that 'there was not a penny to be had'. Only three
days earlier, Giovanni Balbani, of the well-known Lucchese
banking family, had gone bankrupt for 40,000 pounds Flemish,
and confidence in the other Italians had evaporated. From this
ticklish situation he extricated himself, as he sought to show,
with great mastery. There was more borrowing at London,
where he used his personal credit to put £2,000 on the exchange
for Antwerp. But for the most part he solved the Queen's problems by tapping the resources of banking firms outside the
Netherlands. The Welsers of Augsburg had a new agent at
Antwerp; by a great stroke of luck, he proved willing to lend to the
English crown, unlike his predecessor. The representatives of a
couple of other Augsburg finance houses also were found amen-
able. Then there was a promise of something from Maurice
Rantzau of Holstein. In this way, the emergency was tided over,
and after giving a banquet to the Queen's creditors 'both young
and old', Gresham departed after an unusually brief sojourn.[82]

In the ensuing months, a tendency to cut down financial
obligations to Netherlands firms persisted. In December 1566,
Giles Hooftman was dunning Clough hard for repayment of
what was owed to him by the English crown. He had, he alleged,

no other way of satisfying those from whom he in turn, genuine banker as he was, had borrowed the money. 'With much ado', he was persuaded to defer repayment until February.[83] By then, the Queen's liabilities amounted to some 49,000 pounds Flemish, and Clough was urging Gresham that he would have to come in person again.[84] This he duly did, his instructions being dated 22 February 1567. They envisaged his taking up 20,000 pounds Flemish by exchange from London, and thus extinguishing so much of the foreign debt; and providing for most of the remainder by plumbing the money market at Cologne.[85] Fortunately, there was no need to pursue these emergency methods – as Gresham did not fail to point out, the transmission of so large a sum by exchange would have led to a most inconvenient fall in the value of the pound sterling. Most of the old creditors now proved willing to prolong their debts for another six months.[86] This was a surprise, but it may perhaps be ascribed to the deteriorating political situation. The outlook for anyone prominently involved in recent events in the Netherlands was rapidly becoming very bleak. Perez by March 1567 was sounding Gresham to learn if he might seek asylum in England; before the end of the month he had followed Orange to Breda.[87] He ultimately settled as a respectable merchant in the Swiss city of Basel.[88] The position of Giles Hooftman, the largest creditor of the English crown, was very insecure; perhaps he was conscious of the advantage of having so much capital safely lodged in a protestant country – though in the end he reverted to the official religion and, perhaps with the aid of Assonleville, managed to make his peace with the government at Brussels.[89] English crown debts at Antwerp were further diminished during the summer of 1567 by piecemeal remittances.[90] The Queen was turning more and more to the London market for her needs.

The restoration of royal authority over Antwerp and the Netherlands by the summer of 1567 could not prevent some very large wheels from continuing to revolve. King Philip at Madrid had learnt of the Calvinist outbreaks with horror and anger, and in the autumn of 1566 he was moved to take the most far-reaching decision of his life: the cold and deliberate resolution to subjugate the Netherlands by the employment of Spanish troops. For financing this extraordinary operation he had available an enhanced stream of silver from the New World: never enough, but there was further revenue to be extracted from the seventeen provinces. The agent selected by the King for the execution of the project was his intimate councillor the Duke of Alva; once he had done his work, the King proposed to come in person to establish a lasting settlement. The preliminaries mean-while took many months. In December 1566, Alva received his commission and left Madrid to mobilize his troops in Italy.[91] He was served with highly confidential instructions to put an end to local autonomy and to prepare the way for fusing all the pro-vinces into a unitary state of which Brussels was to be the capital 'as Paris in France'.[92] The following summer his army of occupa-tion made its ponderous way northwards, keeping just to the east of the French frontier; he himself, preceded by scarifying rumours that were all too soon borne out by events, reached Brussels in mid August, to meet with a correct but icy reception from the Regent.[93]

Before long, his troops were in possession of all strongholds in the Netherlands. The country lay in the grip of a military government, all constitutional niceties being overridden. The Regent for some weeks continued to protest to Philip II that the merciless measures now being enforced would not stop the flight of the inhabitants who were enriching neighbouring countries with their 'money, bills of exchange, or merchandise and skills', and that only the issue of a general pardon would end the haemorrhage.[94] Her advice was no longer heeded. In October the King accepted her resignation, and at the end of December she left the Netherlands for Italy.

The English reaction to the installation of Alva and his troops in the Netherlands was profound. Elizabeth and her councillors were as much alarmed by the return of Spanish soldiers to northern Europe as they had been relieved by their departure in 1560.[95] They were painfully conscious that once more they had the greatest military power of Christendom as a close neighbour. The Spanish envoy at London, Silva, found in the summer of 1567 that the Queen in conversation with him came back again and again to this topic, and all his skill was needed to assuage her nervousness.[96] News of the occupation of the Netherlands by Spanish forces was received with dismay. Bragging talk on the part of Alva's soldiers against the English was duly reported back to London, accompanied by hair-raising tales of their disci-pline and skill – so precise, that when the cavalry bodyguard of the Duke fired a ceremonial salvo, 'the horses never stirred more than if they had been abroad in the fields'.[97] As to the intentions of Alva, Gresham was able to supply Cecil with authentic details of his purpose to subvert the ancient liberties of the seventeen provinces – which the news of the arrests and executions seemed to confirm.[98] Elizabeth professed to take offence at the failure of Alva to send her any official notice of his establishment as her neighbour until February 1568, when he wrote to announce his accession to the government of the Netherlands, assuring her at the same time of his readiness to do her service and of his concern for the maintenance of the traditional amity.[99] Her acknowledgement was cool. She thanked him for the news of his appointment, adding drily that she 'had heard long since of the same by other means', and warning him of the disruptive tendencies of merchants – i.e., the Antwerp rivals of the Merchants Adventurers – whose devices were undermining the Intercourse.[100] In taking this line, the Queen was hardly being fair, since until the departure of the Regent at the very end of 1567 Alva was no more than captain-general of the Spanish forces in the Netherlands, and in fact he could not have been appreciably more prompt in his address. But the episode added another item to Anglo-Netherlands misunderstandings.

In France, too, the presence of Alva in the Netherlands was similarly misinterpreted, though probably with more reason. In September 1567, the Huguenot leaders felt sufficiently in danger to take to arms and attempt to seize the person of their King, Charles IX. The civil war that followed was ended by the Peace of Longjumeau the following March, but before long the French protestants were again in arms. From September 1568 onwards they had a capital of their own at the Atlantic port of La Rochelle, which now entered upon its stormy career as the headquarters of heresy in France. One powerful stimulus to Huguenot risings was a belief, devoid of a basis of fact but none the less strong, that Catherine de Médicis and Philip II had entered into a murderous conspiracy to extirpate heresy, and that when Alva had completed his task in the Netherlands it would be the turn of France. Similar suspicions mounted in England, where hostility to Alva on religious grounds was not confined to refugees from the Netherlands. There were also those, like Cecil, who felt a political objection to the erection of a centralized catholic state under Spanish control in the Netherlands. Orange, on whom a suspicion of unreliability in politics as in religion had now descended, and who had prudently withdrawn to his estates in Germany, played upon this: in February 1568 he wrote to the Queen to denounce Alva as the tyrant who wanted not merely 'to extirpate the poor Christians and seigneurs who bear some affection to religion and the public weal' but also to reduce the seventeen provinces to 'an extreme calamity and servitude'.[101] When in the following summer the attempt of his brother Louis of Nassau to raise a revolt in the Netherlands came to grief, Elizabeth took serious notice. Cecil was glad to observe that she was now beginning 'to give some hearing to such as think her security can not have continuance'.[102] The presence of Alva in the Netherlands thus conjured into existence a sort of protestant international, overleaping political frontiers, with a membership ranging from Orange and his supporters in Germany to the Huguenot leaders in France and a number of influential persons at the court of the Queen of England.

To the English, the military threat seemed to be underlined by news of the brutality of the Spanish soldiery in the Netherlands, and of the rough handling of inoffensive citizens at Brussels, Ghent, Louvain and elsewhere. Lists of the murders, rapes and pillagings committed by the Spaniards were soon circulating, and were confirmed by the arrival of refugees.[103] Much interest was focussed on the fate of Egmont and Hoorn, the most prominent among the many Netherlanders to be clapped into prison. Merchants acquainted with Antwerp could not fail to be moved by the inclusion in the first batch of arrests of Stralen, who was taken while trying to escape. He could not be proved a heretic, but in implementing the peacemaking policy of the lords of Antwerp he had negotiated with heretics and rebels, and so connived at treason. He was summarily tried and put to death before the end of September. There was a rumour, in time proved false, that a similar fate was reserved for Gresham's friend Jasper Schetz, and other Antwerp notables.[104] To edify the Antwerp populace, four anabaptists were publicly burnt on September 13 – the first martyrs since the execution of Fabricius in October 1564. But Alva was a well-informed man; unlike the ignorant seigneurs who had preceded him in power, he was anxious to avoid damaging the entrepôt traffic of Antwerp. The town was not required at once to house Spanish troops, the relatively well-behaved garrison left by the Regent being allowed to remain.[105] In any case, the business community was not by any means hostile to the new regime, however bloodthirsty and repulsive some of its measures. The Italian and Spanish merchants were not the only inhabitants to welcome a firm government that gave them security. A visible token of this was the castle, whose building was resolutely taken in hand, on a site outside the walls. Alva summoned the lords of Antwerp to Brussels to secure the finance for this project – some doubted if they would return alive – and after receiving some demurs he paid a prolonged visit to Antwerp in person, to press them further and expedite matters.[106]

The English at Antwerp were naturally alarmed by 'a talk that all customs should be risen here, both inward and outward, and no man to be free', in order to finance the erection of the castle. It was known that Alva would not brook denial, and there was news of how he had uttered 'great words' to the lords of Antwerp at their Town Hall.[107] But in the end, it was learnt that the extra taxation was chiefly going to take the form of levies on real property, together with enhanced exise and octroi duties – pressing hardly enough on the people, but not putting the shopsoiled remains of the Intercourse in further jeopardy.[108] When the time for assessment of the new taxes came at Antwerp, every effort was made to spare the English, including those who owned houses there.[109] Thus the cloth traffic was not directly harmed by the fiscal measures of the new government, however harshly they bore on native Netherlanders. The banking world was somewhat more sensitive to events, if only because the imparting of news or opinions on public affairs had become dangerous. The Bourse in the autumn of 1567 hummed with unverifiable rumours, there was a widespread nervousness, and the pound Flemish sank beyond 23 shillings sterling.[110] A small recovery of the pound Flemish in December caused Clough to warn his master to have as little as possible to do with the exchange, its movements being so erratic.[111] Meanwhile, Gresham agreed with Clough that the relatively high value of the pound sterling presented the Queen with an apt opportunity to pay off more of her Netherlands debts.[112] Indeed, the scene was by no means one of unrelieved gloom. There was said to be 'great plenty of money' on the Bourse in early September, and in October Clough was busy operating for Gresham on his personal account as well as on behalf of the crown, and was also taking up sums for the Earls of Pembroke, Sussex and Leicester.[113]

In fact, the nervousness on the Antwerp Bourse was political in origin, and at least in part traceable to fears and rumours of an incursion by Huguenot forces across the Franco-Netherlands frontier. The English at home, even less in contact with reality, developed their own particular bogeys, Gresham going so far as to predict in October 1567 that 'all exchanges and trades of merchandise will grow to nothing' at Antwerp.[114] His reasons for this dismal outlook were emotive and intuitive rather than rational. His agent Dutton had made the unsupported allegation in a letter that 'there is some great mischief meant towards us' in the Netherlands, and Clough was scared by the reports of casual talk among the soldiers to the effect that they would soon 'have a say' with England, and by his observations of how the military strength was building up.[115] But there is not the faintest evidence to suggest that at this time either Alva or his master harboured any hostile intentions. Even if Philip II had not been fully engaged with continental and Mediterranean problems, he was not so foolish as deliberately to antagonize the ally who provided the maritime route linking Spain and the Netherlands with its only friendly coast. As to Alva, he loyally executed the cruel orders of the King. But his purposes were primarily local and political, and he did not consider heresy outside the Netherlands his responsibility. Unfortunately, there was no English envoy at Brussels to interpret the policy of the Netherlands government to the Queen of England, and the English ambassador at Madrid was ineffective and soon to be disgraced. Communication between Philip II and Alva on the one hand, and the Queen of England on the other, thus depended entirely upon the Spanish envoy at her court, Silva. He was an efficient go-between, but unluckily for the smooth conduct of Anglo-Netherlands relations he chose to relinquish his post in the course of the next year.

The failure of the abortive Netherlands revolution that had centred upon Antwerp produced no immediately disastrous impact upon the traffic of the Merchants Adventurers. The English had at the outset of the crisis made an involuntary contribution towards intensifying Netherlands troubles by the diversion of their trade in 1564 to Emden. But the Merchants Adventurers sedulously remained no more than spectators of the cascade of revolutionary incidents two years later. As far as Anglo-Netherlands trade was concerned, the most ominous developments were the precautionary measures adopted on the initiative of the English crown – the resumption of negotiations with Hamburg and the replacement of the two annual cloth fleets by small groups of ships sailing at more frequent

intervals.[116] The events of 1566–7 led also to some slight deterioration of the legal position of the English merchants at
Antwerp, apparent when they made the disconcerting discovery
that they would have difficulty in collecting debts due from cloth
purchasers who had fled or been arrested – their property being
all claimed as forfeited to the King by the government at Brussels. By far the deepest damage was political and emotional.
Opinion in the City and at the court of the Queen was stirred by
news of the arrests and executions carried out on the orders of
Alva, and Elizabeth herself grew anxious at the presence of
the Spanish troops in the Netherlands. All over north-western
Europe, the protestants were alerted to a new sense of danger
and to the need to concert their defences. Before long, rebellion
and battle were to be the common misfortune of all countries.
For what span of time might the peaceful traffic of the merchants between London and Antwerp continue inviolate?

NOTES TO CHAPTER III

[1] There is a survey of the sequence of events at Antwerp in 1566–7 by R. van
Roosbroeck, *Het Wonderjaar te Antwerpen (1566–1567)*, Antwerp and Louvain,
1930, of which use has been made throughout this chapter. There is an interpretation from a different standpoint by P. Mack, 'The Wonderyear. Reformed
Preaching and Iconoclasm in the Netherlands', *Religion and the People, 800–1700*,
ed. J. Obelkevich (Chapel Hill, North Carolina, 1979) 191–220; see also the
essays edited by F. Petri, *Kirche und gesellschaftlicher Wandel in deutschen und
niederländischen Städten* (Köln-Wien, 1980), particularly that by R. van Roosbroeck, 'Wunderjahr oder Hungerjahr? – Antwerpen 1566', 169–96.
[2] Castillo to Granvelle, 31 March and 20 April 1566, Poullet, Granvelle, 183
and 219.
[3] For the Sinksen Mart, at Whitsun, see *ante*, 2.
[4] These points figure in the rebuke of the Regent to the Antwerp chapter, 5
November 1565, Gachard, *Correspondance de Philippe II*, II, 530–1.
[5] Letters exchanged between Regent and Council of Brabant, January–March
1566, *ib.*, 534–50.
[6] *Ante*, 21.
[7] The quotations in the two paragraphs above are taken from the letters of
Fitzwilliams to Cecil, 14 July 1566, KL, IV, 308–11n; Keyle to Cecil, 30 June and
5 July, *ib.*, 305–7 and 308–13; Clough to Gresham, 10 July, *ib.*, 313–15. For a
general narrative, see Rachfahl, *Wilhelm von Oranien*, II, 639 *et seq.*
[8] Keyle to Cecil, 5 July 1566, KL, IV, 305–7, reported how one of the Antwerp
preachers had been 'sent by the Count Palatine of the Rhine'.
[9] Morillon to Granvelle, 11 July 1566, Poullet, *Granvelle*, I, 352.
[10] Fitzwilliams to Cecil, 14 July 1566, KL, IV, 310n.
[11] For an account of the dilemma of the lords of Antwerp, see Rachfahl,
*Wilhelm von Oranien*, II, 650–1.
[12] Morillon to Granvelle, 13 July 1566, Poullet, *Granvelle*, I, 365.
[13] Keyle to Cecil, 15 July 1566, KL, IV, 318–20.
[14] Berty to Cecil, 20 July 1566, *ib.*, 322–3.

[15] Morillon to Granvelle, 31 March 1566, Poullet, *Granvelle*, I, 193.

[16] Clough to Gresham, 22 July 1566, KL, IV, 327–9.

[17] *Ib.* to *ib.*, 11 August 1566, *ib.*, 334–5.

[18] Morillon to Granvelle, 28 July 1566, Poullet, *Granvelle*, I, 388.

[19] Clough to Gresham, 21 and 25 August 1566, KL, IV, 337–9 and 341–4. For Gresham's earlier business at Antwerp, see *ante, passim.*

[20] *Ib.*, to *ib.*, 25 August 1566, *ib.*, 341.

[21] The career of Perez has been examined by P. J. Hauben, 'Marcus Perez and Marrano Calvinism in the Dutch Revolt and the Reformation', *Bibliotheque d'Humanisme et Renaissance*, XXIX (1967), 121–32. Hooftman is noticed in the Belgian *Biographie Nationale*; see also *supra*, 22. Perez had married into the family of Lopez de Villanova, which has been investigated by B. A. Vermaseren, 'De Antwerpse koopman Martin Lopez en zijn familie in de zestiende en het begin van de zeventiende eeuw', *Bijdragen tot de Geschiedenis*, 56 (1973), 3–79.

[22] This and the following two paragraphs in particular owe much to E. Kuttner, *Het Hongerjaar 1566* (Amsterdam, 1949) and E. Scholliers, *De Levenstandaard in de XV$^e$ en XVI$^e$ eeuw te Antwerpen* (Antwerp, 1960).

[23] *Ante*, 275–6.

[24] E. C. G. Brunner, 'Die dänische Verkehrssperre und der Bildersturm in den Niederländen im Jahre 1566', *Hansische Geschichtsblätter*, XXXIII(1928), 97–109. See also H. van der Wee, *The Growth of the Antwerp Market and the European Economy* (The Hague, 1963), I, app. i to v in particular.

[25] On this point see N. Cohn, *The Coming of the Millennium*, rev. ed. (London, 1970), 281–6. H. van der Wee, 'The economy as a factor in the start of the revolt in the southern Netherlands', *Acta Historiae Neerlandica*, V(1971), 52–67, is also relevant.

[26] Guicciardini to Francesco de' Medici, 30 June 1566, Battistini, 266; Keyle to Cecil, same date, KL, IV, 305–7.

[27] Orange to Regent, 14 July 1566, Gachard, *Correspondance de Guillaume le Taciturne*, II, 142.

[28] Morillon to Granvelle, 11 July 1566, Poullet, *Granvelle*, I, 355.

[29] Bertie to Cecil, 20 July 1566, KL, IV, 321–4; Gilpin to *ib.*, 21 July 1566, *ib.*, 324–5.

[30] Regent to Philip II, 19 July 1566, Gelder, *MP*, II, 264.

[31] Orange to Regent, 5 August 1566, Gachard, *Correspondance de Guillaume le Taciturne*, II, 178–9.

[32] Guicciardini to Francesco de' Medici, 4 August 1566, Battistini, 269.

[33] Gilpin to Killigrew, 25 August 1566, KL, IV, 344–5; Castillo to Granvelle, 6 October 1566, Poullet, *Granvelle*, III, 16.

[34] Morillon to Granvelle, 22 September 1566, *ib.*, I, 492.

[35] Castillo to Granvelle, 6 October 1566, *ib.*, III, 16.

[36] Archbishop of Cambrai to Granvelle, 4 October 1566, *ib.*, 2.

[37] Clough to Gresham, 25 August 1566, KL, IV, 341–4.

[38] Orange to Regent, 28 August 1566, Gachard, *Correspondance de Guillaume le Taciturne*, II, 197–8.

[39] *Ib.* to *ib.*, 4 September 1566, *ib.*, 214 – a very notable dispatch. The terms of the agreement with the Calvinists are in *ib.*, 215–18.

[40] *Ib.* to *ib.*, 9 September 1566, *ib.*, 229.

[41] Regent to Orange, 3, 6 and 9 September 1566, *ib.*, 212, 224 and 226–7.

[42] Morillon to Granvelle, 29 September 1566, Poullet, *Granvelle*, I, 500.

[43] Orange to Regent, 5 September 1566, Gachard, *Correspondance de Guillaume le Taciturne*, II, 222–3.

[44] Regent to Philip II, 27 September and 10 October 1566, Theissen, *MP*, I, 170, 188.

[45] Fitzwilliams to Cecil, 12 October 1566, KL, IV, 361–2.

[46] *Ib.* to *ib.*, 19 October 1566, *ib.*, 364–5.

[47] There is a valuable treatment of this large subject by L. van der Essen, 'Les progrès du luthéranisme et du calvinisme dans le monde commercial d'Anvers et l'espionnage politique du marchand Philippe Dauxy, agent secret de Marguerite de Parme, en 1566–1567', *VSWG*, XII (1914), 152–234.

[48] Gresham to Cecil, 9 March 1567, KL, IV, 421–4. A sombre picture of life at Antwerp was depicted in Regent to Philip II, 5 March 1567, Theissen, *MP*, I, 296.

[49] Gresham to Cecil, 17 March 1567, KL, IV, 438–40. The attitude of Orange is discussed by Rachfahl, *Wilhelm von Oranien*, II, 868 *et seq.*

[50] Regent to Philip II, 27 September 1566, Theissen, *MP*, I, 170; *ib.* to Philip II, 18 December 1566. *Ib.*, I, 232, printed also by Gachard, *Correspondance de Guillaume le Taciturne*, II, xxxiii, n.

[51] Regent to Philip II, 27 September 1566, Theissen, *MP*, I, 170.

[52] Morillon to Granvelle, 9 May 1567, Poullet, *Granvelle*, II, 425.

[53] Edict of the Regent for the pacification of Antwerp, 28 May 1567, *CSPF 1566–8*, No. 1236.

[54] Castillo to Granvelle, 1 May 1567, Poullet, *Granvelle*, II, 425n.

[55] Morillon to Granvelle, 9 May 1567, *ib.*, 426. See *ante*, 15.

[57] Intelligence from the earl of Sussex, 5 July 1567, KL, IV, 471–2. He added the qualification 'if the Inquisition be not offered nor they oppressed with Spaniards'.

[58] Marsh to Cecil, 19 September 1568, KL, V, 163–4.

[59] Morillon to Granvelle, 9 May 1567, Poullet, *Granvelle*, II, 425.

[60] *Ib.*, 426.

[61] Morillon to Granvelle, 13 April 1567, Poullet, *Granvelle*, II, 374.

[62] Regent to Philip II, 30 July 1567, Theissen, *MP*, I, 401–2, put their number at 40,000.

[63] *Ib.* to *ib.*, 12 April 1567, *ib.*, 342.

[64] *Ib.* to *ib.*, 24 May 1567, *ib.*, 363; also *ib.* to Nieuwpoort &c., 7 July 1567, Gachard, *Correspondance de Philippe II*, II, 636–7.

[65] Philip II to Regent, 30 June 1567, Theissen, *MP*, I, 382–3.

[66] Royal letter to Antwerp, 23 July 1567, Gelder, *MP*, III, 339–40.

[67] Antwerp to Regent, 7 August 1567, *Bulletin des Archives d'Anvers*, IX(n.d.), 436–7.

[68] R. Boumans, 'Le dépeuplement d'Anvers dans le dernier quart du XVI$^e$ siecle'. *Revue du Nord*, XXIX (1947), 181–94; E. Scholliers, 'Un indice du loyer: les loyers anversois de 1500 à 1873'. *Studi in onore de Amintore Fanfani*, V (1962), 593–617. Cf. H. van der Wee, *The Growth of the Antwerp Market and the European Economy*, I, app. 40/3 and 40/4.

[69] Silva to Regent, 1 April 1566, KL, IV, 276.

[70] Clough to Gresham, 25 August 1566, *ib.*, 341–4; *supra.*, 43.

[71] *Infra.*, 73.

[72] *Infra.*, 74–5.

[73] Fitzwilliams to Cecil, 16 March 1567, KL, IV, 434–8; Gresham to *ib.*, 17 March 1567, *ib.*, 438–40.

[74] Silva to Philip II, 25 May 1566, *CSPSp. 1558–67*, 552.

[75] *Ib.* to *ib.*, 15 July, 6 September, 5 October, 2 December 1566, 18 January 1567, *ib.*, 566, 577, 583, 589–9 and 610.

[76] Clough to Gresham, 6 August 1566, SP 70/85/504.

[77] *Ib.* to *ib.*, 11 August 1566, KL, IV, 333–6; Cecil to Sidney, 19 July and 13 August 1566, SP 63/18/62 and 81; Queen to Gresham, 11 August 1566, SP 70/85/504.

[78] Clough to Gresham, 11 August 1566, *ut supra*. For Pruin, see *ante*, 29, 129 &c.
[79] Clough to Gresham, 25 August 1566, KL, IV, 341–4. Cited *supra*, n. 37.
[80] Gresham to Cecil, 8 September 1566, *ib.*, 352–4.
[81] *Infra*, 124.
[82] Gresham to Cecil, 1 and 8 September 1566, KL, IV, 348–51 and 352–4.
[83] Clough to Gresham, 1 December 1566, *ib.*, 393–6; *ib.* to *ib.*, 5 December 1566, SP 70/87/680.
[84] Gresham to Cecil, 8 February 1567, SP 70/89/759.
[85] Instructions from Queen to Gresham, 22 February 1567, Lansd. 155, f. 310v; another copy at Egerton 2,790, ff. 73v *et seq.*
[86] Gresham to Cecil, 9 and 11 March 1567, KL, IV, 421–4 and 426–7.
[87] Gresham to Cecil, 9 March, *ut supra*; Clough to Gresham, 29 March 1567, KL, IV, 441–5.
[88] P. J. Hauben, 'Marcus Perez and Marrano Calvinism' *ut supra*, 131.
[89] Morillon to Granvelle, 24 May 1567, Poullet, *Granvelle*, II, 467–8 and note.
[90] Gresham to Cecil, 27 June 1567, SP 70/91/1075; Hugh Clough to *ib.*, 1 October 1567, SP 70/94/1347.
[91] Man to Cecil, 19 December 1566, Pepys Papers, I, 655. Philip II announced his appointment as Captain-General of the Spanish forces in the Netherlands in a letter dated 30 December, Theissen, *MP*, I, 240. Since this book was drafted, there has appeared a biography of Alva by W. S. Maltby (University of California Press, 1984).
[92] Printed by A. L. E. Verheyden, *Le Conseil des Troubles. Liste des condamneés (1567–1573)*. Commission Royale d'Histoire (Brussels, 1961), 508.
[93] The mission of Alva was described in some unforgettable pages by J. L. Motley, *The Rise of the Dutch Republic* (London, 1903), II, 112 *et seq.* For the northward movement of his troops see G. Parker, *The Army of Flanders and the Spanish Road 1567–1659* (Cambridge, 1972), 80–101.
[94] Regent to Philip II, 11 September and 4 October 1567, Theissen, *MP*, I, 412 and 418.
[95] *Ante*, 121.
[96] Silva to Philip II, 21 July and 4 August 1567, *CSPSp. 1558–67*, 659 and 671.
[97] Clough to Gresham, 26 October 1567, KL, V, 32–4.
[98] Gresham to Cecil, 16 October 1567, SP 70/94/1373; Alva's alleged instructions are printed by KL, V, 38–41n. On the authority of Alva, see the remarks of Parker, *The Spanish Road*, 106–10.
[99] Alva to Queen, 7 February 1568, KL, V, 66. The original at SP 70/88/752 is misplaced and the calendared version at *CSPF 1566–8* misdated by a year.
[100] Queen to Alva, 21 February 1568, KL, V, 72.
[101] Orange to Queen, 29 February 1568, KL, V, 75.
[102] Cecil to Sidney, 10 August 1568, SP 63/25/63.
[103] List of complaints against the Spanish soldiers, September 1567, SP 70/94/1346.
[104] Clough to Gresham, 2 September 1567, SP 70/94/1284. The printed version, KL, V, 6–8, is wrongly dated.
[105] Dutton to *ib.*, 7 September 1567, *ib.*, 5.
[106] Clough to *ib.*, *ib.*, 15–18.
[107] Clough to Gresham, 28 September 1567, *ib.*, 15–18.
[108] List in *ib.* to *ib.*, 30 November 1567, *ib.*, 49–52.
[109] Antwerp news-sheet, 12 October 1568, *ib.*, 171–2.
[110] Clough to Gresham, 12, 19 and 26 October 1567, SP 70/94/1373 I, and KL, V, 29 and 32.
[111] *Ib.* to *ib.*, 14 December 1567, *ib.*, 55–6.
[112] *Ib.* to *ib.*, 30 November 1567, *ib.*, 49.

[113] Dutton to Gresham, 7 September 1567, SP 70/94/1293 and Clough to *ib.*, 6 and 26 October 1567, KL, v, 20–3 and 32–4.

[114] Gresham to Cecil, 31 October 1567, SP 70/94/1398.

[115] Dutton to Gresham, 28 September 1567, KL, v, 18–19; Clough to *ib.*, same date, *ib.*, 15–18.

[116] *Supra*, 50 and *infra*. 76–7.

# Chapter IV

## *The crumbling of the old order*

In the history of English overseas trade the four calendar years 1565–8 form a well-defined period. The Antwerp mart now entered the final phase of its dominance. It remained the focus of most large-scale foreign trade, only modest portions of English commerce being carried on with Spanish and even French ports, though the centuries-old import of Gascon wine strongly persisted. But the tentacles of English maritime enterprise hardly extended beyond the seas of north-west Europe. A few ships occasionally made their way beyond Portugal to Morocco or further south, but the commercial route to Italy and the Mediterranean normally lay through Antwerp and over the Alps; any ships passing through the Straits of Gibraltar to or from England were likely to be Italian or Ragusan.[1] Transatlantic ventures were usually bound up with the quest for fish, though John Hawkins and his friends organized occasional trading expeditions to the New World; but their immediate economic significance was negligible. There was rather more English enterprise to the east, where the Muscovy Company, chartered in 1555, was developing its activities. The return of English trading ships to the Baltic was encouraged from 1558 by the Russian capture of Narva, a port accessible through the Gulf of Finland; but progress was hampered by the hostility of the Muscovy Company to the interlopers who sought to exploit the trade to Narva without submitting to its regulations. In December 1564 the Privy Council actually tried to suppress the direct traffic to Narva by English merchants, in the interests of Arctic navigation. It was however unable to enforce its prohibition, which in 1566 was reversed, Narva being placed within the privileges of the Muscovy Company.[2]

The wish of the government to learn more clearly which foreign markets were supplied by English merchants and with English products led to the adoption of a much more elaborate system of customs registration in English ports from March 1565 onwards.[3] This inconspicuous administrative reform makes it possible to glean something about the fields in which individual City merchants specialized, though the surviving documents are too sparse and fragmentary to yield more than a few tantalizing glimpses of their activities. Thus in the six summer months of 1565, out of the 354 Englishmen paying customs to the Queen on cloths shipped from London, 246 traded to Antwerp, among them the biggest merchants of the City. 138 others shipped to other destinations, chiefly Spain and the Baltic, though individually in a small way; and 19 out of the 246 dispatched cloths both to Antwerp and elsewhere.[4] If measured by the numbers of cloths rather than the numbers of merchants, the preponderance of the Netherlands market may be confirmed, for during these same six months nearly two-thirds of all cloths shipped from London went to Antwerp.[5] It would however be unwise to assume that this proportion holds good for the complete calendar year, since shipping to long-range markets (other perhaps than Africa) was in abeyance during the winter months, and there were no sailings to the Baltic or Russia when ice covered the seas, while traffic to and from the Netherlands was not normally impeded. It may therefore well have been that in 1565 as in other years taken as a whole the proportion of English cloths sent from London to Antwerp was as much as three-quarters or even 80 per cent or more of total shipments. There was also a lively and well-taxed traffic in goods brought back in return to England, though in this the proportion of foreign merchants, mostly Hanse or Italian, who owned the merchandise unloaded at London, was rather greater than in the export business. A proportion of English merchants, perhaps as much as a third, preferred to take bills on sterling, payable at London, from the purchasers of their cloths, rather than buy foreign wares for import.[6] Unlicenced specie movements were of course illegal.

Upon the re-opening of the Netherlands to English shipping in January 1565 there at once ensued a strong outburst of commercial activity. 'Great quantities' of English woollen cloths were being unshipped at Antwerp during January, even before the sailing of the regular cloth fleet of the Merchants Adventurers from London. With them came a number of senior merchants, unwilling perhaps to trust their large consignments to factors or apprentices. Among them were some cloths sent on from Emden, where they had failed to find buyers.[7] But at Antwerp sales were brisk, and only the unusually severe weather prevented the dispatch of all the cloths in store at London before the end of the month. The exchange veered so far in favour of the pound sterling that Gresham received the order to raise £20,000 for the Queen upon his own credit, payable at London by exchange: his instructions included the caution that 'we require you to use this service discreetly, that you do not impair the exchange', but so buoyant was the market that the proviso was probably not necessary.[8] In February there were further shipments from London, to be followed in March by the organized cloth fleet of forty craft. By March 25, the total value of the cloths discharged at Antwerp since the beginning of January was esimated at 1,700,000 ducats − well over half a million pounds sterling.[9] One observer indeed noted symptoms of glut before long, no doubt because Company restrictions were hard to enforce while the market remained so exuberant.[10]. In time, normality was restored, and in the autumn another cloth fleet dropped anchor in the Scheldt. As measured by the quantity of broadcloths and kerseys exported, 1565 was a record year for the London−Antwerp traffic, making good the shortfalls of 1563 and 1564.

Taken as a whole, the years 1565−8 do not deserve to be written off as a phase of continuous depression in English foreign trade. On cloths shipped from London the Queen's exchequer during the first four years of her reign, reckoning from Michaelmas 1558, had received in tax the gross sum of £131,034 odd, i.e. an annual average of £32,757; for the four years from Michaelmas 1564 the comparable sum received was £128,185 odd, the annual average being thus only very slightly less.[11] But there were fluctuations in the volume of the traffic, and the initial euphoria that marked the early months of 1565 was not sustained. Perhaps the cheerless rumours filtering out from the antechamber of the international commissioners at Bruges in 1565 and 1566 were some discouragement to trade. The gross receipts from the cloth customs at London dropped to £27,879 odd in the twelve months from Michaelmas 1565. There was then a further fall to £23,320 during the next fiscal year, which coincided with the upheavals at Antwerp: for the merchants, they were a sharp discouragement. Business was at a complete standstill for some weeks during the late summer of 1566, and it took months to recover. Early in February 1567, the Deputy Governor of the Merchants Adventurers writing to Cecil from Antwerp explained what a critical moment it was for the members of the Company 'who have no small sums owing to them here, besides a great quantity of cloths remaining on their hands', and he advised some postponement of further shipments.[12] He repeated this warning a little later, stating that existing stocks of cloth would suffice the market until midsummer.[13]

The violent occurrences at Antwerp in the summer and autumn of 1566 could hardly fail to arouse interest and alarm in England, where the Queen must have been ruefully aware of their connection with her dwindling customs revenue. It was perhaps not entirely a coincidence that at this time there were signs of renewed unrest among the artisan clothworkers of the City of London.[14] The dullness of the cloth trade lasted into the summer of 1567, when it was reported at Mercers' Hall that there were three young men of the Company destitute and lacking employment.[15] Nor did the arrival of refugees from the Netherlands relieve tension. Already in May the Lord Mayor had sent a message round to the halls of the livery companies with a warning against the possibility of violence in the City: as he put it, 'an uproar or tumult was suspected to have been practised against strangers, for that certain bills were thrown abroad in the street with a caveat to beware of Ill May Day and such other like desperate words'.[16] Gresham, trying to raise money for the servicing of the royal debts at Antwerp, found it exceedingly scarce there, and in July was forced to take up as much as he could at London, to be dispatched to the Netherlands by exchange.[17] But with the arrival of Alva in August, confidence seems to have returned to the marketplace. The Queen of England greatly resented the presence of the experienced Spanish commander and his troops in the Netherlands, and many of her merchants may have shared her feelings; but the cloth trade was able to climb back to prosperity. The year from Michaelmas 1567 was in fact a buoyant one for the traffic in woollen textiles, the cloth export tax yielding £32,552 gross at London.

Meanwhile on both sides of the sea a debate on the significance of the recent Emden venture was being pursued. More than anyone else, the lords of Antwerp were relieved that the experiment had been abandoned. In their delight at the end of December 1564, when the political arrangements for the resumption of trade were complete, they invited Fitzwilliams and other resident Englishmen to their newly-built Town Hall to

assure them of their good will and to explain at length how they
had been doing all they could to mend the rupture. They also
wrote directly to the Governor and Company of the Merchants
Adventurers at London to the same purpose.[18] They had good
reason to rejoice, though it may be that they felt an added spur
in the knowledge that their ancient rivals of Bruges had also
been angling for the transfer of the English mart to their city,
with the support of the province of Flanders and its governor
the Count of Egmont.[19]

But the pleasure felt at the Antwerp Town Hall was tempered
by some misgivings. The English made no secret of the fact that
they now knew they were not quite so dependent upon the Low
Countries as had long been assumed. This was by far the most
ominous fruit of the whole Emden episode. Years later, it even
seemed to the Merchants Adventurers (or some of them) in
retrospect that if they had only been permitted, they could have
worked their Emden mart up to the Antwerp pitch.[20] Some
humiliation was correspondingly felt on the Netherlands side: as
Fitzwilliams reported from Antwerp, the conclusion of the
agreement 'had brought down a great many of their stomachs,
which had thought it would not come to so honourable an end
for the Queen's Majesty'.[21] But illusions persisted in some quar-
ters. In his remote Burgundian exile, Cardinal Granvelle could
not but wring his hands at the thought that by this premature re-
opening of traffic 'the best opportunity for restoring the commerce of Flanders has been lost'.[22] Nor, as the future was to
show, had Dr d'Assonleville been converted from his former
views. At Antwerp too, Hooftman and his friends were angered
by the course of events, and not minded to give up the struggle
against their English competitors.

On the English side, it was only natural that the rank and file
of the Merchants Adventurers should have sought nothing better than a return to the familiar and profitable traffic in their old
haunts. In a memorandum submitted to the Privy Council late in
1564, the Company plainly stated its wish to go back, though it
recognized that the Emden experiment – even with all 'the very
great charge, loss and damage' it had involved – had been
inevitable. The merchants did not reproach the government for
'provoking' them into it, and indeed admitted that if the mart
for lack of 'surety and quiet' could not be kept at Antwerp, then
it would have to be moved further east – places were not speci-
fied.[23] When pressed for details of this, the Company submitted

that if need be, direct trade could be carried on not merely with northern Europe but also with France, Spain, Portugal, Barbary and the Levant. This was the first hint of a possible revival of seaborne English trade to the Mediterranean, though the Company still envisaged that 'Italy' and even 'Turkey' should be supplied with English manufactures over the Alps. As suggested nearly a year earlier, overseas markets were for the most part to be tapped through Emden or Hamburg.[24] Not everyone thought of these suggestions simply as last resorts in an emergency. Governor Marsh himself opposed the return to Antwerp until in January 1565 he was finally overruled by a vote of the General Court of the Company.[25]

The debate in England was enlivened by some resuscitation of schemes aired in the past, even before 1564. It was no longer possible to revive the project actually envisaged much earlier in the century by Henry VII and subsequently Wolsey, of building up on English soil at Calais an international mart to replace Antwerp, since Calais was now in French hands.[26] But practicable variants were proposed. Gresham's manager Richard Clough had put forward one such, by which the cloth market for exporters should be located at an English port, preferably York or Hull.[27] In May 1564 an Italian at Antwerp passed on the suggestion that London be made a free port, and so a centre of attraction for foreign merchants that might itself rival Antwerp.[28] At about the same time, the Earl of Leicester was expressing an interest in the idea of setting up 'sundry fairs and marts' in England, for the free sale of English products to foreigners.[29] A novel version of this scheme was in circulation probably towards the end of the year, in the form of a project for holding annually 'two free marts' at London, rather after the fashion of the Fairs of Brabant which it was hoped they would supplant: 'by this means might you give checkmate to Antwerp without business and offences of amity and seeking of strange countries'. Indeed, London might emulate not merely Antwerp but also Frankfurt, Lyons and Venice. The plan did not involve any of the tortuous regulation essential to Clough's project, and it was fortified by the argument that the royal exchequer would profit from it.[30]

It is easy to grasp how such schemes might in their different ways have suited the country clothier riding to the market to sell his cloths, but they offered no more than a few crumbs for the native cloth shippers. The Merchants Adventurers were so alarmed by all this talk about the advantages of locating the cloth mart at home instead of in the Netherlands that they marshalled the arguments against it in a paper dating perhaps from very early in 1565. They argued that to keep the mart at home would imply an abandonment of the foreign trade of England to the visiting foreigners, and that English shipping would therefore decay. In addition, they warned that the merchants of the outports (for whom the Company had hardly shown much consideration hitherto) would be brought to disaster, while the ability of foreign governments to damage English trade by unreasonable embargoes would not be lessened.[31] Beyond and above the controversy enveloping the Antwerp mart, Secretary Cecil remained cool and detached. He clearly perceived the perils inherent in over-dependence on the single cosmopolitan metropolis. He feared the excessive import of foreign luxuries; the inordinate growth of the woollen industry, with attendant social and political dangers; the straining of credit among the merchants; the discouragement of shipping because of the short sea route, and so forth.[32] But he stifled his doubts, it may be, because of the wish of the Queen to restore her customs revenue, and played his part in the negotiations for the resumption of the trade to Antwerp, while also encouraging the Merchants Adventurers to continue on occasion to send a few cloths to Emden.[33]

A private contribution to the debate was made by the relatively obscure merchant adventurer George Nedham; it is of sufficient interest to deserve mention. Nedham we have already met as an advocate of the Emden mart and as prominent in its establishment early in 1564.[34] He had presented the Queen with a splendidly-bound manuscript in which his arguments were set forth.[35] The events of 1564 moved him to expound his ideas in a much fuller form, and he was probably still refining the prose of this enlarged second essay when his hopes were dashed by the news that the re-opening of the traffic to Antwerp was about to take place. The political weather favourable to his project was suddenly overclouded, so that instead of heralding a momentous switch in the pattern of English foreign trade he was reduced to supervising the evacuation of the settlement of the Merchants Adventurers at Emden in January 1565, in the capacity of Deputy Governor of the Company there. His mercantile career was in fact broken. His supporters in the City were no longer in the ascendant, and although he had married a widow who owned some property in the Netherlands he was warned by his friends not to show his face at Antwerp, where he was branded as 'the first inventor and discloser of Emden'. His not-quite-finished essay, cast into literary form as 'A letter to the Earls of East Friesland' was put away, and he was careful to suppress any evidence of his authorship.[36]

Nedham in his 'Letter' supplies much curious information about the economic life of Antwerp and the Netherlands in the early 1560s. But he was not content merely to point out the advantages of Emden over Antwerp as the site of an English cloth-distributing centre on the continent. He inveighed sharply against the traditional amity with the House of Burgundy, especially in the person of its contemporary representative Philip II of Spain, and spoke in hostile terms of the papacy. The 'Letter' in fact contained political allegations of a thorough-going anti-Spanish and anti-Habsburg sort that could only bring trouble to its author at the hands of a government at whose centre the Spanish ambassador Silva stood in high favour. No longer could it be a timely act to remind the merchants of the City of the trade stoppages imposed by the Netherlands government in the days of Edward VI and Mary Tudor. Secretary Cecil's sympathy stopped short of allowing Nedham to print his tract; and any ostentatious circulation of the manuscript might have proved dangerous. However, some doors were discreetly left open. As we have seen, trade links with Emden were not completely severed, and neither at the royal court nor in the City was opinion unanimous. Cecil seems to have placed some small pieces of patronage in Nedham's way, and he had other friends at London, from Governor Marsh downwards, who between them saw that he did not starve. Meanwhile, an instructive side of his career lies in the evidence it affords of the persistent tendency in the political world to identify the maintenance of the Antwerp mart with the ancient Habsburg alliance and all that this implied in other fields of policy.[37]

Meanwhile, whatever the ebullience of the market when Anglo-Netherlands trade was restored in January 1565, not far below the surface there lurked some grievances. Whatever the intentions of Queen and Regent, it was beyond their power simply to put the clock of commerce back past the eighteen months of stoppage. The English had seized an initial advantage in the arrangements agreed for the actual re-opening of trade: pending the outcome of the colloquy at Bruges, traffic was to be regulated by the laws in force on either side at the beginning of 1559.[38] A proclamation in the name of the Queen ordered English officials at the ports of her kingdom to permit the transit of goods inwards and outwards 'as the same might have been done' on 1 January in the first year of her reign.[39] It incidentally involved the exercise of the royal prerogative to suspend parliamentary statutes enacted since then.[40] So the English triumphantly maintained their new tax charges and the equally objectionable though ancient Statutes of Employment; for the time being, they agreed to relinquish the navigation regulations of 1559 and the prohibitory laws of 1563.[41] But from the Netherlanders' point of view, these were slight gains, doing little to offset the damage wrought by a year of disarray and disaffection provoked by the rupture. Crown control over the issue of cloth export licences continued to repress the competition offered by foreign merchants in the textile trade. When Giles Hooftman and some other Antwerp cloth dealers tried to circumvent the English merchants by applying direct to Cecil for licences to export, they were not merely refused but rebuked for having kindled political animosity as a result of their manoeuvres.[42]

The Englishmen also felt sore about some things. Their government did not minutely see to all the points made by the Merchants Adventurers late in 1564. In particular, the merchants were disappointed in their demand to enjoy a special period of grace so as to catch the cloth market in advance of their foreign rivals also shipping from London, whatever the position with regard to the licences.[43] Four years subsequently, the Company of Merchants Adventurers ruefully recalled 'the great loss' its members had sustained 'by the sudden opening of the traffic' in January 1565.[44] Before long, the English merchants thought they detected a new fierceness on the part of the Netherlands customs officers, who made searches with iron instruments never before used, and 'picking new quarrels do take from them and detain without just cause' their wares. The remedy open to the Company was to pursue them in the lawcourts, but this did not halt their practices *pendente lite*.[45] The Company, as it complained to the Privy Council, had experience of 'the long and infinite delays and expenses in suit and process' habitual in the Netherlands, and asked for a special letter of recommendation from the Queen to the Regent to hasten the outcome.[46] Wotton, always a realist, no doubt had this situation in mind when at the second adjournment of the Bruges colloquy he gave it as his opinion that the Merchants Adventurers could maintain their privileges only if 'they would now and then send some of their cloths to other places, and make a countenance as though they would not stick to traffic elsewhere', if they were not fairly treated in the Netherlands.[47]

The joyful re-opening of Anglo-Netherlands trade in January 1565 did not therefore entirely banish a certain residual feeling of doubt and even estrangement on either side, though it may not have been much in evidence among either the lords of Antwerp or the Merchants Adventurers so gladly flocking back to their old haunts. When the Company was invited to present its complaints so that they might be put forward at the forthcoming Bruges colloquy it certainly produced a long enough list: but the grievances were all somewhat peripheral, or difficult to substantiate, and certainly outside the power of the municipality of Antwerp to remedy. They concerned such minor issues as the right of Irish merchants to share in the privileges of the Intercourse, the enforcement of the Middelburg wine staple, the obstacles to the transit traffic in German munitions, duties exacted in the province of Flanders, and vague allegations about obstructions in the lawcourts.[48] Before long, matters of more serious concern certainly emerged. Most important among these was a sudden loss of confidence in the social and political stability of the Netherlands arising from the disorders of 1566. These prompted Gresham to urge upon Secretary Cecil the need to look elsewhere for an alternative cloth market – a very ominous piece of advice.[49] And there were other problems.

Consultations between Privy Council and merchants meanwhile were continuing, particularly when in the autumn of 1565 it was evident that the Bruges conference might prove abortive. Representatives of both Merchants Adventurers and Staplers were back in the Council chamber in September.[50] Their problems were formidable – in Cecil's phrase, they provided 'a matter indeed like a maze to walk in' – but the Council tackled them in forthright fashion.[51] The Merchants Adventurers were asked how they felt about trading to the Netherlands without the assurances of the Intercourse, and both they and the Staplers were required to name an alternative place or places outside the Netherlands at which to settle their traffic. The Staplers were in a far weaker position than the Merchants Adventurers, not merely because they were a much poorer and smaller body, but because their wares were chiefly consumed in the Netherlands.

They were floored by the problem and had no constructive suggestion to offer.[52] As to the Merchants Adventurers, they left the Council in no doubt that they too viewed with extreme dismay the prospect of trafficking in the Netherlands without the protection of the *Intercursus*. They were 'very loath' to suggest a substitute for Antwerp. But when pressed they did so, and they were brought – for the third time within two years – to name as their alternative mart towns Emden or Hamburg. They wearily envisaged the transport of cloths from these places further into the interior of Germany 'although not without the great burden, charge and travail of your suppliants'. Western Europe and the Levant, as previously indicated, would have to be supplied with cloths direct by sea. As to the fine cloths of Wiltshire, Gloucestershire and Worcestershire, recently developed as a speciality for consumption in the Netherlands, they could but hope that their manufacturers would return to making other sorts of cloth such as they had done thirty years earlier, which might find a market elsewhere.[53] They had nothing to say about the hardships likely to confront the country clothier and his weavers in re-adapting themselves to this.

The boom that suddenly enlivened the City with the resumption of the cloth trade to the Netherlands at the beginning of 1565 was thus accompanied by anxiety and some tension. There seems to have been a persistent malaise of credit. In April, amid the general scramble to dispatch cloths to Antwerp, the Common Council of London took alarm at the fraudulent way in which some slick creditors had of late been attaching debtors' goods before others were aware of what was happening, and then proceeding to sell them for less than their fair market value. This readiness on the part of some creditors to steal a march at the cost both of the others and of the debtor was noted as a recent phenomenon. It was especially odious since, in the opinion of the Common Council, the debtors in question were mostly 'decayed and fallen in poverty in such wise as then most chiefly pity, compassion and mercy of every good Christian man to them is to be extended and showed'.[54] There was also the persistent incidence of bankruptcy. Bankrupts, who in the preamble to the Bankruptcy Act of 1543 had been stigmatized as deliberate deceivers, were by 1571 being statutorily defined in more neutral terms – a significant shift of opinion.[55] A good reason for this was that, in the language of the later statute, bankrupts had 'and still do increase into great and excessive numbers'. Meanwhile the City did what it could to relieve the plight of debtors by enacting that goods sold by reason of any attachment should henceforth be 'seen, valued and appraised by two good, honest, substantial and discreet Citizens'.[56] Another symptom of uneasiness in trade was to be found in the stricter enforcement of restrictive regulations by the Company of Merchants Adventurers. This was not only with regard to the 'stint' of cloths each merchant might individually ship to each seasonal mart, but also the intake of apprentices. Even the small merchants of the outports were brought within the ambit of enforcement.[57]

The victory of conservative forces over the revolutionaries at Antwerp and in the Netherlands in the course of 1567 produced fresh troubles. 1568 was not a bad year for trade. But a new element of uncertainty was introduced into business relations at Antwerp by the proscription of various merchants who had been prominent in the disturbances of 1566–7, and whose goods had been seized by commissioners acting on behalf of the government at Brussels. Some of these men owed money to Merchants Adventurers, who to their horror discovered that the debts would not be honoured by the sequestrators. Englishmen were well aware that Netherlands laws differed from their own – for instance they had learnt to their cost how the wife of a bankrupt might remove a proportion of his property beyond the reach of his creditors, which in England was not allowed – but hitherto in the Netherlands commercial debts had otherwise enjoyed a priority in payment. This withholding of money, they protested to Alva, who had now succeeded the Regent in the palace at Brussels, was a novel practice that struck at the roots of credit in the marketplace.[58] Apart from this, Englishmen were not directly affected by the proscriptions: whatever their sympathies, they had remained on the side-lines. Among the few exceptions were a couple of Merchants Adventurers, Randal Starkey and George Knightley, who had married and settled down at Bergen-op-Zoom, where they had incautiously allowed themselves to be drawn into the Calvinist church in its brief moment of freedom. Starkey had actually been elected a member of the local consistory. The Company of Merchants Adventurers had prudently ordered any of its members implicated in the disturbances to return home, and this Starkey and Knightley had done, taking their wives and families with them. But thereby they lost their worldly goods, and the chief commissioner of the government at Bergen – none other than Assonleville – proved deaf to their pleas.[59] A letter from the Queen and a recommendation from the ambassador Silva gained them a respite, but could not prevent the forfeiture of all the property they possessed in right of their wives.[60]

The legal basis of the fiscal security whose shelter had enabled merchants from both sides of the sea to develop a flourishing commerce between England and the Netherlands during the previous century or so remained, of course, the *Intercursus*, i.e., the international agreement whose terms had been formulated and accepted in 1496 and on various subsequent occasions restated.[61] But a cloud of uncertainty increasingly enveloped the legal and political validity of this oft-cited instrument. Especially after the adjournment of the Bruges colloquy in June 1566, the English merchants felt in doubt about the protection it afforded. What, if any, validity did it retain? The Merchants Adventurers certainly regarded with thorough dismay any prospect of the abrogation of the Intercourse, which provided their legal protection against heavier taxation in the Netherlands as, for instance, was advocated by Assonleville and his Flemish industrial allies.[62] Queen and Regent had agreed in their initial arrangements of December 1564 that the provisions of the Intercourse should remain in force during the life of the colloquy and for the ensuing three weeks.[63] As to what was then to happen, the only formal assurance lay in the declaration of the Netherlands commissioners at Bruges on the adjournment of the colloquy that issues arising between the subjects of either prince should be judged *statim ac juxta leges aut intercursus de remedio debito.*[64] Events were to show how frail a bulwark this was to provide against the pressures and exactions in the Netherlands during the tumultuous years that lay ahead.

At the back of the minds of the Merchants Adventurers lurked the fear that bit by bit a system of levies would be built up in the Netherlands, with the practical effect of counterbalancing the preferential rate of taxation they enjoyed in England. They were not prepared to compete with the foreign firms on an equal basis. They feared them because of their large stock-in-trade, their more sophisticated organization in companies with ramifications all over western Europe, and their more advanced techniques in book-keeping and accountancy. To cap this, they further alleged the foreigners' ability to undercut them by more frugal living and their smaller expenditure on servants.[65] Cecil seems to have agreed with the Merchants Adventurers here, for while musing upon 'inconveniences likely to follow, if the privileges of the intercourse should cease', he was so far swayed by their outcries as to note that even with the protection of the *Intercursus* 'yet do the strangers with their great purses and spare living even presently oppress the English'.[66] One deterrent applicable to Giles Hooftman and his associates in their efforts to harrass the Merchants Adventurers at Antwerp was the threat to retaliate by the levy of higher taxes from their partners and factors resident at London. These latter were duly assessed for payment of the subsidy voted by parliament in the autumn of 1566, Governor Marsh himself being one of the assessors. He made a declaration at the end of the list of well-to-do foreigners dwelling in the City, certifying that none of the Merchants Adventurers resident in the Netherlands were 'charged with payment of any subsidy, tax or imposition', so that presumably the strangers at London did not have to pay.[67] But the warning cannot have been missed: taxes in the Netherlands would be met by taxes in England.

The most imminent threat seemed to spring from indirect rather than direct taxation, and in the form of the 'double toll'. This was an involved and historically important topic, though founded on very simple facts.[68] The seventeen provinces of the Burgundian Netherlands always retained their individual customs administrations; but shipping between England and Antwerp, which was in Brabant, normally passed through waters in the province of Zeeland, while traffic with Barrow (Bergen-op-Zoom), which was in Zeeland, sometimes passed through Brabant territory. Shipping bound for a destination in Brabant or Holland or even Flanders might well be driven into a Zeeland port. The broad principle that customs charges should be exacted once only on each cargo laden or discharged at a Netherlands harbour had been under discussion during the fifteenth century. It was only by implication included in the *Intercursus* of 1496 but it secured an explicit confirmation when the Intercourse was renewed in 1520.[69] It had been vindicated in a test case as recently as 1555.[70] But uncertainty now reigned again.

Various incidents seemed to indicate some undermining of the right to pay customs once only, and the issue was ultimately joined over three barrels of steel bought by an English merchant at Antwerp. On their shipment for England he had duly paid the Brabant tax, only to have the goods confiscated by the order of the Zeeland customs officer.[71] This became a test case. The Company took up the cause of the Englishman, and thus became entangled in further prolonged and expensive litigation at Brussels. A letter from the Queen of England recommending the cases of the Merchants Adventurers to the Regent was received on her behalf by Assonleville with fair words before the end of 1566, and hopes momentarily rose high.[72] Fitzwilliams spent some weeks at Brussels soliciting such councillors as were to be found there, but his hopes of a speedy and favourable verdict soon evaporated. Amid the political turmoil, a quorum of judges was not available. In any case, the president Viglius 'showed himself but a small friend to Englishmen in their suits'.[73] When the Earl of Sussex on his way to Vienna the following summer took the opportunity in audience with the Regent to mention the pleas of the merchants he met with a polite but evasive reply.[74] The all-important sentence was pronounced against the Merchants Adventurers 'directly against the last compact and against all equity and justice', as Governor Marsh believed. In person, he made his way to Brussels to deliver another letter from the Queen, with a recommendation also from the Spanish ambassador Silva, seeking a revocation of the sentence. He was answered – once more by Assonleville – that this was impossible; and although Assonleville was moved to remark that there was no intention of exacting the double toll, the three barrels of steel were not restored, and the Zeeland customs officers continued to make difficulties. Like Wotton over a year previously, Governor Marsh could see no effective remedy save by trading to some other country.[75]

The degree to which the customary confidence of the Merchants Adventurers had been eroded before the bursting of the storm at the end of 1568 may well be illustrated by one highly significant change in their traditional organization – the abandonment of the regular six-monthly cloth-fleet and its replacement by smaller sailings of four ships at a time at more frequent intervals. So radical an alteration in traditional shipping arrangements seems to have been in execution by February 1567, and was certainly confirmed by a resolution of the Company at Antwerp the next month.[76] There were no doubt good reasons for this levelling-out of traffic. The market at Antwerp had long been virtually continuous. The Fairs of Brabant were now a mere financial convention: the Merchants Adventurers never returned to Bergen-op-Zoom after the resumption of trade in

January 1565 – as they complacently observed, it remained 'by their withdrawing decayed and in manner desolate'.[77] But the chief cause of this new timing of the cloth-ships was a lack of faith in the good will of the government at Brussels which was conniving at the fiscal and other innovations the members of the Company found so harrassing, and the consequent fear that by putting such quantities of merchandise within the power of the Netherlands government to seize at a single stroke it was courting trouble.[78] Besides, the arrests of 1554 and 1563, and the earlier prohibitions too, were not forgotten.[79] At the end of 1568, on the eve of the cataclysm, the misgivings of the Merchants Adventurers reached a good deal further than those they had expressed after the resumption of trade not quite four years earlier. They were clearly set forth in a complaint submitted to the Queen. First and foremost, there was the question of the double toll and other fiscal innovations; then the unfriendly attitude of the judicature at Brussels; arbitrary taxes laid upon some hops the Englishmen were in course of consigning home (a recent episode that had given rise to ill-feeling); the impossibility of recovering debts from persons whose goods had been confiscated; and finally the sad case of Starkey and Knightley. These, they contended, were abuses contrary to the provisions of the Intercourse. Such was the result of carrying on trade without the usual guarantees.[80]

One cloud on the commercial horizon deserves mention – the collapse of the Antwerp alum staple, which may be dated to 1566–8.[81] For fixing dyes, alum was the essential mordant; it was produced within the papal dominions in Italy but marketed in northern Europe by contractors seated at Antwerp. Alum of inferior quality was available from Spain. English efforts in 1564 to supply Emden with alum had involved some infringement of the contractors' monopoly, and by the middle of the next year the Regent at Brussels was alarmed to discover that the English had set up some sort of alum staple of their own there; it supplied Baltic countries as well as England, and alum was actually being smuggled into Holland from Emden. She could not satisfy the Antwerp alum contractors, who complained that for practical purposes their monopoly had been eroded and with it their profits.[82] It was perhaps to break this illicit Emden staple that the Regent now agreed to the shipment of some alum direct to England from Italy or Spain.[83] She also took up the matter with the English at the Bruges colloquy.[84] Then in 1566

Tobia Palavicino, a resourceful Genoese financier, took over the alum farm, in quest simply of profit. But when he sought for a guarantee from the King of Spain that the Antwerp staple would be effectively enforced, he got no answer; and so from at least 1568 he began to allow shipments direct from Italy and Spain to England in place of Antwerp.[85] As early as June 1566 the likelihood of this had been rumoured on the Antwerp Bourse, and it may be that direct English trade in alum with the Mediterranean was not long delayed.[86] It was at least being alleged by mid 1568 that English merchants 'do daily bring over from Rome, Spain and France great quantities of alum' – an exaggeration without doubt, but not devoid of some substance.[87] The traffic in alum possibly provided a magnet to bring English ships once more to trade in the Mediterranean. The importance of this newly-won emancipation from the Antwerp market in so vital a commodity became apparent at the next breach in Anglo-Netherlands relations, soon to occur.

The injuries and forebodings of the merchants were always imparted to the Queen and her councillors; and they had further reasons, especially with the advent of Alva in August 1567, for distrusting the government of the Netherlands. Secretary Cecil was a detached observer of the commercial world, with a sharper insight than the merchants who were themselves involved in it. He believed that the rivalry of the foreign firms, prompted by the policy of the Brussels government while the Intercourse was in abeyance, might in part be met by government action on the English side also. His own inclination was to deal indirectly: by the enforcment of sumptuary legislation to discourage the luxury import traffic, still largely in foreign hands; by keeping a closer watch on the efficiency of the customs officers, so as to prevent organized fraud by foreigners at London; and by encouraging trade with Emden and Hamburg.[88] These were all topics to which the government gave attention. Correspondingly, the merchants also played their part, especially by responding to the invitation of the government to divert at least some traffic to ports that might offer an alternative to Antwerp. This was not simply a matter of shipping a few hundred cloths yearly to Emden or Hamburg, or even of sending factors inland to the fairs of Frankfurt and Leipzig, but of opening up commercial routes beyond north-west Europe. English trade to the Baltic now reached record proportions. The traffic to Barbary was reckoned to absorb a couple of thousand cloths a year.[89] The Muscovy Company was planning to cut out the cosmopolitan firms at Antwerp by organizing the dispatch of silk and spices direct from Persia.[90] Hawkins and others were leading expeditions to Guinea and across the Atlantic.[91] An occasional ship may have reconnoitred the way to the Mediterranean to buy alum.[92] It cannot have entirely been a coincidence that during the years 1564–8 unprecedented quantities of world-maps by Ortelius and other cartographers were being dispatched from Antwerp to England and that discussions on ways and means of sailing to Cathay were being pursued with a new intensity.[93]

It is impossible to be sure how far these tentative gropings are to be linked to any suspicion that the future of the Antwerp mart was in jeopardy. In the light of later events, it is tempting to hail them as pioneering ventures. But in truth all that may be inferred is that there was capital available in the City even for schemes not devoid of considerable risk and that some merchants, as always, were ready to invest in enterprises other than the shipment of woollen cloths to the dominions of Philip II. The wealth of the City was strikingly demonstrated in these years by the erection of a much-admired Bourse at London to enable the merchants to foregather in comfort as they were accustomed to do at Antwerp, sheltered from wind and rain. The stimulus to provide this dated from the construction of the New Bourse at Antwerp, which was in use from 1533.[94] A spirit of emulation helped to prompt the question: why should London not offer comparable housing to its merchants? It was first put by Sir Richard Gresham as early as 1538; but it remained for his son Sir Thomas nearly thirty years later to galvanize the aldermen into providing a site and to spur the livery companies into raising the necessary finance.[95] By the time the Antwerp market had re-opened in January 1565, Sir Thomas had enlisted the experienced and influential Dean Wotton among his allies in promoting the scheme. As the Dean put it, the merchants were to have 'a house and place like unto the New Bourse at Antwerp'.[96] The money for the site, nearly £1,700, was forthcoming chiefly from the major companies, led by the Mercers', in which the Merchants Adventurers were the predominant element, and it was collected during the last weeks of 1566, at a time when the news from Antwerp must have led all merchants of experience to shake their heads in apprehension of what the future there might hold.[97] The Bourse was in use by 1568.[98] But it was ceremonially opened by the Queen in person in January 1571, when it received the new name of 'The Royal Exchange'.[99]

These developments were portents ominous for the future of the Antwerp mart, though the proportion of London traffic immediately affected by them was certainly small. But a quantitative yardstick is sometimes a clumsy tool for the historian. It is in fact difficult to exaggerate the extent of the commercial disintegration wrought by the eighteen months' suspension of Anglo-Netherlands trade and its aftermath. The events of 1563 onwards were no exception to the general rule that crises in the export trade of a commercial country provide a major incentive to argument, experiment and innovation – indeed, the upsets of the 1560s dominated English economic thought until their memory was effaced by the even more blistering troubles of the 1620s.[100] The central point was that the security of foreign trade at the re-opening of Antwerp in January 1565 was less than that of eighteen months earlier. Since the Netherlands government ceased to favour the unconditional continuance of the virtually free port at Antwerp, the conditions under which the Merchants Adventurers had to do business were transformed. They had increasing reason to look further afield. They were no longer willing to accept the Antwerp alum staple. They were supplying themselves with much of their linen imports elsewhere. The English crown was less dependent upon the Antwerp money-market. At home, there were influences at work to reduce the concentration of the cloth industry upon the broadcloths and kerseys that were exported in an unfinished state. Even if there occurred no further political interference with the course of trade, it looks as if the English economy was beginning to free itself from its heavy dependence upon the Netherlands. As it happened, the political interference came, heavy and devastating, near the end of December 1568.

NOTES TO CHAPTER IV

[1] T. S. Willan, 'Some aspects of English trade with the Levant in the sixteenth century', *EHR*, LXX (1955), 399–410.

[2] *APC 1558–70*, 178–9; Willan, *EHMC*, 67 *et seq.*

[3] The 'Port Books': see instructions at SP 12/35/39, *infra*, 163–4.

[4] Figures taken from the London Port Book, March–September 1565, E 190/2/1.

[5] Table printed by B. Dietz, 'Antwerp and London: the Structure and Balance of Trade in the 1560s', *Wealth and Power in Tudor England*, ed. E. W. Ives *et al.* (London, 1978), 190.

[6] No less than 93 of the 246 Londoners exporting cloths to Antwerp in the summer months of 1565 do not appear to have been engaged in the import trade during the fiscal year 1567–8: some doubtless had died or withdrawn from business, but most presumably just preferred to repatriate their money in the shape of bills rather than goods. Names big and small were among them. See *The Port and Trade of Elizabethan London. Documents*, ed. B. Dietz (London Record Society, VIII, 1972) which incorporates a calendar of the import London Port Book for 1567–8, E 190/4/2.

[7] Assonleville, writing to Gravelle on 26 February 1565, Gachard, *Correspondance de Philippe II*, I, 345, mentioned the figure of 24,000 – probably a great exaggeration.

[8] Queen to Gresham, 27 January 1565, Add. 5,755, f. 29v.

[9] By Guicciardini, whose letters of 13 and 28 January, 5 and 26 February and 25 March 1565, Battistini, 244–7, are the sources of statements in this paragraph not otherwise supported.

[10] Sheres to Cecil, 30 April 1565, KL, IV, 201–2.

[12] Figures are conveniently available in Carmarden's statement of c.1582, SP 12/157/59; they vary hardly at all from those enrolled at E 356/28. London customs inwards have much the same tale to tell, Lansd. 14, No. 50.

[12] Fitzwilliams to Cecil, 1 February 1567, SP 70/88/745. The word calendared at *CSPF 1566–8*, No. 923 as 'four' should read 'fewer'. See also KL, IV, 406–8.

[13] *Ib.* to *ib.*, 8 March 1567, KL, IV, 419–21.

[14] G. D. Ramsay, 'Industrial Discontent in Early Elizabethan London', *The London Journal*, I (1975), 235–6.

[15] ACMC 1560–93, f. 107v.

[16] *Ib.*, f. 107. Evil May Day, marked by a riot against foreigners, had occurred in 1517, thus half a century earlier, but was still remembered.

[17] Gresham's list of lenders, July 1567, is at SP 70/92/1103.

[18] Fitzwilliams to Cecil, 30 December 1564, KL, IV, 152–3.

[19] Egmont to Cecil, 3 December 1564, and Bruges to Cecil, 4 December 1564, *ib.*, 144–6.

[20] Merchants Adventurers to Council, undated c. 1578, SP 12/127/88, f. 38v.

[21] Fitzwilliams to Cecil, 30 December 1564, KL, IV, 152.

[22] Granvelle to Perez, 23 January 1565, Gachard, *Correspondance de Philippe II*, I, 339.

[23] Merchants Adventurers to Council, incorrectly ascribed in a later hand to October 1561 but probably written October–November 1564, Cotton, Galba C I, No. 26.

[24] *Ib.* to *ib.*, 10 December 1564, SP 12/35/28; copy at Cotton, Nero B VIII, No. 5.

[25] Smedt, *EN*, I, 293.

[26] *Supra*, 2–4.

[27] *Ante*, 239.

[28] Agorello to Wade, 10 May 1564, *CPSF 1564–5*, No. 387.

[29] Shers to Leicester, 15 May 1565, Pepys Papers, I, 393.

[30] 'Reasons for two Marts in England', undated, Cecil Papers, 3/54.

[31] Merchants Adventurers to Privy Council, undated, KL, III, 662–3. As this document mentions the 'stay of trade' in the past tense, it presumably dates from January 1565 at earliest.

[32] Memorandum by Cecil, undated but probably belonging to September 1564, SP 12/35/33, printed by TP, II, 45–7.

[33] See the reflections on trade with Emden, January 1565, SP 12/36/4.

[34] *Ante*, 261–4 *et passim*.

[35] It is now Add. 35,207.

[36] The letter is printed in G. D. Ramsay, *The politics of a Tudor merchant adventurer* (Manchester, 1979), where further information about Nedham has been assembled.

[37] For the information in this paragraph see Ramsay, *Politics of a Tudor merchant adventurer, ut supra.*

[38] *Supra,* 15.

[39] HL, II, No. 530, bearing date 29 December 1564. The terms as stated in this royal proclamation were not quite identical with those as agreed between Queen and Regent in the statement dated 30 November 1564, Weiss, VIII, 514–15, where 21 January 1559 was set down as the date after which trade offending trade regulations were to be amended. The corresponding edict of the Regent (for the province of Holland), dated 29 December 1564, is printed by Smit, *Bronnen*, No. 1051: it also cites 21 January as the limiting date, after which the offending *edicten, mandamenten ende publicatiën* were to be suspended. For this three weeks' discrepancy no explanation has come to light.

[40] HL, II, No. 530, where the actual word used was 'ordinances'. But the meaning is not to be doubted.

[41] The royal order to suspend these was directed to the Attorney-General, 17 February 1565, SP 12/36/17. The subsequent history of the 1563 prohibitions is considered by Willan, *TBR*, L–LI. For the Statutes of Employment see *supra*, 7.

[42] Fitzwilliams to Cecil, 18 January 1565, KL, IV, 159–61.

[43] They had asked for this in a letter to the Privy Council, 24 October 1564, Cecil Papers, 139/285. The copy at Cotton, Galba C I, No. 26, is incorrectly marked 'Oct. 1561' in a later hand.

[44] Merchants Adventurers to Council, 1 March 1569, Cotton Faustina C II, No. 19, f. 91.

[45] Merchants Adventurers to Privy Council, *c.*1565, Cotton Galba C II, No. 108 *ut supra; ib.* to *ib.*, 6 June 1566, Cecil Papers, 3/74.

[46] *Ib.*

[47] Wotton to Cecil, 24 June 1566, SP 70/84/424. The generally unsatisfactory nature of the situation was expounded in 'The Doleances of the Company in the Low Contrey', undated *c.* early 1569, SP 70/106/175.

[48] 'Complaints of the English merchants', 30 March 1565, *CSPF 1561–5*, No. 1069. Also similar document of about same date, Cotton Galba C I, No. 50.

[49] *Supra,* 50.

[50] *APC 1558–70*, 257.

[51] Cecil to Smith, 16 October 1565, Wright, I, 210.

[52] Staplers to Privy Council, 17 September 1565, SP 12/37/32. See the comments of Rich, *Ordinance Book*, 59–61.

[53] Three memoranda from the Merchants Adventurers to the Privy Council, printed KL, IV, 521–8, from the copies at SP 70, all under the date 25 November 1565. There are other copies at Cotton Galba, C II, Nos. 56, 58 and 65. All doubtless originated at different times in the autumn of 1565.

[54] Journals, 18, f. 318.

[55] 34 & 35 Hen. VIII, *c.* ; and 13 Eliz., *c.* 7.

[56] There is a brief discussion of the bankruptcy problem at this time in *Isham*, liv–lvii. The general development of the law of bankruptcy in England has been examined by W. J. Jones, 'The foundations of English bankruptcy: statutes and commissions in the early modern period'. *Transactions of the American Philosophical Society*, 69 part 3, 1979.

[57] Merchants Adventurers at Antwerp to York, 25 April 1568, Sellers, *York Mercers*, 181–2.

[58] Merchants Adventurers to Alva, undated *c.* June 1568, KL, V, 108–9n.

[59] Starkey and Knightley to Cecil; *ib*. to Privy Council, both June 1568, KL, v, 108–10.

[60] Sheres to Cecil, 12 August 1568, SP 70/101/1924; Marsh to Cecil, 15 and 29 August 1568, KL, v, 145–6 and 153–5. Governor Marsh reported that the proceedings were going ahead very fast, and that small account was made of the Queen's letter.

[61] *Supra*, 3.

[62] Merchants Adventurers to Privy Council, 25 September 1565, KL, iv, 521–3.

[63] *Supra*, 15.

[64] Declaration of 21 June 1566, Smit, *Bronnen*, No. 1109.

[65] Merchants Adventurers to Privy Council, undated but *c*. late 1565, KL, iv, 521–8; printed from copies in SP 70. There are duplicates at Cotton Galba C ii, Nos. 56, 58 and 65.

[66] Memorandum by Cecil, undated but *c*. early 1565, SP 12/38/62.

[67] Certificate of assessment of foreigners at London, undated *c*. April 1567, SP 12/41/60. The Spanish ambassador Silva also helped on this occasion to smooth matters over – Cecil to Winchester, 31 May 1567, SP 46/14, f. 41.

[68] There exists a skilful summary of the complicated situation by S. T. Bindoff, *The Scheldt Question to 1839* (London, 1945). For the 'double toll', see also *ante*, 22.

[69] Smedt, *EN*, ii, 212. See also text of renewal in Rymer.

[70] *Supra*, 10.

[71] Merchants Adventurers to Privy Council, undated *c*. late 1565, Cotton Galba C ii, No. 108; *ib*. to *ib*., 6 June 1566, Cecil Papers, 3/74; Merchants Adventurers to Orange, 29 July 1566, Smit, *Bronnen*, No. 1111.

[72] Fitzwilliams to Cecil, 14 December 1566, KL, iv, 397–8.

[73] *Ib*. to *ib*., 1 February 1567, *ib*., 406–8.

[74] Sussex to Queen, 5 July 1567, *ib*., 468–70.

[75] Marsh to Cecil, 2 September 1567, SP 70/94/1283. Smedt, *EN*, i, 219–24, explains the whole question in terms of administrative efficiency. From the Netherlands point of view this may indeed have been so; but the Englishmen had grounds for suspicion.

[76] Resolution of a General Court of the Merchants Adventurers at Antwerp, 6 March 1567, Sellers, *York Mercers*, 179–80. *Infra*, 56.

[77] Merchants Adventurers to Privy Council, undated *c*. 1565–6, KL, iv, 525. Smedt, *EN*, i, 339.

[78] Merchants Adventurers to Privy Council, 7 January 1569, SP 12/49/14.

[79] Complaints of the Merchants Adventurers, undated *c*. early 1569, SP 70/106/175; cf. *supra*, 8–9.

[80] Merchants Adventurers to Queen, December 1568, SP 70/104B/2271.

[81] J. Delumeau, *L'Alun de Rome* (Paris, 1964), 241, takes 1566 to be 'the turning point'. The English evidence endorses this.

[82] Regent to Philip II, 22 July 1565, Geldern, *MP*, ii, 85; acknowledgment by Philip II, 22 September, *ib*., 117.

[83] Regent to Philip II, 12 January 1566, *ib*., ii, 134–5.

[84] Instructions to Bruges commissioners, 3 August 1565, SP 70/79/1097.

[85] Delumeau, *L'Alun de Rome*, 225.

[86] G. B. Guicciardini to prince Francesco de' Medici, 2 June 1566, Battistini, 263–4. The rumour in due course came to the ears of the Regent, who passed it on to the King – Regent to Philip II, 13 September 1566, Gelder, *MP*, ii, 374–5. See also T. S. Willan, 'Some aspects of English trade with the Levant', *EHR*, lxx (1955), 399–410, and F. Braudel and R. Romano, *Navires et Marchandises à l'entrée du Port de Livourne (1547–1611)*, 49–51.

[87] Petition of Laurence Coxon to Privy Council, undated *c*. early 1568, SP 12/75/25.

[88] Memorandum by Cecil, undated, probably early 1565, SP 12/38/62. Although English administrative reactions to the events of 1564–5 are not directly relevant to the purposes of this study, it may be remarked that the government in November 1564 appointed a commission to enquire into the workings of the foreign exchange, the import trade and the customs system – *CPR 1563–6*, 31–2. Cecil also helped to regularize the customs entries by causing the initiation in 1565 of the series of Port Books that endured until 1799. Instructions for this were drafted in 1564, SP 12/35/38; *supra*, 62.

[89] 'Offers made for carrying on a trade with Barbary', February 1567, SP 12/42/22. See also Willan, 'The foundation of the Barbary Company', in *Studies*, 163–87.

[90] Bannister and Duckett to Muscovy Company, 12 August 1568, *Early Voyages and Travels to Russia and Persia*, ed. E. D. Morgan and C. H. Coote, II, Hakluyt Society, LXXIII (1885), 258–61. The chief merchants of the Muscovy Company were also Merchants Adventurers.

[91] Williamson, *Hawkins*, 142 *et seq.*

[92] *Supra.*, 77.

[93] E. G. R. Taylor, *Tudor Geography 1485–1583* (London, 1930), 87–8 and 99–100.

[94] E. Coornaert, 'Les Bourses d'Anvers aux XV$^e$ et XVI$^e$ siècles', *Revue Historique*, CCXVII (1957), 20–28.

[95] Richard Gresham to Cromwell, 25 July 1538, *LPH*, XIII, i, no. 1453. Materials bearing on the erection of the Bourse were assembled by C. Welch, *Illustrated account of the Royal Exchange* (London, 1913).

[96] Wotton to Vice-Dean and Chapter of Canterbury, 11 February 1565, *Archaeologia Cantiana*, XLII (1930), 103–4. For this reference I am indebted to Mr N. L. Ramsay.

[97] Subscriptions by individual merchants are listed at Journals 19, ff. 15–18.

[98] Stow, i, 201.

[99] *Ib.*

[100] The economic controversialists of the 1620s – Misselden, Malynes and Mun – had an advantage over their predecessors of sixty years earlier in that to a considerable extent they were able to use the printing press to state their various cases. Hence it is that the contribution that they were able to make to the incipient study of economics is now recognized. In the 1560s, the art of printing was much more constricted and less available for use, so that little or nothing of the arguments then employed, illuminating as these sometimes were, has found its way so far into print. But the early Elizabethans did make the effort to dissect the pattern of English foreign trade and its contribution to the well-being of the kingdom. See in particular *ante*, 234.

# Chapter V
## *The breaking of the storm*

Guzman de Silva, Spanish ambassador in England since the summer of 1564, was shrewd in the timing of his request, advanced in February 1568, for a posting to a less disagreeable country. He was able to remind Philip II of some undeniable facts – that in Anglo-Spanish relations the situation was quiet, the friendliness of the Queen not to be doubted, and the traffic of the English with the Netherlands restored – and to deduce the recommendation that his place might therefore easily be filled by someone else.[1] Indeed, it might seem at the time that the rebels and heretics of north-western Europe were being forced back to the defensive. A Spanish general with his soldiery had been installed without overt resistance in the Netherlands, only a few months earlier. When military opposition did take shape a little later, the weight of Silva's arguments was driven home by the failure of Louis of Nassau to withstand the professional troops of Alva. In the next year, the hopes of those who looked for French intervention to rid the Netherlands of the Spanish occupation were dashed when the Huguenots were defeated by the forces of the French crown in pitched battles at Jarnac and Moncontour. Altogether, the late sixties were on land a calamitous interlude for the protestants.

But at sea, the situation was to develop differently. Here, it was practicable for the weaker side to exploit some opportunities. From the summer of 1568 onwards, privateering revived under cover of licences issued in the name of the Queen of Navarre or the Prince of Orange – both of them being legally sovereign princes and therefore entitled to grant letters of marque. The privateers operated from dozens of scattered bases – remote fishing ports in the Netherlands, French harbours held for the Huguenots, especially La Rochelle, and out-of-the-way havens in Cornwall or elsewhere in England. In their wake came as always the pirates, for whom there were fresh pickings. The victims might be French ships manned by papists, Netherlands or Spanish ships carrying on legitimate trade under the protection of Alva, or indeed any ship carrying a tempting freight. The progress registered by the English commissioners for piracy under the eye of Silva came to an end, chiefly in the interval between his recall and his actual departure from England. The merchantmen plying between the Netherlands and Spain, with their often valuable cargoes, became so many ready victims to unidentifiable or elusive plunderers whose language might be French, English or Low German, whatever the alleged source of their authority. There was an unholy international camaraderie that made possible, as in 1562–4, the setting-forth of ships, whether as privateers or pirates, with crews of mixed nationalities, all the less easy to bring to book. The damage being inflicted on the seaborne trade of Antwerp from the summer of 1568 onwards was all the more dangerous from the political point of view since at the same time it affected the maritime life-line linking Alva and his troops in the Netherlands with his ultimate military base in Spain.[2]

There was a simultaneous deterioration of the alternative overland line of communication southwards along the Rhine to Italy. Even in December 1567, Alva could not be certain of the security of his post to southern Germany.[3] Then early in March 1568 the news arrived in the Netherlands that the Elector Palatine, the defiant patron of Calvinism in Germany, through whose territories the Rhine flowed, had stopped a couple of barges at his Mannheim toll-station. They were travelling downstream to the Netherlands with cargoes of Italian luxury wares and a large quantity of silver reals – 200,000 ducats, it was said at first, but later it turned out to be more. The goods were unloaded and taken to the Elector's castle at Heidelberg. His pretext for ordering this was that there was an infringement of the Reich currency laws involved in the dispatch of foreign coins, and as this did not apply to the transit of the commodities they were released after a few days. But he clung to the ducats. At first, he was gratified to think that he had got hold of papal property, but before long he found out that the money belonged to Genoese merchants and was being consigned to Alva for the payment of his troops. There was little that Alva could do about the matter: he protested to the Emperor and to various German princes, with small result. On the Antwerp Bourse there was an immediate panic, and subsequently there was a rumour that the Elector was offering to lend the money to the Huguenot leaders at 16 per cent interest, and to pay the Genoese owners in good bills on Paris.[4] The Queen of England, on hearing of the seizure, was moved to express to Silva her horror.[5] One result of the episode was that for the future Alva was bound to rely more upon the maritime line of communication with Spain, for the use of which it was essential to be on good terms with England. Even if Alva and his master had been single-minded crusaders – which they certainly were not – it would have been witless on their part to provoke the enmity of Elizabeth Tudor and so make the northern coast of the Channel as unsafe as the southern had already become.

The arrival of a new man to succeed Silva as Spanish ambassador in England from September 1568 was bound to be of major interest for Alva – all the more so, since there was still no direct diplomatic link between England and the Netherlands, and with the expulsion of Dr Man there was no longer an English ambassador at Madrid. A peculiarly heavy burden of responsibility therefore rested on the shoulders of Don Guerau Despes, the new envoy, as the one and only official diplomatic intermediary between Elizabeth and both Alva and his master the King.[6] It was reported that he was 'a man of reputation' at the court of Philip II, a member of the royal household, and 'of the President's preferment', i.e. a client of Cardinal Espinosa, President of the Council of Castile, and by implication not a nominee of Alva.[7] There is no evidence to suggest that he possessed any previous experience of life in northern Europe, let alone England. He was a knight of the military Order of Calatrava: Secretary Cecil approvingly reported him to be 'a gentleman well qualified and martial'.[8] Unfortunately, he tended to identify the service of his master the King with the unflagging promotion of his master's religion, in a manner reminiscent not of his predecessor Silva but of the earlier envoy Bishop Quadra. Although tact was not his strong point, he was not lacking in ability or initiative, and unlike Quadra he had a lively appreciation of the importance of commercial questions for the fulfilment of his mission. The instructions he received were plain. He was to explain to Queen Elizabeth why the King had found himself compelled to take action against Dr Man, and to make clear to her that it implied no lessening of his friendship for her. When introduced by Silva, he was 'to salute the queen gaily and graciously' and assure her that he had come 'to serve and gratify her on every possible occasion', as indeed it was his duty to do.[9] In short, he was to keep guard over the maintenance of the Anglo-Burgundian and the Anglo-Spanish alliance, still in seaworthy trim.

The briefing received by Despes proved to be lopsided and probably prevented him from grasping the realities of the English situation. After his appointment, he could hardly avoid the company of the Madrid Anglophils, and he was known to have frequented the society of Sir Francis Englefield, Master of the Court of Wards and influential in the days of Queen Mary, but now enduring a self-inflicted exile for the sake of religion.[10] Such folk, with their nostalgic yearning for pre-Elizabethan England, were as likely to mislead as to help. In July 1568, Despes made his way across France to the Netherlands, there to learn the intricacies of local politics and of the traffic with England. He spent some time, very properly, at Antwerp. Unfortunately, when he arrived, Alva happened to be away, rounding up rebels in the distant province of West Friesland, so that his education in some vital matters fell to Dr d'Assonleville, still a prominent personage in the government at Brussels, and an unrepentant champion of the view of Anglo-Netherlands trade that in 1563 and 1566 had led to such disruptive results.[11] The language used by Assonleville to the new envoy may be inferred from a dispatch sent by Despes to Philip II late in August, in which he naively reported that Assonleville was drawing up for him 'a full statement of the injuries we receive and the terms which were to have been arranged by the Conference at Bruges, which no doubt would have been carried out but for the troubles and disturbances in the Netherlands'. He further assured the King that he had been 'fully informed by the Duke of Alva of the grievances of Your Majesty's subjects both in the Netherlands and Spain, at the hand of those who disregard alliances, ancient friendship and good neighbourship' – a reference presumably to the marauders again at large in the Channel.[12] For the future of the Antwerp mart, it was no good omen that a man thus indoctrinated, and by nature a fighter, should be sent to represent Philip II at the court of Elizabeth.

Despes landed in England on 3 September 1568, and thenceforward was able to judge for himself how greatly the times were out of joint. Hearsay evidence that fed his prejudices he assimilated all too readily. His dispatches home provided a contrast to the shrewd and relatively objective narratives of Silva. It was perhaps only to be expected that he should report to his master within a few weeks of his arrival how the Queen's Secretary Cecil

and the Lord Keeper Bacon – two of the most important personages in her government – were 'among the most bare-faced
heretics here, pernicious and enemies to Your Majesty'.[13] This
was the sort of information that Bishop Quadra had been pur-
veying, years before. It was much worse that he should assert as
his belief that the Queen was helping the Prince of Orange with
money, which was certainly not true, and was the sort of statement that could serve only to poison the Anglo-Spanish alliance.[14] From the outset, his own conduct was, to say the least,
indiscreet. One of his very first acts was to open up communication with the Queen of Scots, now a fugitive half-captive in the
north of England. He was soon in touch with her London agent
the Bishop of Ross, and swimming in the cloud of intrigue that
enveloped her fortunes.[15] It was the fateful first step towards an
alignment of interests between Philip II and Mary Stuart.
Despes came to accept that if only the Queen of Scots could
count upon support from outside, 'it might be easy for her to
change from a prisoner to sovereign of this country' – a most
dangerous line of thought.[16] But, at least for the present, he did
not propose to take up the cudgels on her behalf.

There is evidence that at this time he believed that the restoration of England to papal obedience did not necessitate the overthrow of Elizabeth. It is to be found in the plan of action that he
lost no time in devising, to bring the government of England
back to the fold of catholic Christendom. This was a bold scheme
a draft of which he sent to Philip II in a letter dated 12 December – i.e., just over three months after his arrival. It indicated
how fully he had grasped the fact that the English still depended
upon the Antwerp mart for their well-being. Indeed, all that was
needed for the implementation of his plan was the restoration of
calm in the Netherlands and then an agreement between Philip
and the King of France to suspend all commercial dealings with
England. So dependent were the English upon foreign trade,
especially with the Netherlands, that the rulers of the kingdom
'would be forced to come to reason by pressure from their own
people, who are largely catholics'. And so 'without any necessity
for drawing the sword', Despes foresaw that 'the English will be
forced to adopt the catholic religion'. As to Queen Elizabeth, she
might personally be redeemed from heresy by a timely and
flattering exhortation, embodying the evidence of history, of
natural philosophy and of the fathers of the church, which in
anticipation he had himself drawn up in triplicate for approval

by his master.[17] The economic parentage of this scheme is evident enough: it had no doubt been supplied by Assonleville. It was nothing so complex as a revival of the secret of the cardinal, despite its elaborate and specific form.[18] But it was open to one or two fatal objections. Its execution would have meant very hard times once more at Antwerp, so that the difficulties of Alva in the government of the Netherlands would be all the greater. Most extraordinary of all, its prospects of success hinged upon French co-operation. From an ambassador who in 1568 could seriously adumbrate such a plan, any extravagance might be expected.

Much of the day-to-day business of Despes was concerned with the recent revival of piracy in the Channel, which had already been exercising Silva before his departure. A combination of lawlessness and foul weather made the seas sufficiently unsafe in November 1568 to deter the English wine-fleet from making its usual autumn voyage from west-country ports to Bordeaux.[19] It was under these circumstances that a flotilla of ships, mostly the fast-sailing craft known as *zabras* that relied for security on speed, left Santander in Spain for Antwerp. They carried some wool, but otherwise their cargoes were of a nature similar to those of the Rhine barges detained earlier in the year by the Elector Palatine – luxury commodities, with a quantity of bullion, largely in Spanish silver reals. In both cases, too, the goods were mostly the property of Italian financial houses, and the money was to be handed over to Alva for the payment of his troops. The safe arrival of this treasure was a matter of some moment to Alva, especially since the raising of taxes from the Netherlanders was proving difficult, and it may be imagined that it was also being awaited with anxiety by merchants on the Bourse at Antwerp. The masters of the *zabras* had been instructed at almost any cost to avoid entering a French port, but rather to return; if forced into an English one, they were not to have any truck with the people ashore but merely to explain that they were carrying posts to Alva. If an attempt was made to detain them, they were at once to have recourse to the Spanish ambassador at the court of the Queen.[20] As ill-luck would have it, the Spanish ships met both tempests and Huguenot privateers at the entrance to the Channel. Two of the *zabras* and one other vessel escaped and raced home to port at Antwerp.[21] Another ship, under her master Lope de la Sierra, closely pursued by Frenchmen with obvious designs upon her cargo, found shelter near Southampton. The remaining *zabras* before the end of November made port elsewhere in the west country.[22]

The arrival of these ships in English waters gave rise within a few weeks to some shattering events, whose interpretation from that time to this has been a subject of controversy. But there is not any dispute that the presence of the Spanish vessels provided interesting news and provoked strong currents of opinion. The nature of their cargo was known to Genoese and other merchants at London who did not feel bound to maintain complete secrecy on the point, so that the value of the bullion was heightened by speculation and gossip.[23] As to what if anything should be done about the treasure-ships thus cast by chance upon English shores, views were sharply divided. It so happened that early in December rumours reached London – falsely – that the sea-captain John Hawkins and 'a great number of his men' had been massacred in America by the Spaniards. His brother, writing from the west country to Cecil, put forward the plea that the Queen might 'have stay made of King Philip's treasure here in these parts till there be sufficient recompense made for the great wrongs offered and also other wrongs before that'.[24] The idea must have occurred to plenty of other people, especially to the militant protestants at London and the sea-dogs in the ports of the southern coast.

At the court of the Queen, there were undoubtedly men who shared such an outlook, though it is unlikely that either Leicester or Secretary Cecil were among them. Once it became known to Elizabeth and her Council that the Spanish ships in port along the southern coast were carrying a hoard of treasure, the question was naturally asked – to whom did it belong? Despes sought to cast a protective veil over it by vouchsafing the answer – to his master the King. It could not therefore be touched without very serious consequences. But entirely different information was divulged by the knowledgeable Genoese merchant Benedict Spinola, long resident at London and very well known to most members of the Council. According to his story, it was the property of various Genoese finance houses. It was to be lent to the government of the Netherlands, but had not yet changed hands. When later the treasure was landed, documents indicating the truth of this disclosure came to light. Meanwhile, his words must have altered the legal situation in the minds of Queen and Council. The Genoese were not subjects of Philip II. Might it not be worth while to borrow some of the money from them, perhaps as a reward for preserving the rest from the French? Spinola's partners and associates at Antwerp and Genoa could have no great objection, since the credit of the Queen of England stood far higher than that of the King of Spain. Perhaps Spinola even suggested that the English government might like to take advantage of an unexpected windfall. The Queen was in no desperate straits for money, which in itself must have made her seem preferable to Philip II as a potential debtor in Genoese eyes. Spinola's revelation, whatever prompted him to make it, undoubtedly strengthened the hand of those at the royal court who favoured interference.[25]

But opinion was far from unanimous. In the counting-houses of the City any notion that there should be some tampering with what was virtually Spanish property on the authority of the Queen reeked of disaster. The loose talk favourable to some such action was doubtless one reason why in the course of the month of December 1568 there was a sudden access of tension at London. The English merchants in the City who traded to Spain grew so alarmed by wild reports that on the 28th they actually petitioned the Privy Council to bear in mind 'our poor estates', i.e. the merchandise they owned in Spain, their stock-in-trade, the safety of which would be endangered by any unfriendly act on the part of the Queen.[26] Leading Merchants Adventurers also besought the government not to provoke the King of Spain. The Company itself was so fearful of running risks that a meeting was held to debate whether or not the next batch of four ships with their cloths should sail for Antwerp. The outlook seemed uncertain; but ultimately by 48 votes to 18, prudence was laid aside and it was resolved that in view of the stocks piling up at Blackwell Hall the merchants should accept the risks and the ships should depart.[27] A pervasive fear of trouble looming ahead may possibly explain the unusually long interruption in the meetings of the Court of Aldermen, from 16 December to 12 January.[28]

As to the Spanish ships, they continued at anchor in English waters because of the persistent presence of the Frenchmen lying in wait for them on the high seas. They were in effect being blockaded. Since the Channel was likely to remain infested by Huguenot privateers for the indefinite future, how was the treasure to be conveyed to the Netherlands? The alternative courses appeared to be either to carry it overland to Dover and there to embark it by the short sea route to Antwerp; or for the

Queen to provide an escort from her own warships to protect the Spanish ships for the remainder of their voyage. On the Spanish side, no fear for the safety of the treasure while in English hands was at this stage expressed.[29] Despes had been prompt to enquire of Alva which alternative he preferred, but Alva not surprisingly proved slow to declare his mind.[30] Thus the days and the weeks passed, while the Spanish ships with their precious freight lingered in their English refuges. As late as 14 December, Despes had audience of the Queen, but he did not, as far as the evidence goes, tax her with further demands.[31]

Meanwhile, events in the Channel did not stand still. A tense drama was being played out in the murky winter weather at the entry to Southampton Water, where the largest treasure-ship lay in imminent danger of attack from the pursuing Frenchmen, under the guns of Calshot Castle. These gave small protection during the hours of darkness, which was naturally when the French launched a surprise attack in expectation of seizing the bullion. They were beaten off, with casualties on both sides; the Mayor of Southampton was 'severely wounded' while attempting to restore the peace.[32] At Saltash and Fowey, where the other four treasure-ships had sought shelter, their plight was similar though less immediately perilous. The Frenchmen, foiled in direct attacks, were ready to use other methods to attain their purpose and offered bribes to the English officials, who were not immune from the temptation to accept them. The general situation was thus at best unstable. It was at this point that the English government intervened with an action that has been variously interpreted. Mr Secretary Cecil, presumably acting on instructions, wrote to the local admiralty representatives to ensure the safety of the cargoes carried by the Spanish ships by having them put ashore. His letters have unfortunately not survived, but from the terms in which they were acknowledged it is possible to deduce one important point about their contents.[33] The treasure was to be landed as an act of Anglo-Spanish collaboration, to preserve it from the French, and force was not to be used.

At Southampton, Lope de la Sierra had unintentionally smoothed the way for the landing of his freight by asking for protection for it. He was genuinely grateful for assurances that this would be forthcoming. But as Sir Edward Horsey, the recipient of Cecil's instructions, reported, he was at first reluctant to see the treasure landed and agreed only when Horsey pointed out to him that its safety could not otherwise be assured. It was therefore removed with his consent but not without misgivings on his part, and by 20 December was in the custody of the Mayor of Southampton. At Saltash and Fowey the landing was delayed until some days later. But however peaceful these deeds may have been, and however non-committal or even friendly the intentions of the Queen and Cecil, Horsey and his colleague Sir Arthur Champernowne at Saltash and Fowey took a relish in the proceedings for reasons of a very different hue. Champernowne was hand-in-glove with the Huguenots and his nephew was actually at the time at La Rochelle. He would have been willing to connive at a Huguenot seizure of part of the treasure, provided the rest came into English hands, though he would rather have seen everything pass to the Queen – as he put it to Cecil, 'so great a treasure is most fittest for her grace'. Horsey expressed himself more guardedly, but if Lope de la Sierra had not agreed to the landing of his freight, Horsey would have laid hands on it even at the cost of bloodshed. Champernowne too was prepared to use force and to brave the momentary anger of the Queen in order to land the bullion; at Saltash, he reckoned upon local opposition only from the servants of the papist Sir John Arundell of Lanherne. In short, neither the political scruples of the English government nor the dismay of City merchants were matters to trouble overmuch either Champernowne or Horsey.[34]

As to Despes at London, he could as late as 18 December still refer in a dispatch to the landing of the money from the treasure-ships for safety's sake without apparent alarm.[35] But in a protestant environment teeming with refugees from the murderous regime of Alva, there must have been no lack of fire-eaters hopefully and loosely talking of the possible confiscation of the treasure-ships by the government – enough assuredly to enhance the atmosphere of crisis. To all this, Despes could not but be sensitive. The political tension at London evidently took on a new and sinister significance for him as he pondered further on the implication of the news that the treasure had been removed from the ship at Southampton. He learnt of Lope de la Sierra's misgivings.[36] He himself subsequently alleged that he was told by 'many persons of position' (not however named) that the Queen was going to lay hands on the bullion because she knew that it was private property.[37] He was aware how vital its safe arrival was to the government of the Netherlands. What could possibly deter Elizabeth from seizing it? True, he had no

definite information that this was her intention. He was relying
on hearsay evidence. But it sufficed, we must suppose, to fill him
with dread. And so he abruptly changed course and on 21
December committed himself to an extreme step from which
there could be no withdrawal. He sent a message to Alva urging
him to seize at once all English shipping and merchandise in the
Netherlands, 'particularly at Antwerp', and to forward information of his action swiftly to Spain 'as there are valuable English
ships at Bilbao and Laredo'.[38] It was one of the most decisive
and fateful deeds in the annals of diplomacy.

Having thus applied the match to the fuse, Despes did not
envisage his action as being merely defensive. He sought to
improve the occasion by clearing the way for the execution of
the far-reaching plan he had submitted to the King of Spain
earlier in the month – a joint trade boycott of the English by
order of the French and Spanish governments working hand-in-
hand.[39] In pursuit of this project, only a day or two after writing
to Alva, he paid a call on the French ambassador to the court of
Elizabeth, La Mothe Fénélon. Within the walls of the French
embassy, he unfolded his scheme for concerted action – first for
the removal of the heretic Cecil from power, then for the restoration of catholicism in England by joint commercial pressure. The Frenchman, a cool and sharp-sighted *politique*,
reported these advances to the Queen-Mother of France without
enthusiasm. As far as French interests were concerned, he commented, there could be worse ministers than Cecil; as to the
suggested boycott, as soon as the King of France had become
embroiled with the Queen of England, the English and the
Spaniards might well come to terms, leaving him in the lurch.[40]
This was not a groundless fear. Indeed, while Despes was en-
gaging himself in this large project he did not cease to address
himself to Elizabeth, asking her that the money that had been
safely landed at Southampton and placed in the custody of the
Mayor there should be 'restored' to Lope de la Sierra, though
not necessarily put again on his threatened and vulnerable ship:
as previously broached, it should either be sent overland to
Dover or escorted by her warships to Antwerp.[41] It is astound-
ing that he should have believed that the arrest of all the English
in the Netherlands would encourage the Queen to follow one or
another of these courses. What a misreading of the tempera-
ment of Elizabeth, and what a miscalculation of her attitude to
the merchants and their traffic![42]

On 22 December, thus the day following the dispatch of his message to the Netherlands, Despes went to court to seek audience of the Queen. It was not granted; but in the grave though uninformative demeanour of Cecil and Leicester he read the confirmation of his fears. He therefore sent his secretary with another more urgent letter to Alva, re-iterating his call for instant action.[43] On 29 December, exactly a week later, he at length saw the Queen. According to his story, she told him at this audience that in order to save the treasure from the pirates she was having care taken of it. When he produced a letter of credence from Alva asking that it should be sent under escort to Antwerp, she then retorted that 'she had decided to avail herself of it', to quote the phrase employed by Despes.[44] But according to the version published by her command just over a week later, her words were different. She told Despes that if the treasure really belonged to King Philip she had done him a great service in preserving it from the French, 'showing him therein some particularities of the diligence of her officers'. But, she continued, she was informed that it belonged to merchants. He should know her mind further in four or five days' time. She ended by giving him an assurance 'on her honour, that nothing should be herein done that in reason should miscontent the king her good brother'.[45] Whichever account of what passed at the audience was the truer, the somewhat Delphic flavour of the royal utterance provided the first scrap of direct evidence given to Despes for inferring that perhaps not all the money would immediately be forwarded to the Netherlands.

Whatever the ultimate intentions in the mind of the Queen at this last audience with Despes may have been will never be known; probably she had not formulated any. Given her financial dependence upon the City of London and its merchants, and especially her fiscal interest in the smooth conduct of the cloth trade, it is inconceivable that she would knowingly have risked the provocation of a catastrophe of the size of that now about to break. While ready money was always welcome, she was not in any dire financial need, though Despes might delude himself into the belief that she was.[46] Indeed, when the bullion ultimately passed into her direct custody it remained for long unused and sterile. Some was possibly disbursed in the winter of 1569–70, but Gresham in March 1571 was lamenting to Cecil what 'a great pity' it was that so much Spanish money should lie in the Tower of London 'dead and put to no use'.[47] If no crisis

had been precipitated in the Netherlands by Despes, it is unlikely that Elizabeth would for long have held on to the treasure,
or most of it. To regulate its release by dribs and drabs, or at
most to have retained some of it perhaps on the plea of covering
costs of transport, would not have been out of keeping with her
ways of conducting affairs. Certainly it would have pleased her
to give a rap on the knuckles to remind Alva and Philip II of
their dependence upon her good will and to indicate her distaste
for the presence of Spanish troops and methods in the Netherlands. But this is mere speculation. What Elizabeth and her
councillors may have debated in December 1568 bore only a
limited relevance to the mighty train of events set in motion by
the missives of Despes dispatched on the 21st. and 22nd. of the
month.

When Alva received the dispatches, he was aghast. That the
Queen of England could wish to break with the King of Spain he
found hard to believe.[48] He was aware of the economic consequences for the Netherlands of the action he was now called
upon to execute. However, he could not disregard the urgent
and explicit request of the chosen envoy of his master at London, so that his own course of action was plain and unavoidable.
But he interpreted the message in his own way and acted gently.
For the arrest of the Merchants Adventurers he used as his
agent not the municipality of Antwerp, whose lords would have
been embarrassed in the extreme, but the military commander
of the new castle, Count Lodron, who was instructed to proceed
with all possible courtesy.[49] Over 120 English subjects were
involved, mostly young men not in business on their own but
serving employers at home. They were summoned on the afternoon of 28 December by Lodron, who informed them that he
had orders to arrest them and their goods; considerately, he
gave them until the next day to move into the English House.
Here they were required to reside, no doubt in very cramped
conditions, though they were allowed to walk about the town
during the day. But the keys of their warehouses were taken
from them, their counting-houses were sealed up, and a guard
of soldiers was placed at the entrance to their enforced residence.[50] Two English ships held up by ice on their way downstream to the sea were made to return, and another two laden
with merchandise riding before the city were also detained.[51]
Never before had English merchants been molested, in their
persons and their property, in this wholesale way. The manner

of the arrest might seem mild and gentlemanly enough, but its ultimate consequences would be hard to exaggerate.

Besides, while the Merchants Adventurers at Antwerp comprised by far the most important settlement of Englishmen in the Netherlands, they did not include all subjects of the Queen there. There were also Englishmen scattered here and there in lesser towns throughout the country. Alva was unable to intervene quickly enough to protect them from the brutality and roughness from which the Merchants Adventurers were shielded. Opinion in England was subsequently stirred by various stories of the indignities they suffered, and in particular by the evidence that when Despes had sent off his secretary to Alva, that same secretary on landing in the Netherlands lost no time in seeing to the arrest of all the Englishmen in the Flemish towns through which he passed. Even the ship on which he had travelled was seized in harbour at Dunkirk, and its crew sent to prison. Among those arrested were the interlopers at Amsterdam and even the Staplers at Bruges, where there was some trouble in distinguishing the wool and wool-fells belonging to Englishmen from the property that had passed to Italian and German buyers.[52] Only the little colony of papists at Louvain went unscathed. But in Flanders the English sailors and merchants suffered most, as a result of the attentions of the malevolent secretary, for there they were thrust into the common gaols.[53]

Intelligence of the arrests reached London late in the evening of 3 January 1569, thanks to the carelessness of a special courier sent by Alva to Despes.[54] At midnight the news was broken to the Lord Mayor Thomas Rowe, by 'certain worthy English merchants' who called upon him 'suddenly and very fearfully'. The story lost nothing in the telling: as Rowe passed it on to Cecil, all the English at Antwerp 'be kept prisoners in the English House there, and that by the guard of a thousand men, and all their goods attached, and none of our nation whatsoever to depart upon pain of death'.[55] Rowe was himself an important personage in the Company of Merchants Adventurers, and fully alive to the intense gravity of the situation. He kept his head sufficiently to stop the departure of the post that was just about to set out for the Netherlands; the packet of letters was sent instead to Cecil to be investigated 'to the intent that the Queen's Highness may have the better intelligence what goods king Philip's subjects have here'.[56] There can have been few in the City who in one way or another did not stand to lose by the

renewed interruption of trade with the Netherlands, from the
big merchant trafficking to Antwerp who was brought so much
nearer to bankruptcy, to the humble porter in Cheapside whose
employment was in jeopardy and who could see starvation
looming ahead. The streets that night were alive with people, as
the resident Spanish merchants fled with their goods for safety
to the house of Despes and hostile crowds gathered to demonstrate against foreigners. The aldermen and constables were
called out to patrol their respective wards; even Despes thought
that they did their job effectively and prevented the situation
from getting out of hand. Secretary Cecil himself was in the City,
but when morning came he made his way back to Hampton
Court, where the Queen was in residence.

What counter-measures could be taken? We may imagine the
problem being debated by the privy councillors at court from
the morning of 4 January onwards. Before long, the Queen
signified her agreement that the first step must be an immediate
retaliation in kind upon the merchants resident in England but
owing allegiance to the King of Spain. To prevent their escape,
messengers were dispatched at once to close the ports, and the
command went forth that no post-horses were to be issued to
anyone. A royal proclamation dated 6 January gave order that
all subjects of the King of Spain together with 'their goods,
merchandises, ships and vessels' should be 'arrested and stayed,
to be forthcoming and answerable as well for the indemnity of
her majesty's subjects already without any just cause detained, as
for other necessary consequences': this was to be effected without any use of violence, and was not to apply to the many
refugees from the Netherlands who had come for the sake of
religion.[57] If there were to be arrests on either side of the North
Sea, Cecil felt certain that the balance of advantage lay with the
English. It was regrettable that the Merchants Adventurers in
their short-sighted pursuit of mere profit had recently allowed
the four cloth ships to sail and thus presented Alva with extra
pledges; for this they were berated in Council and made to offer
an apology.[58] But their debts at Antwerp were believed to
exceed their assets there by £100,000, while as to Netherlands
and Spanish property in England, in Cecil's words, 'I think a
great richness is now in our ports'.[59] This was soon to be augmented as ships from Spain on their way to the Netherlands
unsuspectingly put in at English harbours, only to find themselves interned there. Alva was alive to this danger and wrote to

warn the King; but before the end of February there were fourteen more such vessels in detention along the south coast.[60] The English fared better: most of their trading ships got away from Spanish ports before any embargo was applied there, and Hawkins limped back before the end of January without sustaining any further damage in the final weeks of his voyage.[61]

At London, the arrests proceeded methodically. The Lord Mayor lost no time in reporting to the Privy Council that the goods in the warehouse of Jan della Faille, one of the richest Antwerp merchants trading to England, had been placed in the safe-keeping of the alderman of his ward and that his factor 'Harman Peter' had been confined in the house of Alderman Allen. The della Faille firm had been singled out for immediate action because the Lord Mayor had been informed that it possessed 'more goods here at this present than any one merchant else hath by £1,000 and better' – as it turned out, this was not quite accurate, since although della Faille property to the value of over £3,000 Flemish was sequestrated, even more valuable hauls were made from a couple of other firms.[62] But while a simultaneous arrest of all merchants professing allegiance to Philip II would if only for mere administrative reasons have been impracticable, a speedy inventory of their goods and debts could be made. Two petitions from the City urged that this should be done, and doubtless as a result of these the Privy Council authorized the Lord Mayor and aldermen to commission forty knowledgeable citizens to investigate the property of Netherlands and Spanish concerns.[63] Among these City commissioners were John Fitzwilliams, long resident at Antwerp, Thomas Starkey, probably a relative of the Starkey whose property at Barrow had been seized by the Netherlands government, Thomas Aldersey, who had led the Emden voyage of 1564, and many other prominent Merchants Adventurers.[64] Not much is likely to have eluded them: after all, they were hastening the discomfiture of their trade rivals and at the same time ensuring for themselves the existence of compensation at hand in London to offset any losses that might accrue through the action of Alva at Antwerp. The unhappy foreigners concerned, naturally enough, were believed to be neglecting no device, within or without the law, to convey their goods to others exempt from the enquiries of the commissioners.[65] To prevent collusion of this sort, the Lord Mayor was a little later told to put a stop to the issue of attachments of goods or debts of subjects of the King of Spain.[66]

The events of January 1569 fairly certainly constituted the
most damaging blow ever to be inflicted upon the cosmopolitan
Antwerp firms with branch offices at London. Their trade was to
lie at a standstill for nearly five years, during which their capital
was immobilized and they had to participate in wearisome and
expensive negotiations. Even foreigners not directly involved
were not spared loss. The Italians, though they and their goods
might escape arrest since they were not subjects of the King of
Spain, found that their transit trade with the Netherlands was
abruptly brought to a halt. They were thus sundered from their
headquarters and confronted by a new challenge to their in-
genuity and technique. The Genoese, Florentine and Lucchese
merchants resident at London were in particular affected. It also
happened that just at this moment there were two great ships of
Venice, each of 900 or 1,000 tons, at anchor off the Kentish
coast at Gore End, peacefully taking on cargo delivered to them
from both London and the Netherlands. The Admiral of England, Lord Clinton, at once had his eye on them. He argued that
if the Queen did not at least prevent them from sailing they
would simply fall into the hands of the King of Spain and be
used for the carriage of his subjects' merchandise to and from
the Netherlands, if not for a more hostile end. Since the two
big ships of the royal navy, the *Jesus of Lubeck* and the *Minion*,
were both absent with Hawkins and the date of their return still
uncertain, the situation in his opinion demanded action.[67]
The Doge might lodge a protest, but the two Venetian ships
were held and not allowed to depart until the summer, when
they were released to transport English cloths direct to the
Mediterranean.[68]

As to the bullion whose movement had occasioned the fresh
rupture of trade, there could be no question, after the arrest of
the Englishmen in the Netherlands, of forwarding it to its intended destination. Instead, it was transported from the several
west country ports to the Tower of London – 155 chests of
Spanish silver reals, reckoned ultimately by Gresham to be
worth £85,000 odd in sterling.[69] The merchandise taken from
Netherlands and Spanish shipping was stored in official custody
at London and elsewhere, while the crews were left to languish
ashore – Despes reported in February 1569 that seventy or
eighty mariners had been put into Bridewell, there to listen to
the sermons of a heretic Spanish minister, while others in the
western ports were 'worse treated than Turks'.[70] As already

remarked, the bullion remained in the Tower, locked away for some years. It was not needed to buttress the royal credit; Gresham was confident of his ability to grapple with the debts of the crown. In the summer of 1569 he was pleading in vain that the Queen should put the treasure 'to use of some profit, as to mint it into her own coin'.[71] Its significance lay in politics, in its value as a pledge for the restoration of the property seized at Antwerp and elsewhere in the dominions of the King of Spain.[72] The Queen was at pains to demonstrate to the world that she was keeping it under lock and key in the Tower because the English merchants had been arrested and their belongings seized – emphatically not the other way round. This was the essential point clearly stated in the long proclamation speedily drawn up and published in her name on 6 January.[73] Every effort was made to secure international publicity for it. In addition, a very full account of events was sent to her ambassador in France, who was instructed not only to inform the French King and his council but also to pass on the information to the Spanish ambassador there so that the unvarnished story might be transmitted direct to Philip II.[74]

It did not take long for the Queen and her Privy Council to deduce that the whole episode had been precipitated by one man only – Despes. Writing on 5 January, the Lord Keeper Sir Nicholas Bacon was quick to point out to his colleagues how the timing indicated that the arrests in the Netherlands must have been made without any order from the King of Spain, and that the Spanish envoy should therefore be taxed with the responsibility to see if he accepted it. If he did, then the Lord Keeper could see no reason for the further sojourn of Despes in England.[75] In fact, at the first arrival of the news from the Low Countries the ambassador had feigned surprise and, in Cecil's words, 'imputed the faults to hasty councillors about the Duke d'Alva'.[76] This was not a pretence that could be long maintained, for within a couple of days there arrived the hair-raising information of how his secretary had personally been responsible for having Englishmen in Flanders flung into prison, and some grim details were supplied by a couple of Staplers who had managed to get away from Bruges.[77] Not surprisingly, Despes at once wrote off to warn his secretary not to return to England, and prepared himself for a riposte from the English government.[78] Since the King of Spain had very recently provided a precedent for taking action against an ambassador who was alleged to have misused his privileges, there was no reason for the Queen to hesitate about the matter.

So without loss of time the Lord Admiral Clinton accompanied by Mr Secretary Cecil called in the early afternoon of 8 January upon Despes at his lodgings in Paget House, in the Strand at the Temple Bar end.[79] They were escorted by a large train including most of the aldermen of the City: we may imagine the tense atmosphere as the procession made its way, with the scarlet gowns of the aldermen enlivening the wintry day. Inside the embassy, there was an angry confrontation. Clinton at first addressed the ambassador, to explain the Queen's 'misliking of the Duke of Alva's proceedings against our subjects, and his also'. The topic was then taken up by Cecil, who enlarged upon the English grievances against the King of Spain, from the days of Bishop Quadra onwards, and taxed Despes with direct responsibility for the arrest of the Merchants Adventurers at Antwerp. When he denied this – it must have been a stormy scene at this point, perhaps audible to the crowd outside – proofs of his complicity were adduced, relating particularly to the dispatch of his secretary just over a fortnight previously, and he was put under what might be described as house arrest. The order was that no Spaniard might leave the embassy. The papist English servants were sent away, and other Englishmen of good birth were appointed to take charge of the household and to remain with the ambassador 'as well to see him and his defended from the violence of any of our subjects being irritated by reason of the arrest of their friends, servants and goods on the other side, as also that neither he nor his should depart'. The correspondence of Despes in future was to be put under surveillance. When he protested at this, he was informed that by his conduct he had forfeited his rights as an ambassador, and he was further reminded of the fate of Dr Man. Fortunately for Despes, the English did not yet know the full extent of his machinations – that only a day or so earlier he had numbered among his visitors not merely the Bishop of Ross, agent of the deposed Queen of Scots, but also the Earl of Northumberland, who had come in disguise and given an assurance of his adhesion to the King of Spain – though they may well have had some suspicions.[80]

Despes though now caged was not in the least silenced. He evidently enjoyed a fight. He had taken care to get rid of incriminating papers, so that the English could find nothing in his house that could be used as evidence against him. Amid the confusion that prevailed during the visit of the Lord Admiral and Secretary Cecil, he had even managed to smuggle off a courier to the Netherlands. His defiant strategy was fortified by information of proceedings at the Privy Council board where one of the members, as he explained to his master, told him all.[81] For the future, he planned to elude the English censors by sending dispatches in the bag of the French ambassador, who was embarrassed by the request that he should connive at this.[82] Meanwhile, he scored some neat points by composing letters duly left open for perusal by the privy councillors. One was directed to Alva, and contained not only various sardonic and offensive remarks about Cecil, but also the forthright statement that while he was in power there could never be a lasting peace.[83] Another was addressed by Despes to his banker at Antwerp, to tell him not to take alarm at the news of his detention 'since the enchantments of Amadis still exist in this island and Archelaus is still alive. Nevertheless here I am, safe and sound, a prisoner of Queen Oriana, and I have no doubt … this will all end in a comedy'.[84] An important purpose of these letters was to provoke debate in the Privy Council and supply ammunition for any enemies of Cecil within it; it is possible that they achieved some small success in this.[85] On the other hand, Despes further annoyed the Queen, who took umbrage at the implied comparison with the mythical Oriana. There followed an acrid exchange of missives between Despes and the Council, in which the ambassador gave as good as he got.[86] But controversy of this sort could only help to worsen relations between Elizabeth and Philip II. This was clean contrary to the purpose for which Despes had been sent to England.

Meanwhile, Alva in the Netherlands was taken aback by the sudden and decisive English reaction to the arrest of the Merchants Adventurers at Antwerp. As we have seen, he had himself acted with all moderation possible, and probably with great reluctance.[87] He remained unable to believe that the English sought a rupture with the Netherlands.[88] Any prolonged estrangement between the two countries could only be to his disadvantage. He therefore resolved without delay to dispatch an envoy to the Queen, to urge the restoration of the old amity and of the normal traffic. If the Queen would but release the bullion and the ships, he would at once free all Englishmen under arrest; and if this point were amicably agreed, it might even be possible to go further and iron out some of the causes of the friction that had marred Anglo-Netherlands relations before the crisis. This dispatch of a deliberate olive branch was not regarded by everyone at the court of Brussels as an opportune step.[89] It was to some extent a confession of weakness and certainly so interpreted by Elizabeth and her entourage.[90] To achieve anything, much dexterity was required. But whatever faint hopes of success might in the abstract have attached to the project, they were entirely nullified by the choice of an envoy. Alva looked for someone well acquainted with the English and their ways. It was therefore perhaps only to be expected that he should have lit on Assonleville, still considered at Brussels to be an expert on Anglo-Netherlands problems.[91] But neither in mentality nor manner was Assonleville a fit harbinger of conciliation. He remained a stern critic of the unrestrained import of English cloth, while to the English he was fatally associated with the train of events that had led up to the first rupture at the end of 1563, and with the failure to reach any understanding at the Bruges colloquy in 1565 and 1566. From the first, his mission proved ill-starred.

On his way to England, Assonleville was held up by contrary winds at Calais, where he learnt from some Frenchmen that the English, greatly embittered by the news from Antwerp, had arrested the subjects of his master and closed their ports: it seems to have encouraged him in his opinion that the English needed firm handling.[92] Tactless words of his to this effect subsequently got to the ears of the English government.[93] When at length he landed at Dover, he was at once identified by the representative of the Lord Warden of the Cinque Ports as the trouble-maker of 1563, and he had got no further than Rochester when he was met by a messenger and stopped. Here, he was informed that permission would have to be secured before he might make his way to the court of the Queen – a rebuff at which he manifested great annoyance.[94] The comedy had indeed begun, though not as Despes had imagined. It was the belief of the French ambassador that the Queen deliberately made Assonleville wait at Rochester for a couple of days so that he could observe how her great ships of war were being fitted out at the neighbouring arsenal.[95] During this interval of enforced inactivity, he sent off two letters, one to Despes via the French ambassador, and another to the Queen to request audience.

On the resumption of his journey, he was met at Gravesend in the name of the Lord Mayor of London by two notable members of the Company of Merchants Adventurers – John Gresham, a brother of Sir Thomas, and Thomas Aldersey, whose identification with the Emden experiment five years earlier must have marked him out as hardly a friend. In their company he was escorted to the City, where on 23 January he was put to lodge in the mansion of Mr Alderman Bond, recently sheriff, another Merchant Adventurer.[96] Here he remained, half prisoner and half guest, while his nine servants were accommodated in adjacent houses. The Queen, with a characteristic sense of irony, had decided that while in England he should stay in the charge of those very cloth merchants whose traffic at Antwerp had in the past so often excited his denunciation. Neither he nor his suite were permitted contact with any other subjects of the King of Spain, so that he could not establish a personal touch with Despes, whose embassy was little more than a few minutes' walk distant.[97] Worse still, the Queen persistently refused to receive Assonleville, on the legal ground that his commission came from Alva only and not from the King of Spain, though he was informed that he might if he wished declare his message to the lords of her Council. This, as the Lord Mayor reported, was 'very ill taken' by him, 'as might seem by his countenance'.[98]

A couple of days now passed, during which the wrath of Assonleville at his semi-captive status mounted and he plied the Lord Mayor in vain with requests for an answer to his demand for an audience, or alternatively to be allowed to confer privately with Despes. Then on 26 January a formal invitation arrived for him – to appear before the Privy Council. It was conveyed by two functionaries, one of whom by a further appropriate touch – we may be sure it was no coincidence – was none other than his old acquaintance John Marsh, Governor of the Company of Merchants Adventurers. How many times in recent years had Marsh been a suppliant at Brussels for the favour of the powerful Dr d'Assonleville in the petitions and lawsuits of the Merchants Adventurers we do not know; but this time the roles were certainly reversed. On the arrival of Governor Marsh and his colleague, the indignation of Assonleville burst forth. He agreed that the merchants who escorted him to London had been 'very honest gentlemen' and that he had 'found very good entertainment' in the house of Mr Alderman Bond, but he protested that he had not been allowed his rights as an international envoy, nor

even allowed the liberty of an ordinary individual. His letters to
the Queen and the Lord Mayor had not been answered. He
flatly refused to appear before the lords of the Council, 'for my
commission is first to confer with the Spanish ambassador and
then to have talked with the queen's majesty herself'.[99] Voluble
and assertive in speech as he was, Assonleville must have made
quite a scene. But in fact he was greatly taken aback by the
reception he was meeting in England.[100]

Two or three days later, after a further interval of reflection,
Assonleville relented so far as to agree to meet some of the lords
of the Council to explain why he had come to England. A
conference therefore took place at the London house of Lord
Keeper Bacon, attended also by the Lord Admiral, the Duke of
Norfolk, the Earl of Leicester, Secretary Cecil and two other
privy councillors. Despes had been invited, but was unable to
appear because of *ung flux de ventre*. It was again explained to
Assonleville that his credentials were insufficient. The extent of
English resentment at the arrest of the Merchants Adventurers
was then driven home. At this, he became somewhat crestfallen
– in the words of Cecil, 'he seemed sorry for things past'.[101] His
renewed request to meet Despes privately was turned down until
the Queen should declare her pleasure. This was made known a
few days later: the two envoys might be allowed to foregather
under the roof of Sir Thomas Gresham.[102] When Sir Thomas
duly appeared to escort him to his mansion across the way,
Assonleville poured out to his old acquaintance a tale of woe:
'never', as Gresham reported it, had Assonleville 'heard nor saw
ambassador so hardly kept and so straitly dealt withal' as himself
and Despes. Unhappily, neither envoy had the least notion of
using their conference to devise some imaginative suggestion
that might have moved the Queen to soften her attitude. Instead, they played into the hands of the enemies of Anglo-
Netherlands reconciliation by producing the unseasonable
requests that Assonleville might lodge in the Spanish embassy
and that the Queen might either grant him an audience or
licence him to depart.[103] Throughout February, while the tonnage of captured merchant ships from the Netherlands–Spain
trade route was piling up in English harbours, and the requisitioned bullion was methodically being stacked in the Tower,
Assonleville therefore remained, indignant and restless, dangling in the house of Alderman Bond. He was able to seize some of
the realities of the situation – not all – and apprehend that

Elizabeth intended to exploit his presence to wrench all possible concessions from Alva and the King of Spain.

In fact, it suited both Alva and the Queen, for not very dissimilar reasons, that Assonleville should persist in his mission. Too late, Alva had grasped the situation. His conviction that Elizabeth did not desire a permanent break with Philip II remained firm.[104] He was ready for his part, in order to end the paralysis of trade at Antwerp, to sink matters of etiquette, even to the point of administering a snub to Despes, and to make far-reaching concessions.[105] Before the end of January, the Merchants Adventurers arrested at Antwerp had begun to trickle back to England, having given bond to their captors.[106] On the English side, there is nothing to suggest that the Queen envisaged a prolonged interruption of trade, though she was aware of the imprudence of appearing over-eager: as Cecil wrote, 'in these matters we have cause to be somewhat slow to satisfy them, lest they should according to their accustomed manner grow too audacious'.[107] Sir Thomas Gresham remained in touch with Assonleville, who was also visited by the Lord Admiral and Secretary Cecil.[108] A long vista of further negotiations was opened up when on 25 February Gresham once more escorted the envoy to a meeting of privy councillors at the house of the Lord Keeper, there to listen to a statement on behalf of the Queen – that whatever her feelings about Alva she intended to remain the friend of his master the King of Spain.[109] A little later, there came another royal message, to the effect that the release of the bullion now in the Tower would have to be accompanied by a wider Anglo-Netherlands settlement clearing up the points left unresolved at Bruges in 1566. This could not have been entirely unwelcome to Alva. Subsequently, Gresham plied Assonleville with arguments to demonstrate the strength of the English position, assuredly in the hope that he would pass them back to Brussels. But Gresham was not a born diplomat, and his brags that the Queen could borrow a million ducats from her subjects at 10 per cent if she wanted, and that not so long ago the English had conquered half France, seem to have misfired. Assonleville failed to perceive how an avenue of conciliation was covertly being indicated.[110] Perhaps, given his prejudices and his rigid cast of mind, he was incapable of envisaging it.

Instead, what he passed on to Alva was a series of confused and incomplete dispatches, coupled with requests, more and more insistent, for his own recall.[111] So much did he assume that his own departure homewards was growing imminent that he explained how he was reserving important points until he could report them by word of mouth – to the indignation of Alva, who for the present had no intention of recalling him and was meanwhile deprived of the information needful for assessing the situation in England.[112] But however thick-skinned Assonleville may have been, and however much he may have appreciated the good cheer in the house of Alderman Bond, he had come to understand how much he and the cause he represented were disliked in the City, even by those who had not personally been injured by the arrests and confiscations at Antwerp. In addition, feeling must have been running high in February as details of the misfortunes of Hawkins and his little flotilla of ships in Spanish-American waters at last became public property at London.[113] Assonleville was hardly the man to remain calmly at his post as excitement grew in the City and danger mounted, and his nerve seems to have ebbed away. Without waiting for any authorization from Alva, and without audience of the queen, he made up his mind to depart, 'much miscontented'.[114] On 5 March he set out for Dover, fussing to the last about a safe-conduct from the Queen and the provision of an English naval escort to protect him from the Huguenot privateers in the Narrow Seas.[115] As Alva disdainfully informed Philip II, Assonleville had returned to Brussels from England on 14 March without his permission, so great was the fear he had conceived for his own person.[116] Since there was now no English representative at the courts of either Brussels or Madrid, and since Despes was henceforth little more than a tolerated conspirator on English soil, without access to the royal presence, the flight of Assonleville removed the last chance of mending the Anglo-Netherlands rupture before an entirely new configuration of international trade had taken shape. What the misplaced zeal of one diplomatic agent had precipitated, another in his ineptitude had failed to mitigate.

The Anglo-Netherlands trade stoppage of 1569, like its less serious predecessor of 1563, thus occurred without any direct participation on the part of Philip II, although it deeply affected his most vital interests. Its immediate origins lay in the adjustment of his method of government in the Netherlands from the autumn of 1566 onwards, and more particularly in his unwise appointment of Despes to the London embassy in 1568. Elizabeth took good care, as we have seen, to ensure that her version of events was made available to the King, through her envoy in France. But in addition, she wrote directly in person to the King to ask him to believe that she was not at fault and that it remained her very great wish to retain his friendship. She exonerated him personally from any responsibility for events, and put the blame for the rupture squarely on Despes, *quod plane perspicimus*, with some share of responsibility falling on Alva.[117] In this last point, she was of course misinformed, doubtless because she lacked any channel of communication with the government of Brussels other than Assonleville. Alva by mid February had certainly come to the conclusion that the personal projects and problems of Despes were irrelevant if not harmful to Netherlands interests and had even gone so far as to instruct Assonleville to rebuke the ambassador for holding up urgent Netherlands business.[118] Perhaps Philip, with both sides of the case before him, may have regretted that he had not clarified the standing of Despes and Alva each in respect of the other, though since he viewed trade and politics as separate fields it may have taken some time for the significance of the arrests to penetrate his slow-moving mind.[119]

On full consideration, Philip did not – indeed he could hardly be expected to – disapprove of the arrests in the Netherlands, which in February he had extended to Spain. But he instructed Despes for the future to take his cue from Alva; and the far-reaching schemes of Despes for the overthrow of Elizabeth and her replacement on the English throne by the exiled Queen of Scots he referred to the judgement of Alva, which was virtually equivalent to putting them in very cold storage. He agreed with Alva that Elizabeth Tudor could not wish to fall out with him, and he ascribed her actions to the influence of heretics and evil councillors. Meanwhile, he pathetically pinned some hope on the mission of Assonleville.[120] Indeed, when he learnt that Assonleville was in difficulties and that the Queen was refusing his requests for an audience on the ground that his commission came only from Alva, he formally issued an authority to the latter to treat in his name with all other sovereigns – alas, many weeks after the return of Assonleville to Brussels.[121] Subsequently, when Philip learnt of the failure of Assonleville to achieve anything, he lost little time in sending instructions to Alva to continue to negotiate – not indeed by using Assonleville again, since they thought so little of him at London, but by dispatching someone of more weight.[122] But by now the cloth fleet was ready to sail to Hamburg, and the Queen was too deeply committed to her course of action to agree to any more parleys with Netherlands envoys. Philip was never abreast of the course of events in north-western Europe, where his one genuine ally had been the Queen of England. Now, by the sheer bungling of his agents, he was about to lose her.

## NOTES TO CHAPTER V

[1] Silva to Philip II, 21 February 1568, *CSPSp. 1567–79*, 10. Silva had other more private reasons: *cf. ante*, 100.

[2] This paragraph is largely based on material in the first two sections of J. C. A. de Meij, *De Watergeuzen en de Nederlanden 1568–1572* (Amsterdam, 1972).

[3] Silva to Philip II, 20 March 1568, *CSPSp. 1568–79*, 13.

[4] Antwerp Newsletters, 8, 15, 21 and 28 March 1568, KL, v, 77, 80, 82, 83; Guicciardini to Francesco de'Medici, 7 and 14 March 1568, Battistini, 309–10; Frederick III, Elector Palatine, to Landgrave Wilhelm of Hesse, 5 March 1568, A, Kluckhorn, *Briefe Friedrich des Frommen, Kurfürsten von der Pfalz*, II (2) (Braunschweig, 1872), with appendix, 193–6.

Alva was trying to raise the matter at the Reichstag meeting in 1569, without success. See report of Mundt to Cecil, 31 May 1569, KL, v, 393–4.

[5] Silva to Philip II, 20 March 1568, *CSPSp. 1568–79*, 13.

[6] The letter of Philip II to the Queen announcing the appointment of Despes, 24 June 1568, is at *CSPF 1566–8*, No. 2297. While the mission of Despes in these pages is considered only in its bearing upon Anglo-Netherlands relations, it was no less important as an episode in Anglo-Spanish dealings, for which see the study of J. Retamal Favereau, *Diplomacia Anglo-Espanola durante la Contrarreforma* (Ediciones Universidad Catolica de Chile, 1981).

[7] Man to Cecil, 24 June 1568, *ib.*, No. 2277; Alen to Cecil, 30 July 1568, SP 12/47/27.

[8] Cecil to Sidney, 12 September 1568, SP 63/25/85.

[9] Instructions to Despes, 28 June 1568, *CSPSp. 1568–79*, 66–8.

[10] Man to Cecil, 18 June 1568, *CSPF 1566–8*, No. 2277.

[11] Silva to Philip II, 31 July 1568, *CSPSp. 1568–79*, 62.

[12] Despes to Philip II, 25 August 1568, *ib.*, 69–70.

[13] Despes to Philip II, 23 October 1568, *ib.*, 79.

[14] *Ib.* to *ib.*, 9 October 1568, *ib.*, 76.

[15] *Ib.* to *ib.*, 18 September and 30 October 1568, *ib.*, 71 and 81.

[16] *Ib.* to *ib.*, 12 December 1568, *ib.*, 85.

[17] Despes to Philip II, 12 December 1568, *CSPSp. 1568–79*, 85; the draft of the proposed address from Despes to the Queen, urging her to order a return of England to the papal obedience, is at 85–8.

[18] *Cf. ante*, 194–6.

[19] 'Divers of the Bordeaux fleet have unladen and mind no further to proceed in that voyage', Champernowne to Clinton, 2 November 1568, SP 12/48/37.

[20] Instructions to two *zabras*, *c.* November 1568, *CSPF 1569–71*, Nos. 2218 and 2219.

[21] Despes to Philip II, 12 December 1568, *CSPSp. 1568–79*, 83–4.

[22] This and subsequent paragraphs in this chapter owe a good deal to C. Read, 'Queen Elizabeth's seizure of Alva's pay ships', *Journal of Modern History*, v (1933),

443–64. The conclusions drawn from the evidence are however not quite identical, and fit rather with the narrative of Williamson, *Hawkins*, 210 *et seq.* See also the analysis by W. MacCaffrey, *The Shaping of the Elizabethan Regime* (London, 1969), 188–95.

[23] The figure of £400,000 was being bandied around – several times the actual value of the treasure: Champernowne to Cecil, 19 December 1568, SP 12/48/60.

[24] William Hawkins to Cecil, 3 December 1568, Williamson, *Hawkins*, 216. The irrelevance of the Hawkins misadventures to the course of events at London has been shown by J. Retamal Favereau, 'El incidente de San Juan de Ulua y la pugna Anglo-Espanola de fines del siglo XVI', *Historia* (Santiago, Chile), 1966, 171–89.

[25] Alva, who had his own means of unearthing secrets, opined that it was Benedict Spinola who provided the inspiration for the actions of the English government – Alva to Philip II, 13 June 1569, *CSPSp. 1568–79*, 162–3. Formal written proof that the money at Southampton belonged to private merchants and not to the King was not forthcoming until late in December – see Horsey to Cecil, 24 December 1568, *CSPF 1566–8*, No. 2685.

[26] London merchants trading to Spain to Privy Council, 28 December 1568, SP 70/104/2170.

[27] Merchants Adventurers to Privy Council, 7 January 1569, SP 12/49/14; La Mothe Fénélon to Catherine de Médicis, 10 January 1569, MF, I, 97. For Blackwell Hall, see *ante*, 37–9.

[28] Rep. 17, f. 431v.

[29] Despes to Philip II, 12 December 1568, *CSPSp. 1568–79*, 85: 'the queen consented to give me a passport for the money to be brought overland'.

[30] *Ib.* to *ib.*, 29 November 1568, *ib.*, 83.

[31] The audience on the 14th is mentioned in Despes to Philip II, 27 December 1568, *ib.*, 94.

[32] Lope de la Sierra to Horsey, 19 December 1568, *CSPF 1566–8*, No. 2678; Despes to Philip II, 12 December 1568, *CSPSp. 1568–79*, 84.

[33] The acknowledgments are the letters of Champernowne to Cecil, 19 December 1568, SP 12/48/60; Horsey to *ib.*, 20 December 1568, SP 12/48/62; and Champernowne *et al.* to *ib.*, 1 January 1569, SP 12/49/1. They provide the evidence cited in this and the next paragraph.

[34] It is incorrectly stated in HL, II, 303n. that the Spanish ships 'were ordered seized (*sic*) by Privy Council order' in late November 1568. Whatever Horsey and Champernowne may have hoped, the landing of the bullion was not equivalent to appropriation.

[35] Despes to Philip II, 18 December 1569, *CSPSp. 1568–79*, 88. The negative significance of this dispatch is great. As he told his master 'the money is safe, with the queen's letters and authority to land it if necessary'.

[36] Despes to Queen and to Cecil, both 21 December 1569, *CSPF 1566–8*, Nos. 2679 and 2681.

[37] Declaration of Despes, January 1569, *CSPSp. 1568–79*, 102–4.

[38] Despes to Alva, 21 December 1568, *ib.*, 90; notes also by Gachard, *Correspondance de Philippe II*, II, 52.

[39] *Supra*, 89.

[40] La Mothe Fénélon to Catherine de Médicis, 28 December 1568, MF, I, 69–72.

[41] Despes to Queen, 21 December 1568, *CSPF 1566–8*, No. 2679.

[42] *Ib.* to Alva, 27/30 December 1568, *CSPSp. 1568–79*, 92.

[43] Despes to Alva, 22 December 1568, *CSPSp. 1568–79*, 91.

[44] *Ib.* to *ib.*, 30 December 1568, *ib.*, 93.

[45] Royal proclamation, 6 January 1569, HL, II, No. 556. Despes boldly issued a public defence of his actions on 10 January 1569, in reply to the above document. In this, he took his stand on the palpably false assumption that he had urged Alva to arrest the Englishmen only after the allegedly unsatisfactory audience with the Queen on 29 December, whereas he had in fact done so over a week earlier – Despes to 'all and singular', 10 January 1569, KL, V, 229–32. But historians seem still bemused by this distorted recital of events.

[46] Despes to Philip II, 27 December 1568, *CSPSp. 1568–79*, 94.

[47] Gresham to Cecil, 7 March 1571, SP 12/77/30. See also C. E. Challis, *The Tudor Coinage* (Manchester, 1975), 194, note 188 and the references there.

[48] Alva to Philip II, 4 January 1569, Gachard, *Correspondance de Philippe II*, II, 52–3.

[49] *Avec toute la douceur et les menagements possibles*, *ib.*, 53.

[50] Report of Robert Harrison, 10 January 1569, KL, V, 235–6; memorandum by Cecil, 18 January 1569, *ib.*, 253–62.

[51] Margrave of Antwerp to Alva, 4 January 1569, AGR, Papiers d'Etat et de l'Audience, bundle 403, No. 1.

[52] The reports of the municipality of Bruges to Alva, explaining how his order had been effected, dated 9 January and later, are at AGR, Papiers d'Etat et de l'Audience, bundle 403, No. 9.

[53] For examples of harsh treatment, see Henry Lucas *et al.* to Privy Council, 25 January 1569, Smit, *Bronnen*, No. 1163; Smedt, *EN*, I, 347–9; in general, Norris to Alava, undated February 1569, *CSPSp. 1568–79*, 114–22. News of the acts of the Spanish secretary was conveyed by Rowe to Council, 7 January 1569, SP 12/49/12.

[54] Despes to Philip II, 8 January 1569, *CSPSp. 1568–79*, 95.

[55] Rowe to Cecil, 4 January 1569, KL, V, 211.

[56] Despes to Philip II, 8 January 1569, *CSPSp. 1568–79*, 95.

[57] Royal proclamation, 6 January 1569, HL, II, No. 556.

[58] Merchants Adventurers to Council, 7 January 1569, SP 12/49/14; *supra*, 92.

[59] Cecil to Sidney, 6 January 1569, SP 63/27/2.

[60] Alva to Philip II, 11 January 1569, *CSPSp. 1567–79*, 104; Despes to Alva, 29 February 1569, *ib.*, 111.

[61] Cecil to Norris, 30 January 1569, *Cabala*, 148.

[62] Rowe to Council, 6 January 1569, SP 12/49/11; Brulez, *De firma della Faille*, 29–30 and 565 (where the year is incorrectly stated in the margin). 'Harman Peter' is to be identified with Herman Pottey, the London manager for Jan della Faille.

[63] Merchants Adventurers to Council, SP 12/49/15; 'a remembrance of the lord mayor and other merchants', both dated 8 January 1569, KL, V, 218–19.

[64] List of commissioners appointed by the City, undated, SP 70/104A/2194.

[65] Merchants Adventurers to Council, 8 January 1569, SP 12/49/15; Rowe to Cecil, 14 January 1569, KL, V, 244–5.

[66] Rowe to Cecil, 23 January 1569, *ib.*, 266–7.

[67] Clinton to Cecil, 9 January 1569, SP 12/49/16.

[68] Doge of Venice to Queen, 11 February 1569, *CSPF 1569–71*, No. 110; Despes to Philip II, 12 March, 9 and 29 May and 1 July 1569, *CSPSp. 1567–79*, 138–40, 149, 153 and 169–71.

[69] Account of Gresham for Spanish monies, 23 May 1572, SP 70/123/178.

[70] Despes to Philip II, 14 February 1569, *CSPSp. 1568–79*, 107–8.

[71] Gresham to Cecil, 14 August 1569, Ellis, *Original Letters*, second series, II, 315–9. *Supra*, n. 47.

[72] *Cf. supra*, 97.

[73] Text at HL, II, No. 556, with some questionable footnotes.

[74] Cecil to Norris, 8 January 1569, *Cabala*, 147; Queen to *ib.*, 11 January 1569, SP 70/105/43. This latter presents the fullest and clearest account of English actions.

[75] Bacon to Cecil, 5 January 1569, SP 12/49/10.

[76] Cecil to Sidney, 6 January 1569, SP 63/27/2.

[77] Rowe to Cecil, 7 January 1569, SP 12/49/12; Offley to *ib.*, same date, SP 12/49/13. *Supra*, 89.

[78] Despes to Curiel, 8 January 1569, SP 70/105/19.

[79] It had long been the London residence of the bishops of Exeter before its occupation by Lord Paget, and had been known as Exeter House – Stow, II, 92.

[80] The two accounts of the arrest of Despes are in his own letter to Philip II, 8 January 1569, *CSPSp. 1568–79*, 95–8; and in Queen to Norris, 11 January 1569, SP 70/105/43.

[81] Despes to Philip II, 8 January 1569, *CSPSp. 1568–79*, 96.

[82] La Mothe Fénélon to Catherine de Médicis, 10 January 1569, MF. I, 98.

[83] Despes to Alva, 10 January 1569, *CSPSp. 1568–79*, 98–9; original text to KL, V, 233.

[84] Despes to Curiel, 12 January 1569, *ib.*, 105; KL, V, 234–5.

[85] La Mothe Fénélon to Charles IX, 17 January 1569, MF, I, 115.

[86] Privy Council to Despes and Despes to Privy Council, 14 and 16 January 1569, KL, V, 242–7.

[87] *Supra*, 97.

[88] Alva to Philip II, 4 January 1569, Gachard, *Correspondance de Philippe II*, II, 52–3; *ib.* to *ib.*, 11 and 19 January 1569, *CSPSp. 1568–79*, 104 and 106.

[89] Morillon to Granvelle, 29 January 1569, Poullet, *Granvelle*, II, 456.

[90] La Mothe Fénelon to Charles IX, 30 January 1569, MF, I, 158.

[91] Instructions to Assonleville, 9 January 1569, KL, V, 220–6.

[92] Assonleville to Alva, 14 and 17 January 1569, KL, V, 239–241 and 249–50.

[93] Cecil to Norris, 7 March 1569, *Cabala*, 149.

[94] Taylor to Cobham, 20 January 1569, KL, 264–6 (two letters).

[95] La Mothe Férélon to Charles IX, 30 January 1569, MF, I, 158–9.

[96] It is likely that the residence of Alderman Bond was the famous mansion house known as Crosby Place, still surviving though on another site. It had passed into his possession in 1567 – *CPR 1566–9*, No. 631. This was first pointed out by Burgon, II, 295–6.

[97] Rowe to Cecil, 23 January 1569, KL, V, 266–7. Alderman Bond is noticed in the *DNB*.

[98] Rowe to Cecil, 25 January 1569, KL, V, 269; Cecil to Norris, 30 January 1569, *Cabala*, 158.

[99] 'A true report of the speech used by Assonleville...', 26 January 1569, KL, V, 270–1.

[100] Assonleville to Alva, 31 January 1569, KL, V, 277–80.

[101] 'Matters to treat of with Assonleville', 29 January 1569, Cotton, Galba C III, No. 83, mostly but not entirely printed by KL, V, 272–3; Cecil to Norris, 30 January 1569, *Cabala*, 147–8; Assonleville to Alva, 31 January 1569, KL, V, 277–80.

[102] La Mothe Fénélon to Charles IX, 15 February 1569, MF, I, 194–5.

[103] Gresham to Cecil, 6 February 1569, KL, V, 288.

[104] Alva to Philip II, 11 and 19 January 1569, *CSPSp. 1568–79*, 104 and 106.

[105] Alva to Assonleville, 14 February 1569, KL, V, 296.

[106] La Mothe Fénélon to Charles IX, 30 January 1569, MF, I, 160.

[107] Cecil to Norris, 30 January 1569, *Cabala*, 148.

[108] Statement of Gresham, 19 February 1569, KL, v, 299; Assonleville to Alva, 20 February 1569, *ib.*, 302–4.

[109] Council to Assonleville, 26 February 1569, *ib.*, 311–15.

[110] Statement of Assonleville, March 1569, *CSPSp. 1568–79*, 122–32; Despes to Philip II, 27 February 1569, *ib.*, 112–13.

[111] Assonleville to Alva, 7, 23, 25 and 27 February 1569, KL, v, 289, 306, 310–11 and 316–20.

[112] Alva conveyed his rebukes in letters dated 7 March 1569, KL, v, 323–6, which was too late to affect the situation.

[113] News of the arrival of Hawkins reached London towards the end of January – Cecil to Norris, 30 January 1569, *Cabala*, 148.

[114] Cecil to Norris, 7 March 1569, *ib.*, 149.

[115] The final correspondence about the departure of Assonleville is at KL, v, 326–9. He was escorted across the Channel by four English warships – Morillon to Granvelle, 20 and 21 March 1569, Poullet, *Granvelle*, III, 520. Assonleville's passport remains at AGR, Papiers d'Etat et de l'Audience, 401, f. 103.

[116] Alva to Philipe II, 18 March 1569, Gachard, *Correspondance de Philipp II*, II, 74.

[117] Queen to Philip II, 18 January 1569, SP 70/105/56; see also Queen to Norris, 11 January 1569, SP 70/105/43; Norris to Cecil, 24 January 1569, KL, 243–5n; statement to Alava, Spanish ambassador at Paris, February(?) 1569, *CSPSp. 1568–79*, 114–22.

[118] Alva to Assonleville, 14 February 1569, KL, v, 296.

[119] *Supra*, 30–1.

[120] Philip II to Alva, and *ib.* to Despes, both 18 February 1569, *CSPSp. 1568–79*, 108–10.

[121] Grant of authority to Alva to treat in the name of Philip II, 9 May 1569, Gachard, *Correspondance de Philippe II*, II, 88.

[122] Philip II to Alva, 15 May 1569, *ib.*, 91.

# Chapter VI
## Hamburg, the new rival

The Anglo-Netherlands trade rupture in 1569 was much more open and brutal than that of 1563. No courtesy-saving device such as the allegation of plague infection was employed. Further, the international situation in early 1569 was more menacing: Alva, backed by Spanish troops, was ruling the Netherlands, while in France the Huguenots were still fighting for their existence. Not only was Antwerp closed to the Merchants Adventurers, but English foreign trade was also bereft of its second-best market, Spain. To crown all, a trade embargo was imposed on the English in Normandy, where in mid January, following some friction the previous autumn, there was a seizure of English merchandise at Rouen. Subsequently, the clerk of the Privy Council introduced to the French ambassador a deputation of merchants from the City, whose grievances came as a surprise to the envoy. He wrote home for instructions, pointing out that if the English were provoked into taking offence they might well hasten to bury the hatchet with Alva.[1] The French government was not in fact implicated, and it gave prompt instructions for the release of the English goods.[2] But its authority over provincial governors was far from complete, and in March some Englishmen on crossing the frontier from the Netherlands were held at Boulogne, while Gresham's Antwerp manager, with his bag of letters, was arrested at Dieppe.[3] Negotiations to reach an agreement in Normandy were long drawn out, and not until late summer did they achieve their end.[4] Cross-Channel trade was never considerable, so that City merchants were not greatly damaged by this local difficulty; indeed, from the trade point of view, the episode mattered chiefly because it removed Rouen from the list of possible substitutes for Antwerp as a mart town. But its political significance was immense. Particularly in February, before the assurances from Paris had been received at London, it was impossible to feel secure from the danger that the French government might align itself with Philip II and Alva in a great anti-English and anti-protestant confederation, thus bringing into existence the coalition for whch Despes was still scheming.[5]

The anxiety generated among privy councillors by this spectre of a continental alliance against England was paralleled by the dismay widespread among City merchants at the course of events. The sangfroid of Governor Marsh, Aldersey and other protestant stalwarts at the prospect of another protracted exclusion from Antwerp does not seem to have been shared by the rank and file of the Merchants Adventurers, who sourly recollected the trials and tribulations of the Emden mart in 1564.[6] The Company in December 1568 had already done its best by petition and remonstrance to head the government away from an international rupture.[7] In the first few weeks of 1569 it was not yet evident that the value of Netherlands and Spanish property sequestrated in England would ever suffice to yield compensation for the English merchandise seized at Antwerp and elsewhere in the dominions of King Philip. There were therefore good reasons for alarm both in the City and at court; in mid January, the French ambassador observed how in all ranks of society many men had lost their assurance and were 'crying loudly for the ancient alliance with the House of Burgundy'.[8] Great faith, and great zeal for the reformed religion must have been needed to persuade men that not merely the prosperity of the City of London and the cloth trade, but the future of the existing ecclesiastical settlement and the political security of the kingdom itself had necessarily to be placed in such jeopardy as they now evidently stood. Indeed, so serious did the situation seem that a palace revolution involving the downfall of Secretary Cecil was narrowly averted.

The crisis precipitated among the closest advisers of the Queen by the rupture with the Netherlands was none the less severe because it was muffled and not known to the outside world. A sharp division of opinion at the Privy Council board first made itself felt when some of the councillors began to absent themselves and hold their own meetings, to which Cecil was not invited. The dissidents varied in the strength and nature of their dissatisfaction, from old Winchester who doubtless as in 1564 regretted the impending loss of revenue, and Leicester who liked to swim with the tide, to such middle-of-the-road magnates as Pembroke and Shrewsbury, who feared the catastrophe that might spring from any prolonged interruption of the Anglo-Burgundian or Anglo-Spanish alliance. None of these had any wish to impair the authority of the Queen: what they sought was the overthrow of Cecil and the reversal of the policy with which he in particular was associated. The ill-advised Norfolk was drawn into their conclave. Outside the council there was a more extreme conspiratorial wing, reaching to Northumberland and other papist lords in treasonable contact with Despes and his Florentine banker Roberto Ridolfi. As on other occasions, political, economic and ecclesiastical grievances were linked in varying proportions. The flickers of resistance at the heart of the government seem to have been snuffed out by decisive action on the part of the Queen before the end of February, but beyond the court the plotting grew more active until it finally burst forth into the rebellion of the northern earls in the autumn. The establishment of the Merchants Adventurers at a new mart town alternative to Antwerp in the course of 1569 thus took place against a background of high political tension in England, both at the Council table and in the country.[9]

In the City too, the winter of 1568–9 was an uneasy season. Already during the autumn of 1567 the government had taken alarm at the afflux of strangers to London. Some, perhaps most, were English, but there were also many Netherlanders.[10] Twelve months later, the Privy Council ordered the Lord Mayor to see that no 'stranger or alien born', refugees for the sake of religion excepted, lingered for more than one day and one night within the City.[11] Then in November 1568, on royal instructions, a systematic search was instituted for 'masterless men, suspect persons and idle vagabonds' in the City – an order twice repeated before the end of the year.[12] In the following March, the government was still prodding Lord Mayor and aldermen into action to search out the beggars, loiterers, vagabonds and rogues, including those who had come 'out of foreign parts'.[13] Next, in June it issued a lengthy reprimand to the Lord Mayor for alleged slackness in the execution of these orders.[14] Although this was a period of relatively cheap corn, the month of December 1568 was marked by snow and frost, which gave point to the measures of the Lord Mayor to restrict the prices of fuel – candles and beer were also controlled.[15] Intervention whether by government or City in these social matters was nothing novel, but during the winter of 1568–9 it seems to have been unusually frequent – a point that might seem to suggest some fear of popular unrest. Prices were still rising, there was visible evidence that the beggars were coming to town, and there was uncertainty

about the trustworthiness of the strangers who had made their
way from the continent. All classes were doubtless bewildered by
the news coming of late from the Netherlands. An expression of
the restlessness and discontent abroad in the City is perhaps to
be traced in the deliberate defacement of the arms of Sir
Thomas Gresham recently 'set upon the west door of the stairs
at the new Exchange'; Gresham himself was said to be greatly
pained.[16] To allay the feeling of insecurity the City now instituted nocturnal policing by a couple of bellmen.[17]

The situation must have grown more tense when the tidings
of the arrests at Antwerp became known on the night of 3/4
January 1569.[18] Only a few hours before the arrival of the news,
the Lord Mayor had enjoined upon the aldermen, on behalf of
the Queen, the duty of preventing any 'interlude or other sort of
play in any house, inn or brewhouse' used as 'a common resort
of people' after 5 p.m.[19] There was evidently some nervousness
at the royal court and probably at the Guildhall, lest tumults
might arise from an unauthorized concourse of people. A
month later, the order was repeated in a more elaborate form:
plays and interludes might only be acted in the hours of daylight
– a severe limitation at such a season – and householders on
whose premises performances were held should give bond to
permit no casual spectators.[20] In May, the prohibition having
presumably lost much of its force with the long evenings, the
Common Council intervened to forbid altogether any 'stage
plays, interludes and other disguisings' until the end of September.[21] This was perhaps prompted by a scene that had occurred
a few days earlier, when the ill-humour of the populace had
found an ominous outlet. The house of Anthony Guaras, the
foremost Spanish merchant in the City, had been closed by
order of the government: it was now invaded by the crowd,
crucifixes and other looted property being flung on the street
and a mock procession organized. Anti-foreign cries were raised
as the furniture was burnt in Cheapside before an excited populace. Despes saw the hand of the Privy Council in this, though in
so sultry a political climate an outside stimulus was hardly required.[22]. Meanwhile, in view of the threats multiplying at home
and abroad, the government took practical steps to re-activate
and strengthen the City militia. As supervisors, eight Commissioners of Array were appointed. In addition to the Lord Mayor
in office, they comprised three of his predecessors and also Sir
Thomas Gresham; the remaining three were men of military

experience. Of the eight, half were members of the Company of Merchants Adventurers, and another a prominent Stapler.[23]

The commissioners sat at the Guildhall. On 4 April they summoned before them 'all the constables of the several parishes and wards of the City and a great number of the best commoners thereof', and methodically set about the examination and distribution of weapons. Citizens were required to replenish their stocks of arms if necessary by purchases from the arsenal at the Tower. Then on 27 April a formal inspection was held simultaneously throughout the whole City, so as to render impossible any 'chopping and lending of armour amongst neighbours'. Defaulters were found to be 'very few', though the commissioners in their report noted a shortage of horses. But they thought fit to warn the Privy Council of the danger of drawing 'apprentices and handicraftsmen' from their toil for military training, since there was a likelihood that they 'would thereby fall into such idleness and insolency that many of them thereby would never after be reduced again into any good order of service or labour'.[24] Fears of social trouble in the City were not confined to the leading merchants. A foreign observer very little later confessed to detecting symptoms of an approaching social upheaval at London, where there were '30,000 poor folk seeking nothing better than plunder'.[25] This was a highly inflated estimate, since the total number of able-bodied men duly mustered – citizens being householders, their servants and sons – amounted to only just over twelve thousand. [26] But it was not devoid of some element of truth. The Privy Council itself, as we have seen, was well aware of the swarm of beggars in the City, 'apt to attempt any stirs or other mischievous enterprises'.[27] The arming of the people has always had its perils.

While these discontents were simmering in the City, the Privy Council addressed itself to the problem of locating the new mart town. After the fashion of five years earlier, it lost no time in consulting the Merchants Adventurers, who answered much as they had done in January 1564, pointing to 'Hamburg and Emden or either of them' as possible alternatives to Antwerp. They added a rider, born of their experience in that year, that it would be necessary to impose an effective ban upon trade with the Netherlands to protect any new mart.[28] As far as Emden was concerned, there was not the faintest reason to doubt the readiness of the government of East Friesland to welcome back the English merchants; indeed, Count John having learnt of the

rupture of Anglo-Netherlands relations was already hastening
to offer his services to Queen Elizabeth.[29] Conditions had however changed during five years, and any notion of reviving the
Emden mart was quickly dropped for simple military and political considerations. In 1564, the Netherlands had been a poorly-
armed country, and its Regent could count upon only a meagre
body of soldiers, insufficient for interference beyond the frontier. But the situation was now transformed. In place of the
Duchess of Parma there ruled the Duke of Alva, a highly competent and experienced soldier. To enforce his will, he had at his
command a striking force of moderate size but proven effectiveness, including some trained Spanish regiments. He had a garrison at the stronghold of Delftzijl, commanding the Ems estuary.
East Friesland lay open to his troops.[30]

This point had been very recently demonstrated. In the
summer of 1568, Alva had suppressed an attempted rebellion
led by the Prince of Orange and his brother Louis of Nassau.
The north-eastern provinces had been a main theatre of the
conflict, and they were now occupied in force by his victorious
soldiers. Indeed, the final defeat of Louis of Nassau had actually
occurred on East Friesland soil, which Alva had violated in order
to overtake and disperse the rebels. As a mere military operation
a Spanish occupation of East Friesland would not have presented any great problem; indeed, in July 1568 the rumour was
current in Antwerp that Alva was about to turn upon Emden,
notoriously a nest of Netherlands refugees.[31] The sons of the
Lady of Emden were greatly alarmed and sent envoys to the
Queen of England to seek her protection and to ask her to
intercede on their behalf with the King of Spain. They were
fearful that there might be retaliation for their admittance of
English cloths when their import in 1564 had been prohibited in
the Netherlands. Elizabeth raised the matter with the Spanish
ambassador Silva, who pooh-poohed the fears of the Counts of
East Friesland, but pointed out that they would need to walk
warily and not allow the Netherlands rebels any succour, since
Philip II held the imperial title of perpetual Vicar-General of all
Friesland – a vague but ancient office.[32] Clearly, it would not
have been difficult to trump up a colourable legal excuse for a
Spanish occupation of East Friesland. What caused Alva to stay
his hand was in all likelihood only the fear of giving offence to
the major princes of Germany.[33] From the English point of
view, to direct the cloth fleet of the Merchants Adventurers to

Emden while East Friesland lay in the shadow of Spanish might would have been rash in the extreme. Hence the lack of any further mention of the re-establishment of the mart there.[34]

With Hamburg, English relations though slender were ancient and not without economic significance.[35] Hamburg was in law a free city of the German Reich, but for practical purposes its own political master. It was ruled by an enterprising mercantile oligarchy, whose chief organs of government were the Burgomasters and Senate. Hitherto, the commercial interests of Hamburg had been served by membership of the Hanseatic League, and there were usually some representatives of Hamburg firms in residence at its London agency, the Steelyard. In the early sixteenth century, Hamburg interests in England had centred on the sale of German linens and Iceland stockfish there, and on a modest share in the export of English woollen cloths to Germany. Hamburg profited from the great upsurge of Anglo-German traffic in the second quarter of the century. Hamburg merchants were drawn into the busy vortex of international trade that centred on Antwerp, and the pattern of their activities became more complex. But Hamburg, like Cologne, continued to maintain its own cloth-finishing industry.[36] Indeed, the dyeing and dressing of English cloths shipped by Hanse merchants to Hamburg reached proportions sufficient to arouse the jealousy of the Merchants Adventurers, who in the fifties were professing to fear that Hamburg, served by their rivals of the Steelyard, might actually compete with and even eclipse their own mart at Antwerp.[37] It was certainly as well placed for serving the consumers of English cloth in Germany.[38]

With the removal of Hanse fiscal privileges in England in 1552, the Hamburg cloth-finishing industry noticeably declined, and with their temporary restoration in 1554–7 it only recovered partly.[39] Hamburg cloth merchants in the 1560s retained some independence of the Antwerp mart, their agents at the Steelyard dispatching the unfinished English fabrics either home directly or via Amsterdam, where they were presumably transferred to barges for the remainder of their journey.[40] Occasionally a native London merchant might take advantage of the departure of a Hamburg-bound ship to load a few cloths upon it, though never in any quanitity.[41] In fact, there was not much direct traffic between England and Hamburg: when Gresham in 1560 was trying to arrange for

the shipment of German munitions down the Elbe, he discovered that not more than ten or twelve ships in a year used to
sail for London.[42]

The Hamburg merchants who dealt in English cloths were a
powerful influence in their city, closely linked with the gild of
cloth dyers and finishers there. Some of them were without any
doubt very rich men: the outstanding example was Paul Snepel,
whose shipments from London in 1545/6 reached the considerable total of 1,567 cloths, so that in working capital he can have
been surpassed by no more than a handful of Merchants Adventurers.[43] When early in 1564 the news reached Hamburg that
English cloths were being denied entry into the Netherlands, it
was pressure from the cloth-dealing and cloth-finishing interests
that induced the rulers of the free city to address letters to both
the Queen of England and the Merchants Adventurers, urging
that the cloths should instead be shipped to the Elbe.[44] So keen
were Burgomasters and Senate to attract the Englishmen that
they offered them in general terms the same freedom to traffic
in their city as the native merchants. They thus flouted the
principles for which the Hanseatic League was still contending
at London.[45] This offer was welcomed by Governor Marsh, who
informed Cecil that the Company favoured the traditional
policy of maintaining twin mart towns, so that Emden and
Hamburg might as a pair follow Antwerp and Barrow, one
being played off against the other.[46] But the Hamburgers were
too late. By now, the English were too deeply committed to the
Emden mart to consider the diversion of any of their cloth
exports to Hamburg in the immediate future. Queen and Merchants Adventurers in separate letters therefore wrote at the
end of April 1564 to explain that before the arrival of the
Hamburg offer it had been fully concluded that the cloth fleet
should sail to Emden, so that the voyage could not have been put
off without incurring some stigma of faithlessness. However,
they expressed their willingness to treat at some time in the
future for the dispatch of English cloths to Hamburg and a
settlement of the Merchants Adventurers there.[47] After this,
there was no further diplomatic move for over two years. But
the offer was not forgotten.

Meanwhile, the cloth-dealers and cloth-finishers of Hamburg
continued to benefit from the keeping of the mart at Emden,
where at the outset there were large purchases on behalf of
Hamburg firms.[48] Perhaps with the assistance of immigrant

artisans from Antwerp, the quantity of English cloths dyed and finished at Hamburg approximately doubled from September 1564 onwards, and even when Antwerp was re-opened to the English at the beginning of 1565 the cloth-finishing did not fall back to its earlier level.[49] On the English side, the enthusiasm of the merchants at the resumption of traffic to the Netherlands cooled as the increased insecurity of their status became evident, while little hope was offered by the progress of the conference at Bruges.[50] When it adjourned for the last time in June 1566, the ever alert Dr Wotton urged that the English merchants would do well 'now and then to send some of their cloths to some other places and make a countenance as though they would not stick to traffic elsewhere, if they be not well used and enjoy their privileges here'.[51] This advice was reinforced some ten weeks later by Sir Thomas Gresham, who on visiting Antwerp after the iconoclastic outbreak took alarm at the prospect of serious political troubles 'and great mischief' in the Netherlands.[52] As a result in all probability of these warnings, the English government renewed its interest in Hamburg, and it was almost certainly on its prompting that Governor Marsh now sent George Gilpin, the Secretary of the Company, to explore the possibilities there.[53] Not much time can have been lost, since the Burgomasters and Senate of Hamburg responded with a friendly letter to the Queen dated 13 October 1566.[54] This time, the threads of diplomacy were not allowed to drop.

By January 1567 the rumour had reached the Steelyard at London that the Merchants Adventurers were about to acquire a settlement at Hamburg – an item of news unlikely to please any inmates whose connections were with Danzig, Cologne or Lübeck.[55] Early in March, the Company wrote to Hamburg to announce the dispatch of two London merchants, Francis Robinson and Francis Benison, to pursue negotiations there on its behalf; the letters of the Governor and the Company were accompanied by a formal safe-conduct from the Queen and another curiously apologetic royal missive commending the two envoys of the merchants and explaining that the Company had but meagre proficiency in matters of diplomacy. Even without this double-edged comment, it would have been difficult to disguise the complete dependence of the Company upon the government, which from the start had guided the negotiations and was pressing for the settlement of the mart town at Hamburg for ultimate reasons of political security. The letters purporting to emanate from Governor and Company as well as those sent in the name of the Queen were alike cast into Latin, always the language of Anglo-Hanse diplomacy, by Roger Ascham, the Queen's Latin secretary. They were probably drafted by the same hand and scrutinized by the Queen herself before dispatch.[56] At the beginning of May the English delegation reached Hamburg and entered upon negotiations of over two months' duration. It so happened that not far distant, at Lübeck, a Hanse Congress under the aegis of Dr Suderman, Secretary of the League, was at the same time being held. Suderman would dearly have liked to wreck the Anglo-Hamburg discussions, which he must have followed with horror. In vain he adjured the Hamburgers to respect the common interests of the League, to remember the damage and loss that would accrue to the Hanse settlements at London and Antwerp if the English had their way, and not to throw to the wind the 20,000 *talers* that since 1553 had been expended in efforts to secure recognition of the ancient rights of the League in England.[57] Letters from the Hanse Congress and from the Emperor himself were sent without effect to the Queen.[58] Despite all obstacles, an Anglo-Hamburg agreement, lengthy and complete, was produced on 19 July 1567.

For the English, the importance of this cunning move in commercial diplomacy would be difficult to over-estimate. At one stroke, Antwerp and the Netherlands were outflanked, the Hanseatic League disrupted and pushed further into angry impotence, and the Merchants Adventurers assured of a new continental mart equipped with cloth-finishing facilities, if need should be. Within two or three days, information of the agreement reached the Netherlands and found the Regent in residence at Antwerp after its recent pacification. The news doubtless added to the alarm among the merchants on the Bourse.[59] Five years earlier, Stralen on the first rumour of an Anglo-Hamburg arrangement had taken it as a threat more serious than the Emden voyage. The damage the agreement was likely to wreak upon Antwerp became at once a topic of discussion. Someone – could it have Viglius or Assonleville? – suggested that it would be appropriate to reply by forbidding the use of English cloth throughout the dominions of the King but to this extreme counsel the Regent demurred, arguing that if Netherlands cloth was to replace English it would be necessary first to make sure that an adequate supply of wool from Spain would be forth-

coming for the local manufacturers.[60] After all, the English were
not threatening to leave Antwerp. Besides, public attention was
riveted upon the final discomfiture of the iconoclasts and the
impending arrival of Alva, to be followed, it was expected, by the
King himself from Spain. Subsequently, when Alva had installed
himself in power, his hands were full enough with other matters.
But the English did not disregard their new rights at Hamburg,
where they did not wish to leave the impression that 'we used
them rather for a refuge in time of necessity than of a plain
meaning'. Accordingly, as the bi-annual cloth fleet had now for
security reasons been replaced by sailings of no more than four
ships at a time, the order was issued by the Company of Merchants Adventurers that the first four cloth ships to sail after the
end of March 1568 should make for Hamburg, not Antwerp.[61]
There is evidence to indicate that the order was duly executed.[62]

The Anglo-Hamburg agreement was to be valid in the first
instance for a period of ten years. Its fifty-seven clauses ranged
over many aspects of the business of the Merchants Adventurers.[63] On the English side, they represented an attempt to
reproduce at Hamburg the state of affairs for which the
Company had always striven at Antwerp: no doubt the presence
of Secretary Gilpin in the English delegation for at least part of
the negotiations was a help in clarifying this. The English were
promised, free of charge, the equivalent of their House at Antwerp, with suitable exhibition space for displaying their cloths.
These they might sell wholesale not merely to Hamburg citizens,
but to anyone they wished – a most important concession. They
might live where they chose – another right not unquestioningly
accorded to visiting merchants in great cities at this epoch. Once
they had paid the modest octroi duty, their goods were not to be
subject to any other levy. The Englishmen themselves were to be
exempt from personal taxation and from liability to watch and
ward, nor were they to pay groundage, wharfage or anchorage
money. The great crane by the waterfront they might use freely,
and if it proved insufficient the city promised to erect a larger
one. The Company was to appoint its own packers, binders and
measurers up to a fixed number, and to arrange for the presence of sworn brokers – evidently cast for the role of the *maklers*
whose contacts oiled the dispatch of business at Antwerp.[64] The
English merchants were not to be pursued for faults discovered
in the cloths they had sold after the lapse of three months. A
number of clauses dealt with the problems of making payment,

not forgetting cases of bankruptcy. Others covered the organization of the English settlement: their general intent was that while
equity should prevail, the English as far as practicable should
live by their own laws. Official recognition was given to the
authority of the Governor of the Company, who was to be
entitled to call upon the government of Hamburg to enforce his
will and maintain the peace. This last was more than had been
allowed at Antwerp.

Historians commonly date the rise of Hamburg to its position
as one of the greatest trading cities of the western world to the
agreement of 1567 with the English. It made practicable the
diversion of a major stream of commodity traffic to the Elbe.
The main architect of the agreement on the Hamburg side was
Dr Wilhelm Müller, the town clerk or *Syndicus*, who was no
doubt alive to the broader issues involved as well as to the
prospect that the city finances, whose plight was none too
healthy, would benefit from the afflux of strangers.[65] But the
topics upon which the Hamburg negotiators dwelt were varied
and sometimes parochial. They wanted to make sure that the
advent of the Englishmen would not affect the staple rights they
enforced over all navigation on the Elbe. They further required
that any Englishmen responsible for discharging into the river
the sand carried as ballast should be 'severely punished'.[66] Nor
were the English to enter into competition with the shopkeepers
of their city by selling their cloths by retail. In the interests of the
ecclesiastical order, a special clause forbade the English to crit-
icize the church services or to disseminate the opinions of Calvin
or Zwingli – Hamburg being now a strict Lutheran city. What
the Hamburg city government seems to have envisaged was that
the English merchants would come with their cloths – giving
three weeks' notice of their arrival, so that the necessary preparations might be made for their reception – that they would
sell some of them there and then, but that others they would
employ the local cloth-finishers to dye and dress. When the
Englishmen had done their business, they would either sail back
home or whisk the finished cloths off to the fairs at Frankfurt,
Leipzig or elsewhere far to the south.[67] For all its length, the
agreement was marked by some significant gaps. One was its
small mention of specific purchases that the English might make
at Hamburg, other than corn, which they might not export, and
munitions of war, which they might. Another was its silence with
regard to the rights of Hamburg merchants in England.

No doubt these were matters much discussed behind the scenes. We may guess that the Hamburgers promised to do what they could to attract the south German and Italian merchants with their wares, as the counts of East Friesland had done in 1564. But any grant of reciprocal Hanse rights in England posed a delicate question. The agreement was a formal document framed so as to pass the scrutiny of the other Hanse cities, so that it would have been impossible to mention any privileges which Hamburg firms might come to enjoy in England, but in which the Lübeckers and other old comrades would have no share. Indeed, the Burgomasters and Senate had been very bold in committing their city to this its first independent international treaty and thereby infringing the alignment which for so many centuries had bound it to its sister-cities of the Hanseatic League. In particular, since the city of Danzig had very recently reached a new pitch of bitterness in its relations with the English, the agreement by admitting them to a settlement at Hamburg could there be regarded only as an act of sheer treason. This treachery to fellow-Germans for mere selfish ends was only superficially mitigated by the two clauses in which both the Company of Merchants Adventurers and the City of Hamburg severally bound themselves to the statement that their agreement was not to be to the prejudice of the ancient rights of the Hanseatic League in England.[68] In any case, the Company had no legal right to offer anything of substance to the Hamburgers other than the traffic it might bring – it was, after all, no more than a trading corporation with its seat at Antwerp. The only other major inducement that must have been dangled before the Hamburgers was presumably a reciprocal freedom for Hanse merchants to buy and sell at London – i.e., in practical terms, the right to buy cloths direct from the country clothiers at Blackwell Hall. This concession was indeed made, though by a municipal and neither a royal nor a Company act.[69] But the blunt truth was that Hamburg by making the agreement had enabled the English to turn the tables on the Germans. Hitherto, it had been the rights of the Hansards in England that bulked in negotiations; henceforth, it was to be the rights of the English in Germany.

With the arrest of the Merchants Adventurers at Antwerp in January 1569 the full significance of the agreement was laid bare. Sometime in February, probably after the failure of Asson-leville and Despes to produce any offer after their meeting

under the roof of Sir Thomas Gresham, the English government made up its mind that Hamburg should be the next destination of the Merchants Adventurers.[70] They formally conveyed
their acquiescence in this decision by a further letter to the
Privy Council, dated 1 March.[71] In this missive they pressed in
fuller detail for a number of safeguards whose need had been
demonstrated to them by their experiences at Emden in 1564.
They wanted to be assured of escort by warships of the Royal
Navy on both the outward and return voyages; they urged the
extreme necessity of putting a stop to traffic by any other route
with the Netherlands, so that the concentration of trade at
Hamburg should be complete; they were willing to allow the
Italians at London to trade concurrently through Hamburg,
using English shipping if they liked, but they insisted that English traffic with France should be limited to Rouen and ports
further west, so that any indirect commercial contacts with the
Netherlands through Artois and Picardy should be impracticable. Their major argument was that the existence of any
loopholes, such as would be created by the issue of licences to
permit favoured individuals to trade with the Netherlands,
would bring about the ruin of their projected Hamburg mart.
There is good reason to assume that these requests fell upon
receptive ears. But Governor Marsh and his colleagues re-
frained on this occasion from suggesting that the Company of
Merchants Adventurers should nominate some of its own members to supervise the making of entries in the customs houses.
Perhaps they felt that the experiment had given more trouble in
1564 than it was worth.[72] Or possibly the government had made
it clear that it intended to perform the increased administrative
supervision for itself.

The assembly of the cloth fleet in the Thames was meanwhile
proceeding under the noses of the French and Spanish ambassadors and their agents. The Frenchman was not displeased that
the English connection with the Netherlands should thus be
interrupted, but he feared that the sales of cloth at Hamburg
would enable the Queen to borrow from her merchants sufficient foreign currency to give help to the Huguenots in the
recruitment of foreign mercenaries – a fear that proved well
grounded.[73] On Despes, under restraint in his embassy as he
was, none of the significance of the expedition was lost. Any
mishap to the cloth fleet would, he believed, turn the disquiet of
the Londoners to anger and provide an opportunity for the

papist and other enemies of the Queen – with whom he boldly maintained touch – to take to arms.[74] He perceived clearly that the future of the heretical regime in England was bound up with the success of the Hamburg mart, and urged with all his vehemence that Philip II should not merely hold firm with the trade embargo but also make a naval demonstration from Spain to deter the cloth fleet from putting to sea. Or, failing this, surely Alva could arrange to have it intercepted at the mouth of the Elbe. Or at least the Emperor could make his power sufficiently felt in Germany to punish the Hamburgers – using their Calvinism as a pretext.[75] At this point Despes displayed some ignorance, since not only was the authority of the Emperor in northern Germany little more than nominal, but Hamburg was still Lutheran.

By the end of March 1569 the freighting of the cloth fleet for Hamburg had been completed.[76] It carried not only cloths but some wool, which the Staplers were now licenced to dispatch – possibly in the expectation that it might find its way overland to Italy rather than past Alva's guards into the Netherlands.[77] According to reports reaching the French ambassador, the value of the goods carried by the fleet was close on a quarter of a million pounds sterling, so that the anxiety of the Londoners for a safe journey may readily be imagined.[78] Everything depended upon the ability to beat off any attacks that might be made by Netherlands ships believed to be lurking for that purpose by order of Alva. The merchantmen numbered in all rather less than thirty, including a few fitted out by the Hanse merchants of the Steelyard, so that the fleet was somewhat smaller than those which until 1566 had usually sailed twice a year to the Netherlands. It was manned by some 2,500 of 'the best mariners of England', who might expect to have to fight as well as sail their ships; they were reinforced by a number of gentlemen well armed and said to be positively hoping for battle.[79] Contrary winds held up the departure of the fleet for some weeks, but early in May it left the Thames and then put in to Harwich to pick up an escort of six of the Queen's warships.[80] As it happened, Alva made no attempt to hinder the voyage, though the ships must have passed at no great distance from the many ports of Holland; whether they thundered en route a ceremonial greeting to the coast of the Netherlands 'with the greatest bravado possible', as was the boast before departure, we do not know.[81] On May 23 the fleet sailed intact up the Elbe to anchor at Hamburg, 'not a little welcome to them of this town', as Killigrew the English envoy there reported to Cecil.[82] A major hurdle had been surmounted.

Even more than the Emden expedition, the Hamburg voyage was essentially political in its implications. Apart from Governor Marsh and his knot of enthusiasts, the merchants of the City were reluctant if not sullen. Less than two years later, the Chancellor of the Exchequer, Sir Walter Mildmay, recollected how by the order of the Queen the Privy Council had after the breach with the Netherlands treated with the merchants 'to direct their trade to Hamburg: whereunto at the first they were nothing inclined, the place being far distant, unknown to them, and no great appearance of any good vent there, as they alleged'.[83] A cloud must have hung over London as preparations for the voyage went forward, despite the full political encouragement from the government. The Deputy Governor of the Merchants Adventurers at Hamburg, and thus the leader of the expedition, was in fact none other than Gresham's erstwhile Antwerp manager Richard Clough, assuredly no zealot but a man of means and experience, whose presence well indicated the official patronage, not to say direction of the venture.[84] Clough in 1564 had been a vehement opponent of holding a cloth mart at either Emden or Hamburg; he had condemned Hamburg as lying too distant from the main trade route to Germany and Italy and its citizens because they were 'enviously and beggarly both of goods and wits'.[85] More than three years later, he was still branding the Hamburgers as 'knaves without honesty', no better than the Netherlanders.[86] It may be inferred that now he was acting under some pressure.

It is not surprising that in these circumstances the co-operation of Court and City temporarily broke down. The government for the moment was short of supplies, owing to the interruption of the customs revenue, though the international credit of the crown stood high. But the Antwerp money market was inaccessible, and with so many perils external and internal threatening the kingdom it was impracticable to summon a parliament to vote a subsidy. Accordingly the Queen in May authorized the levy of a large forced loan from all her subjects capable of payment. Among these, wealthy Londoners figured prominently: thirty-four of them, headed by Sir Thomas Gresham, were put down for £100 each, and about 250 more for 100 marks – £66 13s. 4d.[87] The Queen also expected as usual to collect a loan of ready money from the Merchants Adventurers when they had disposed of their cloths at the new mart town. But on this occasion the Company was to prove recalcitrant, even when the unprecedented concession of an advance in sterling at London was offered. Instead of the customary private arrangement between Gresham and Governor Marsh, there were attempts at evasion on the part of the Merchants Adventurers, followed by argumentative meetings of the whole body of freemen of the Company. The royal demand was openly debated, there was strenuous opposition, and a negative vote was taken. Cecil in the name of the Privy Council delivered a stinging rebuke, pointing out that such behaviour was 'an usage unmeet for princes' cause', and all the worse because the Queen's offer of repayment 'was generally rejected not only by the youth whom you the elders are commonly wont to blame to us for all disorders in your absences, but by yourselves also the heads' – i.e. the established merchants who usually remained in England, being represented by their factors at the General Courts of the Company held at Antwerp.[88]

The first information from Hamburg after the arrival of the cloth fleet there seemed to confirm the fears of the pessimists. Cloth sales, it was said, had been slight, or confined to the coarser sorts, or with small profit.[89] But before long, the news was much better. All the cloths were sold. By the middle of August, the French ambassador was reporting how the fleet of the Merchants Adventurers had returned to the Thames, 'laden with much merchandise, to the great content of the merchants and the marvellous delight of the protestants, who argue that by the opening of this trade they can for the future dispense with Antwerp'.[90] Even before this, the government had been prodding the merchants into the organization of a second fleet; the preparations were pushed forward in some haste, so that before the end of the month a further thirty ships had been freighted with another thirty or forty thousand cloths as well as other goods.[91] If broadcloths for the German market had been the chief cargo on the first fleet, the second undoubtedly carried kerseys in quantity, destined chiefly for transalpine consumers.[92] Not only was the transcontinental route to Italy open, but despite the gloomy predictions the Englishmen were to discover that Hamburg in some respects might actually be preferable to Antwerp as a terminal port in northern Europe for the Italian traffic, being both quicker and less expensive.[93]

The government was thus relieved of its greatest fear, that the Merchants Adventurers for lack of sales abroad would be unable to buy up the cloths offered by country clothiers coming up to London. But its financial apprehensions also were allayed. Gresham as early as 14 August had sought to comfort Cecil by the forecast that the second cloth fleet would carry merchandise to a total value of £200,000 or more, including at least 30,000 cloths, so that the Queen could count upon £10,000 in customs duties in the immediate future. She could, he argued, therefore afford to service the royal debts both abroad and at home.[94] In fact, during the fiscal year ending at Michaelmas 1569 the total number of notional 'short cloths' shipped from the port of London – for the most part, it may be assumed, to Hamburg – must have been over 111,000, with a gross customs yield of nearly £39,000.[95] A third fleet sailed early in 1570, by when it could be reckoned that the new mart town had established itself.[96] Thus the reasons that five years earlier had led the Queen to call off the Emden experiment were no longer operative.[97] But it had been a close shave. There had been a short-lived disturbance in some manufacturing areas of Norfolk and Suffolk, in which discontent at the momentary interruption of cloth sales and the consequent loss of livelihood had been mixed up with ecclesiastical grievances.[98] And in the City, the merchants were still not content.

Nevertheless, for all its drawbacks, Hamburg for the better part of ten years remained the chief continental market for English foreign trade, and for nearly five it served the Merchants Adventurers as virtually their only mart town. Between the Englishmen there and the Burgomasters and Senators, points of friction from time to time inevitably cropped up. The most serious concerned the occasional complaints of the Hamburgers about piracies alleged to be committed by English ships, or about the sale of pirates' ill-gotten plunder in England.[99] The English, on their side, were nervous at the threats to the security of their settlement at Hamburg emanating from intrigues or actual military threats to the city on the part of Alva, or the Duke of Holstein, or the King of Denmark.[100] A continuous irritant was supplied by the Lutheran ministers of the established church of Hamburg who in their sermons denounced the English as heretics and thereby provoked, 'grudgings and murmurings' among the common people against them. When an Englishman died, there was much difficulty in procuring burial

in consecrated ground for his body. Later, the Merchants
Adventurers in a vain attempt to appease the preachers went so
far as to suspend the reading of Church of England services at
their headquarters.[101] This lack of tolerance in matters of
religion led some of the Englishmen to recall the comparative
freedom of Emden, and from 1572 onwards some cloths were
being shipped there from London, with the authorization of the
Company.[102] But none of these troubles provoked a major crisis
at Hamburg. On either side, benevolent gestures were made to
placate feeling. At the opportune moment, the English government at a time of general corn scarcity in north-western Europe
was prepared on request to stretch a point and allow some
export specially for the relief of Hamburg.[103] Or the Burgomaster would explain to the anxious Deputy Governor that the
military movements outside the walls meant nothing and that
the English merchants could count on full security.[104] Invita-
tions to a banquet were sent out, first by one side, then by the
other, with a marked improvement of relations as a result.[105]
The continuance of the mart was too advantageous to both
parties for either to allow it to be endangered.

However, Hamburg never seemed so convenient for the Englishmen as Antwerp. They had to make the best of a number of
shortcomings lying outside the scope of any conceivable agreement with Burgomasters and Senate. To begin with, the longer
sea voyage meant that freight charges would be a good deal
higher than on the Antwerp route. Further, since the Merchants
Adventurers were so nervous as to require an escort of warships,
which the Queen after the initial voyage was not willing to
provide free of charge, the Company had to take a levy from its
members to pay for this service. The charge was sufficiently
heavy to be noted by the French ambassador at London.[106]
Then there was the problem of establishing direct contacts with
the market in the German hinterland. Since the Emden expedition of 1564, individual Merchants Adventurers had begun to
frequent the fairs of Frankfurt-on-the-Main and Leipzig to sell
their cloths and make purchases; indeed, there were English
merchants who had made their way to Frankfurt in the autumn
of 1568 via Antwerp who returned home next year through
Hamburg.[107] This sort of journey now became much more a
part of the ordinary business of the Merchant Adventurer,
since the cloth-finishing facilities at Hamburg, rapidly as they
expanded from 1569 onwards, never seem to have been equal to

the demands put upon them. Hence a supplementary centre for dyeing and finishing English cloths sprang up at the free city of Nuremberg, intended in all likelihood to serve the Italian as well as the south German market. It was fostered by the Nuremberg city government, which granted fiscal privileges to English merchants.[108] Aggressive marketing tactics thus preserved the German and transalpine markets for English goods, and with the further help of modest sales in Russia, the Baltic lands and Barbary, any disaster to the English woollen industry was averted. But the vending of cloths had become a much more complicated business.

The new and artificial pattern of trade now enforced brought a substantial cut in profit margins. By mid February 1569, Despes was joyfully reporting how since the rupture some six weeks earlier, the prices of broadcloths, kerseys and wool had already fallen by some 15 per cent and that as a result there was no little discontent.[109] Much the same information, more modestly phrased, was repeated by the French ambassador in April.[110] Even with the successful voyages to Hamburg in the summer, prices remained depressed, and it cannot be doubted that the pinch was being felt in turn by the country clothiers, their weavers and spinners, the sellers of wool and ultimately all with a stake in the countryside.[111] Further, although the new mart absorbed the output of cloths, it only partly resolved the complementary problem of imports. This continued to baffle court and City alike. The English economy in the later sixteenth century habitually absorbed exotic wares in quantity, not all of them luxuries, and its need of these had mostly been satisfied at Antwerp or in Spain. As we have seen, the Merchants Adventurers had always insisted from the start that if the Hamburg mart were to have any chance of establishing itself all commercial dealings with the Netherlands would have to be prohibited. And the prohibition would need to be rigidly enforced – without the issue of any licence by the crown that might infringe it.[112] Alva for his part had obligingly forbidden any dealings with the English, by a proclamation in March.[113] Before long, prices of imported commodities on the London market began to rise and in time shortages developed. The higher level of import prices was in part due to the greater cost of shipping goods from the Elbe, with the longer sea voyage and the less developed organization of transport, and to that extent proved permanent. The Hamburg mart in fact meant for the English a lasting deterioration in the terms of trade.[114] The scarcity of certain commodities was in many cases alleviated by enterprise and invention, but in others remained to challenge the merchants. Efforts to remedy it soon produced effects of high economic and political significance.

From Hamburg, the English could replenish their stocks of German linens and fustians, and they could also lay hands on timber products and naval stores, though these were also available, perhaps more cheaply, in the Baltic and northern Russia. There is evidence to suggest that southern silks and satins were soon making their way along the re-aligned transcontinental route to the Elbe, though never in abundance.[115] Elsewhere, traffic with the western coast of France remained open, so that wine from Bordeaux and salt from Brouage – the two foremost items – remained in supply, as did Toulouse pastel.[116] The alum farmers had now established London as a distributing centre, though there existed problems in the transport of papal alum from Civitavecchia. As to specifically Netherlands products, costly tapestries of Brussels or Oudenarde might well be foregone; but this was less true of the more common Netherlands wares habitually imported into England – hops, madder, pins and fine linens.[117] To tap fresh sources of supply, or to encourage home production, would take time. It was even more awkward to do without certain Spanish goods, especially the iron imported from the Basque ports, and the oil that was needed both in soapmaking and for cleansing wool before it was spun. Early in August 1569, Despes was gleefully reporting that the English needed oil so urgently that they were trying to extract it from rape-seed to dress their wool, and even attempting to utilize the oil to be got by boiling sheeps' feet.[118] As to the currants, raisins, almonds and other goods usually shipped from southern Spain to England, there were hopes that shortages might be made good by the occasional arrival of great Venetian ships with alternative supplies from the Adriatic and Ionian Seas, and sweet wines from the eastern Mediterranean; several of these anchored in English waters in September, to the great satisfaction of their hosts.[119]

The most teasing problems of supply were provided by sugar and spices, both of them habitually acquired by the English for the most part at Antwerp. Sugar was produced on the Portuguese Atlantic islands and in the western Mediterranean, and in the 1560s it was sometimes brought home by English ships trading to Malaga, Alicante and elsewhere on the Spanish coast.[120] It was also fetched from Barbary, where it remained available.[121] One result of the closure of Antwerp therefore was to give the London merchants who dealt in Barbary sugar a sudden fillip to their traffic, all the greater because sugar might now in addition be re-exported to Hamburg.[122] Their ranks were soon reinforced by some wealthy newcomers whose un-practised ways provoked an outcry from the old hands and a demand for a monopoly company to organize the trade.[123] More serious was the political offence that English activities in Barbary gave not merely to the King of Spain but also to his nephew the King of Portugal, a potentate whose grip extended over the spice as well as the sugar trade. Indeed, as a result of the Turco-Venetian war, the Portuguese hold on the spice trade was appreciably tightened. Spices from the East Indies, valued among other things for preserving food throughout the winter, were available in north-western Europe in the 1560's from two separate intercontinental lines of traffic. One, recently revived, led through the Turkish dominions to Alexandria or some other Mediterranean port, whence the goods were transported to Europe chiefly by the Venetians.[124] They supplied Germany and occasionally even Antwerp with spices, with the aid of large-scale merchant firms seated at Augsburg and other south German cities. After the outbreak of the Turco-Venetian war, some of these Swabian firms with commendable initiative set about importing spices themselves through Marseilles, though not with any lasting success and probably in lesser quantities than the Venetians.[125] The other intercontinental line of traffic consequently became more important than ever. It led round Africa to Lisbon. In the early 1570s, therefore, the King of Portugal controlled the supply of spices for northern Europe to a degree unsurpassed since the first years of the Portuguese domination of the East Indies.

The smooth supply of wares carried by Venetian ships came however to an end with the outbreak in 1570 of the Turco-Venetian war caused by the Turkish invasion of Cyprus. Venetian trade with the Levant was suspended, and until the restoration of peace there were no further Venetian sailings into the Atlantic. To fill the gap in Anglo-Mediterranean trade there remained only the merchants of the Adriatic city-state of Ragusa, whose republic had agreed to pay tribute to the Sultan at Constantinople. This secured them freedom to traffic during the Turco-Venetian war. While it lasted, the Ragusans enjoyed a brief and precarious golden epoch as the chief intermediaries not merely between east and west, but between England and the Levant.[126] Their ships were the universal tramps of the age, flexible in their choice of cargoes and destinations.[127] At London, there had for some time been a tiny colony of resident Ragusan merchants, one of whom, Austin de Nale, had in 1566 secured letters of denization.[128] The business of these Ragusans in the City was maintained by the occasional arrival of one of their big ships – 'argosies' – bearing a miscellany of wares that might include not only currants and oil, hitherto procured from Andalusia, but also gall, cotton-wool, brimstone and even armour. The Ragusans were men of small capital, anxious for a quick turnover, and the presence of an argosy in the Thames was apt to flutter the City with rapid price fluctuations, as they sold off their goods and hastened to stock up with English products and so be gone.[129] Like the Venetians, they were always made welcome; there is record of a ship, probably Ragusan, that arrived off the Downs in January 1570 and was specially provided, by government order, with convoy and pilotage to London.[130]

Once the Hamburg mart had actually materialized, the pressing importance of the trade with Lisbon became apparent at London. With Antwerp henceforth inaccessible, where else could supplies of spices and sugar, adequate and assured, be available? In addition, Portugal provided a market for the coloured cloths made in Suffolk and other counties. Finally, in the minds of some merchants there lurked the hope that Portugal might provide a clandestine means of access to the now closed Spanish market. In the summer of 1569, when so much in the world of international traffic seemed at stake, the alluring nature of the Portugal trade was inescapable. It was reckoned that every year in spices, drugs, sugar, bullion, precious stones and other exotic wares, freight to the value of around two million ducats – about £600,000 sterling – was conveyed from Portugal to Antwerp. This was why the Portuguese merchants there received such consideration. Only a very short further step was needed to ask the question – why should not the staple for Portuguese spices and sugar be transferred from the Netherlands to England? The English might then become the distributors of spices and sugar for northern Europe, with all the profits attaching to the business, while the Portuguese merchants could be promised lower taxation and greater security by land and sea than they enjoyed under the heavy hand of Alva at Antwerp. Besides, the worsted cloths sought by the Portuguese in the Netherlands were now happily being manufactured in England.[131] The idea of establishing a spice staple in England was already familiar to City merchants interested in the Muscovy trade. Just a year earlier, the hopes of their agents had risen high: their aim had been to divert the spice and silk traffic of the Indies to a more northerly overland route via Persia and Russia to the Baltic at Narva, outflanking Portuguese and Venetians alike, and supplanting the Antwerp entrepôt.[132] This visionary project haunted the Muscovy merchants for some years to come. But meanwhile, why should not Lisbon offer a more practicable alternative to Narva as a staging-post for an English spice staple?

Unfortunately, there were political differences between England and Portugal that stood in the way of so advantageous an adjustment of the paths of trade. Resentment was caused at Lisbon by the belief, not without good ground, that the English were welcomed in Barbary because they supplied the sultan with arms. Penetration by English merchants further south along the African coast was even more disliked. Guinea had been known to the English in the fifteenth century; then, after a long intermission, they began to trade there in a more persistent and methodical fashion from 1553. They sought to sell coloured cloths and metal trinkets, and to obtain gold dust, ivory and pepper; Hawkins in particular added to this list slaves, for shipment across the Atlantic to Spanish America. The presence of strangers in these forbidden waters was always resented by the kings of Portugal. The stock English defence of these intruding voyages was formulated as early as 1555 and rested on two main arguments – first, that English trade was not conducted in districts under Portuguese control, and secondly, that the English were doing no more than the French, whose incursions the kings of Portugal were equally unable to curb.[133] From time to time, there were clashes between the English and the Portuguese on the West African coast, accompanied sometimes by fighting and bloodshed. The protests of the King of Portugal were conveyed to the Queen of England either by a special envoy or through the Spanish ambassador at London. During the sixties, grievances were amassed on either side.[134]

The English chose an injudicious moment at which to aggravate their existing difficulties with the Portuguese – January,

1569, at almost the moment of the closing of Antwerp, when it might have been thought they had sufficient trouble on their hands. In that month a licence was issued by the Admiralty, in favour of the sea-captain William Wynter and his brother, entitling them to take possession of goods to the value of £7,600 out of Portuguese ships, in compensation for a vessel of theirs that had been sunk off the coast of Guinea, with the loss of its cargo, nearly six years previously.[135] Admittedly, the Portuguese government had refused any indemnity. Nevertheless, such an action was hardly compatible with the professions of the Queen, who when writing at this time to the King of Portugal had prudently declared herself anxious to avoid any disturbance of the alliance so ancient and so needful to both kingdoms.[136] As things were, the Wynter brothers did not even have to go to the trouble and expense of fitting out a privateer or two: all that was necessary was to identify Portuguese property on board the Peninsular shipping now perforce piling up in English ports, and lay claim to it. The Portuguese envoy was quick to protest.[137] By the summer of 1569 Cecil was understandably fearing a further 'jar' in Anglo-Portuguese relations.[138] There is evidence to indicate a short-lived seizure of English goods in Portugal just at this time.[139] However, this was the moment at which not only the City merchants had come to grasp the extreme importance of the trade to Portugal, but also a Portuguese agent was at work at London, attempting to find a basis for settlement.[140] For a while, normal relations were ostensibly restored.

But not for long. Further English voyages to Guinea and seizures of Portuguese ships at sea were reported at Lisbon, so that near the middle of 1570 the patience of the Portuguese government gave way. At the end of May two English ships sailed unsuspectingly into the Tagus, laden with wheat, coloured Suffolk cloths and wax; the gross market value of these goods was put at only a little less than £8,000. They had been dispatched by a group of Ipswich merchants on whose behalf Lawrence Coxon, citizen of London and Merchant Adventurer, was travelling as agent in charge. The purpose of the voyage was to buy spices with the money raised by the sale of the commodities brought in the ships. In this, there was believed to be 'great gain'. But the Portuguese proved worse than unwelcoming. In the Tagus but outside Lisbon, the ships were warned to drop anchor; then, after much delay, their sails and armament were removed and their cargoes impounded. Coxon to his chagrin could meanwhile observe brisk business proceeding ashore – there were some Bretons selling corn at a good price, while other Bretons, Basques and strangers were likewise offering English cloths for sale. Some of the English sailors who disobeyed Portuguese orders and ventured on land were committed to prison 'amongst felons and thieves as if they had been grievous malefactors'; then at last the crews were taken off and told to make their way home best as they could, 'having neither penny nor pennyworth given them for their succour and relief'.[141] High feeling was at once aroused in England at the news of this harsh dealing by the Portuguese government, and the Privy Council lost no time in demanding restitution.[142] In default of this, it gave orders, first for the seizure of Portuguese goods, and subsequently for the arrest of Portuguese subjects, mostly to be found in London.[143] Later, it instructed that compensation for the Ipswich merchants and others should be taken from the Portuguese wares now impounded.[144] A breach in Anglo-Portuguese relations comparable to the Anglo-Netherlands rupture two years earlier had thus been precipitated.

However, negotiations between London and Lisbon continued. Near the end of 1571 they actually seemed to be on the brink of success, despite Spanish efforts to hinder them. Neither the letters of marque issued to the Wynter brothers and the Ipswich merchants, nor the arrests and seizures of goods on either side provided an insurmountable obstacle. Even the Barbary trade might at a pinch be ignored. The fatal stumbling-block lay in the chronic Portuguese objection to any English voyages to Guinea and other territories forbidden to European traders by the King of Portugal – in broad terms, his 'Indies'. This point was appreciated in the City, where the clash of interests between the merchants with a steady long-term interest in the market for Suffolk and Devonshire coloured cloths in Portugal and the speculative adventurers to Guinea was delineated in a petition presented by the former to the Privy Council in December 1571. Their ranks were headed by two or three prominent Londoners, but they also numbered many small men from the western outports – Bristol, Barnstaple, Exeter, Totnes and Dartmouth. They pointed to the excessive cost of the voyages to Guinea, in terms of ships wrecked and mariners dead, some by violence but most through disease, and went on to argue that the gold dust of the Sahara could more easily and peacefully be obtained by selling cloths at Lisbon, where the market was easy. The only result of injudicious attempts by untrained and selfish interlopers to trade direct with the Portuguese 'Indies' since 1553 had been international strife and now, for two years, a complete stoppage of trade between England and Portugal. There were losses to the Queen's customs, to the clothmakers and indeed to everyone save those who secured authority to help themselves to Portuguese goods in England – a wry dig at the brothers Wynter. This common-sense paper was given the weighty support of Governor Marsh 'not as a merchant trading Portugal but understanding their minds and the necessity of the matter'.[145] But there were sea-faring, shipping and mercenary interests on the side of the traffickers to Guinea, with influential friends in the Privy Council; and they were to prevail.

The consequences of the Anglo-Portuguese rupture were alleviated by the persistence of clandestine trade between the two countries. There may have been others like the merchants of Morlaix who made a regular practice of transporting English manufactures to Portugal;[146] nor do we know how far English ships venturing into Portuguese or Spanish waters to trade were able – as one or two at least were – to masquerade convincingly as Flemish or belonging to Emden.[147] Equally unknown but probably more significant was the traffic maintained by the Marranos with their well organized commercial network of agents. When early in 1571 the forty-odd Portuguese residents at London were being identified by the English government for the purposes of the arrest, it was discovered that many of them were unsure of their allegiance to the King of Portugal: they were crypto-Jews, ambiguous in their politics as in their re-ligion.[148] The Portuguese Jews at London could not afford to avow their faith; this might serve to incriminate their relatives in Portugal and the Netherlands, as well as leading to trouble with the English. But they were ready to collaborate in drawing the spice trade to England and away from an Antwerp purged by Alva. They had supported, if they did not instigate, the project aired in the summer of 1569 for establishing a staple for spices in England.[149] Alva himself suspected as much, and observed to his master that many of the Antwerp Portuguese might well like to go to England to live there 'in the law of Moses', taking their spice trade with them to hearten the English in their mal-practices.[150] One of them, a member of the wealthy family of Mendes, certainly went out of his way at the time of the rupture to oblige Lionel Duckett, a leading merchant of the City, soon to be Lord Mayor, by finding a way to collect his debts in the Netherlands for him and transmit them to London.[151]

The Marranos resident at London included some large-scale merchants, active in business with relatives both at Antwerp and in Portugal, and in touch with associates from Barbary to the Levant. Prominent among them was Dunstan Ames, a freeman of the Grocers' Company from 1557, who later set up his second son as his agent at Lisbon; other members of the family also were interested in the spice trade. But the most striking personage among them was Hector Nunez, widely known at the royal court as a doctor of medicine – a fellow of both the Royal College of Surgeons and of the College of Physicians. He was also a merchant on no mean scale, with apprentices both English and Portuguese to serve him. He traded in concert with his relatives at Antwerp and Lisbon as well as conducting ventures on his own.[152] His business resembled that of the Italian firms at London; like them, he dispatched woollen cloths to Antwerp, dealing not in the fine broadcloths destined for nothern Europe but in the kerseys and 'cottons' serving southern markets.[153] In 1565, he was also shipping cochineal from London to Antwerp – a reversal of the usual current of traffic, since such small quantities of this Mexican dye as reached England normally would come via Spain and the Netherlands.[154] After the rupture of Anglo-Netherlands trade relations in January 1569 he was able to maintain touch with relatives at Antwerp who were importing sugar and other wares from Barbary; he also helped them by arranging, with groups of English merchants at London, for the insurance of their property while in transit. Hector Nunez or Dunstan Ames are the most likely persons to identify with the 'Portuguese' merchant who in the summer of 1569 suggested that a spice staple should be established in England.

A further reason for the continued arrival of Portuguese spices in England was provided by the renewed prevalence of violence at sea. From the autumn of 1568 onwards, this was springing from two distinct sources.[155] One was the open revolt of the Prince of Orange and his brother in the Netherlands; on land, it was crushed by Alva, but at sea it was continued by privateers whom Orange as a sovereign prince claimed the right to authorize with letters of marque. The other was the outbreak of the third war of religion in France, where the Prince of Condé, leader of the Huguenot cause, was able in September to seize and hold the Atlantic port of La Rochelle, which entered forthwith upon its lively sixty years as a protestant stronghold. It was henceforth a nest for the privateers whom Condé in the name of the Queen of Navarre was also licensing. One of their earliest exploits was the attempted interception of the Spanish *zabras* carrying bullion to Antwerp, which unluckily had to race for shelter in English ports.[156] The general upshot of these events, capped by the Anglo-Netherlands, Anglo-Spanish and Anglo-Portuguese ruptures, was that the waters of western Europe became unprecendentedly dangerous for peaceful traders of any nationality or faith. Anyone with capital sufficient to arm and send out a ship could purchase a letter of marque from the agents of Orange or Condé and try his luck. For instance, Thomas Bowes, the shady but ingenious son of Sir Martin Bowes, Lord Mayor of London in 1545–6, hastened in partnership with the more reputable London merchant John Foxall, Mercer and Merchant Adventurer, to activate early in 1569 the *Barcke Bowes*. She had been lying idle at Southampton for the past year. They made her seaworthy, provided her with a crew and letters of marque emanating from Condé, and sent her forth. As chance would have it, she fell in with a Frenchman carrying wine; she promptly seized her prey and brought it into Portsmouth to dispose of the cargo.[157] It had been a sheer plundering foray 'against the papists' in name, in fact directed against any tempting victim.

The effect of irresponsible actions of this sort, multiplied a hundred-fold, may be imagined. The great maritime artery of European commerce along the western shore of the continent for the moment lay open to any well-armed marauder. New patterns of trade arose, as piracy and privateering were supplemented by fraud and collusion. Above all, under the shadow of the great protestant fortress at La Rochelle, normal trade was replaced by a traffic in sugar, molasses and other wares hitherto unfamiliar. Such goods might re-enter the world of legitimate commerce by transhipment from a privateer to some pacific vessel belonging to a respectable merchant, perhaps in harbour or perhaps at some discreet rendezvous in the Downs.[158] They might even be sold on English soil, perhaps at some remote haven. A flourishing market in goods from despoiled ships grew up at Mede Hole – now Osborne Bay – on the Isle of Wight. It was fed by the 'sea rovers' of various nationalities who found an anchorage not far away at Newport, where the inhabitants were alleged greatly to 'favour, relieve, maintain and succour' them. At this market it was possible to pick up all sorts of commodities, from spices and sugars to ivory, wine, figs, raisins and even English cloth and wool. Well-known sea-captains were to be met there, including John Hawkins, as also sharp City men prepared to face the risk of legal action on the part of legitimate owners when their purchases were offered for re-sale.[159] Close contacts between the sea-captains and some traders of London there must have been, though it is unlikely that the former were financed by commercial speculators on the massive and systematic scale accepted by bold City merchants during the Spanish war twenty years later.[160] But it is scarcely possible to doubt that the deficiencies of the Hamburg mart in spices, sugars and other goods were to an appreciable extent made good by the operations of the privateers during the years 1569–72.

The worsening of the terms of trade was bound sooner or later to affect all ranks of English society. It was bad enough that cloths, wool and other English exports were fetching less in the foreign market.[161] But consumers too were affected. They might know little about either Antwerp or Hamburg; but they could not fail to resent the discovery that imported commodities in general were costing too much. No doubt this was particularly true of spices, sugar and other Atlantic commodities. But the prices of goods produced in the interior of Germany were also raised. The merchants of the Steelyard pointed out that as they could no longer convey various sorts of merchandise down the Rhine to the Netherlands for shipment, but had to bring them to Hamburg in order to secure unhampered entry to England, at their 'great and intolerable charges', they had to ask higher prices simply to avoid loss. They instanced steel, bowstaves, Rhenish wine, Cologne hemp and 'battery wares', i.e. metalwares probably from Nuremberg.[162]

A symptom of the anxiety provoked by this maladjustment of prices is possibly to be discerned in the output of statutes dealing with mercantile disorders, for which the Parliament that sat for a few weeks in the spring of 1571 was responsible. Among these acts were measures to prevent debtors from cheating their creditors by means of fraudulent gifts or alienation, a further development of the law of bankruptcy, the legalization of interest at not more than 10 per cent (characteristically entitled 'an act against usury'), and efforts to encourage sea-fishing, tillage and shipbuilding.[163] Among the acts whose validity was prolonged was one against the venerable offences of forestalling, regrating and engrossing, with a significant proviso exempting wines, oils, sugars, spices, currants and other foreign victuals, i.e. goods imported chiefly from the Netherlands and Spain.[164] This gave rise to controversy at the time of the next Parliament, which sat during May and June 1572, when it was argued that the exemption was ill-timed because the prices of these wares had approximately doubled within recent years.[165] Some members evidently vented their irritation on the dealers in these goods, for the session was also marked by the introduction of an abortive bill 'against merchants, to be purchasers of lands or leases'.[166] A little later, some great landowners who were hit in their pockets by the squeeze in the profits of wool production took offence at the lavish feasts reported to take place in the halls of the City livery companies, at a time when prices of luxury foods had never been so high; and an appeasing act of Common Council was accordingly drafted to forbid this sort of conspicuous consumption.[167] No doubt there were other longer-term reasons for this friction between merchants and landlords. It has been observed in a different context that these were years marked by a suspension of intermarriage between noblemen and the daughters of rich Londoners.[168]

Thus, although the Hamburg mart enabled the Merchants Adventurers to dispose of their cargoes of cloths and other wares, the circumstances of their trade were not so attractive as they had been in the good old days at Antwerp. We need not doubt the eagerness of most Londoners to return to their mart in the Netherlands whenever the political situation should make it possible. In fact, the Hamburg mart was to survive the re-opening of Antwerp, but only because of a series of violent happenings in the Netherlands to which we must now turn.

NOTES TO CHAPTER VI

[1] La Mothe Fénélon to Catherine de Médicis, 30 January 1569, MF, I, 163.

[2] *Ib.* to Charles IX, 8 March 1569, *ib.*, 217–21.

[3] *Ib.* to Catherine de Médicis, 21 March 1569, *ib.*, 274–5.

[4] Details in the letters of La Mothe Fénélon from June to August 1569, MF, II, 19–166 *passim*.

[5] *Ib.* to Catherine de Médicis, 30 January and 10 February 1569, MF, I, 166 and 190.

[6] See discussion in *Isham*, lxxxi–lxxxv.

[7] *Supra*, 92.

[8] La Mothe Fénélon to Charles IX, 17 January 1569, MF, I, 114.

[9] The main source of information about the top-level political crisis of early 1569 is the dispatches of the French ambassador, especially his

letter of 13 March to Catherine de Médicis: MF, I, 258–62. The whole episode was carefully examined by C. Read, *Mr. Secretary Cecil and queen Elizabeth* (London, 1955), 440 *et seq.*, to whose analysis this paragraph is indebted. Read took the rupture with the Netherlands and the stoppage of the Antwerp trade as the starting-point of the attempted upheaval. W. MacCaffrey, *The Shaping of the Elizabethan Regime* (London, 1969), 199–246, follows a divergent approach.

[10] Privy Council order, October 1567, Journals, 19, f. 81.

[11] *Ib.*, f. 132v.

[12] *Ib.*, ff. 134, 136 and 138.

[13] *Ib.*, ff. 158v, 162v, 164v–5.

[14] *Ib.*, ff. 171v–2.

[15] *Ib.*, ff. 134, 138v, 143, 145.

[16] City proclamation, 16 February 1569, Letter Book v, f.3322.

[17] Their first appointment was decided on 7 December 1568, their stipend was fixed at 5 marks each *per annum* on 18 January 1569, and on the 24th it was resolved that their cry should be REMEMBER THE CLOCKES. LOKE WELL TO YOUR FYER AND YOUR LIGHT AND GOD GEVE YOU GOOD NIGHT, FOR NOWE THE BELL RINGETH — Rep. 16, ff. 422v, 433v and 439.

[18] *Supra*, 99.

[19] Order of Lord Mayor to aldermen, 3 January 1569, Journals, 19, f. 138v.

[20] *Ib.*, 143v.

[21] Journals, 19, f. 167v, printed by E. K. Chambers, *The Elizabethan Stage*, IV (Oxford, 1923), 267.

[22] Despes to Philip II, 9 May 1569, *CSPSp. 1568–79*, 144–8; La Mothe Fénélon to Charles IX, 12 May 1569, MF, I, 374–5.

[23] See certificate of musters, and also London commissioners of musters to Privy Council, both 15 August 1569, SP 12/58/13 and 14. Archery practice was being resuscitated from 10 January 1569, Rep. 16, f. 431v.

[24] Report of the London Commissioners of Array, 15 August 1569, SP 12/58/14; on the general issue, La Mothe Fénélon to Charles IX and Catherine de Médicis, 1 September 1569, MF, II, 197–8.

[25] Andrio to Cecil, *c.* August 1570, SP 70/115/971.

[26] Certificate of London musters, 15 August 1569, SP 12/58/13.

[27] *APC 1571–5*, 52–3 and 72–3.

[28] Opinion of Merchants Adventurers, 19 January 1569, SP 12/49/30.

[29] Count John of East Friesland to Cecil, 16 January 1569, KL, v, 248–9.

[30] Merchants Adventurers to Privy Council, undated *c.* 1578, SP 12/127/88.

[31] Guicciardini to Francesco de'Medici, 25 July 1568, Battistini, 319.

[32] Queen to Count Edzard, 11 July 1568, KL, v, 122–4; Silva to Philip II, 17 July 1568, *CSPSp. 1568–79*, 55–6.

[33] See the petition of Electors to Emperor Maximilian II, September 1568, *CSPF 1566–8*, No. 2487.

[34] This explanation was put forward in the Antwerp newsletter *c.* 18 February 1569, KL, v, 297. See also Despes to Alva, same date, *ib.*, 297.

[35] Hamburg–England trade in the first half of the sixteenth century has been investigated by W. Friedland, 'Hamburger Englandfahrer, 1512–1557', *Zeitschrift des Vereins für Hamburgische Geschichte*, XLVI (1960), 1–42. To this work the following paragraph is indebted.

[36] *Ante*, 63.

[37] Declaration of Merchants Adventurers, undated *c.* 1554, Rawl., C 394, p. 114; *ib.* to *ib.*, similar date, SP 11/4/36; *ib.* to *ib.*, *c.* February 1555, SP 11/5/5; Paget *et al.* to King Philip, undated *c.* March 1556, SP 69/8/492.

[38] Further information about the potential rivalry of Hamburg and Antwerp

before 1569 may be found in W. Brulez, 'Les routes commerciales d'Angleterre en Italie au XVI$^e$ siecle', *Studi in honore de Amintore Fanfani*, IV (Milan, 1962), 178–81.

[39] Figures printed by Ehrenberg, *EH*, 327.

[40] Entries in London Port Book, 1565, E 190/2/1.

[41] During the months May to September 1565, 97 cloths were thus entered with the customs, *ib.*

[42] Gresham to Cecil, 16 and 19 April 1560, SP 70/13/473 and KL, II, 335.

[43] Friedland, 'Hamburger Englandfahrer', 27.

[44] Ehrenberg, *EH*, 78–80.

[45] Hamburg to Queen, 17 March 1564, SP 70/77/874. The calendared version, *CSPF 1564–6*, No. 1050, was misdated by a year, as was pointed out by Ehrenberg, *EH*, 76n.

[46] Marsh to Cecil, 9 April 1564, SP 12/33/50; Ehrenberg, *EH*, 79.

[47] Merchants Adventurers to Hamburg, 30 April 1564, pr. *The Whole Works of Roger Ascham*, ed. J. A. Giles, II (London, 1864), 87–9.

[48] *Ante*, 262–3.

[49] Table printed by Ehrenberg, *EH*, 327.

[50] *Supra*, 30–1.

[51] Wotton to Cecil, 24 June 1566, SP 70/84/424. *Supra*, 71.

[52] Gresham to Cecil, 8 September 1566, KL, IV, 352; quoted by Ehrenberg, *EH*, 82.

[53] See the comment of Ehrenberg, *EH*, 82.

[54] Acknowledged in letter from Queen to Hamburg, 9 March 1567, Royal, 13 B 1, f. 178.

[55] Alderman of Steelyard to Suderman, 18 January 1567, Höhlbaum, I, No. 2986.

[56] The four letters from Queen, Governor and Company to Hamburg, dated 8 and 9 March 1567, were all entered in Ascham's letter-book, Royal, 13 B 1, ff. 177v–9v. The Hamburg side of the diplomatic correspondence was known to Burgon – II, 319–20 – a short time before the destruction of the municipal archives by fire in 1842.

[57] Protest by Suderman, 9 June 1567, Höhlbaum, I, No. 3122 and 590–3; Ehrenberg, *EH*, 83 *et seq.*

[58] Maximilian II to Queen, 10 May, and Hanse Congress to *ib.*, 14 May 1567, Höhlbuam, I, Nos. 3097 and 3098. On Suderman, see *ante, passim.*

[59] Stralen to Gilis, 13 July 1564, *Bulletin des Archives d'Anvers*, VIII (n.d.), 83–5.

[60] Regent to Philip II, 12 July 1567, Gelder, *MP*, III, 302.

[61] Entry in Minute Book of Merchants Adventurers, 6 March 1568, pr. Sellers, *York Mercers*, 179–80; oath to be administered to Merchants Adventurers, *c.* June 1568, *ib.*, 183; Ehrenberg, *EH*, 101–2.

[62] Ehrenberg, *EH*, 102, pointed out that the four ships did not sail until July.

[63] The text of the Anglo-Hamburg agreement was printed by Ehrenberg, *EH*, 312–26, from the copy in the Lübeck archives. To this, and to his discussion, *ib.*, 93–100, this and the succeeding paragraph are indebted. A second copy in the Danzig archives was calendared by Simpson, No. 5176. Yet another copy of the agreement, not known to Ehrenberg, has survived and is now at Add. 48,010, ff. 446–59.

[64] Article 19; *ante*, 11. Attention had also been given to this need at Emden: *ante*, 260.

[65] Lafarten to Suderman, 30 July 1567, Höhlbaum, I, No. 3147, referred to him as *hujus tragediae principalis actor*; Ehrenberg, *EH*, 85.

[66] *A nobis graviter punietur*, article 15.

[67] Specifically mentioned in article 9.

[68] Articles 55 and 56.

[69] The withdrawal of the concession in 1578 was a mere act of the Lord Mayor and aldermen, though the Privy Council subsequently required them to justify their action – *APC 1577–8*, 418–19.

[70] *Supra*, 107–8; La Mothe Fénélon to Charles IX, 20 February 1569, MF, I, 201; Despes to Alva, same date, KL, V, 302.

[71] Merchants Adventurers to Council, 1 March 1569, Cotton, Faustina C II, No. 91, ff. 90–2.

[72] *Ante*, 268–9.

[73] E.g., La Mothe Fénélon to Charles IX, 30 April 1569, MF, I, 355.

[74] Despes to Philip II, 12 March 1569, *CSPSp. 1568–79*, 133–7.

[75] Despes to Philip II, 9 May 1569, *CSPSp. 1568–79*, 144–8.

[76] Despes to Alva, 23 March 1569, KL, V, 339; *ib.* to Philip II, 2 April 1569, *CSPSp. 1568–79*, 138–40.

[77] Licence to Staplers, 24 April 1569, *CPR 1566–9*, 358.

[78] La Mothe Fénélon to Charles IX, 30 April 1569, MF, I, 355, put the value at 700,000 *ecus*.

[79] La Mothe Fénelon to Charles IX, 13 April 1569, MF, I, 313; *ib.* to Charles IX and Catherine de Médicis, 20 April, *ib.*, 326; *ib.* to Charles IX, 24 April, *ib.*, 339.

[81] This is the figure quoted by Cecil writing to Norris, 4 June 1569, *Cabala*, 152. The French and Spanish ambassadors reported larger ones.

[81] For the boast, La Mothe Fénélon to Charles IX, 21 March 1569, MF, I, 272.

[82] Killigrew to Cecil, 25 May 1569, Cecil Papers, 156/28.

[83] Opinion of Sir Walter Mildmay on Mr Garrett's licence, 8 December 1570, NRO, F. (M) P. 171.

[84] Ehrenberg, *EH*, 116, accepted Burgon, *Gresham*, II, 357 ff., where the evidence for Clough's tenure of the office of Deputy Governor is given. A conclusive item was supplied by M. Sellers with the printing of a letter from Clough to the York Merchants Adventurers dated 21 February 1570, *York Mercers*, 185–6, in which he signed his name as deputy governor. See also Clough's will, PCC 37 Lyon.

[85] Clough to Gresham, January 1564, Cotton Galba B XI, No. 67; quoted by Ehrenberg, *EH*, 66–7. *Ante*, 239.

[86] *Ib.* to *ib.*, 6 October 1567, KL, V, 20–3.

[87] Names of persons to whom privy seals were directed, 20 May 1569, SP 12/49/87; La Mothe Fénélon to Charles IX, 19 September 1569, MF, II, 238–9. Basically, the royal finances were sound enough: the fact that the Queen had now to tap her reserves did not supply any justification for the opinion of Despes the previous autumn that she was in straits for money. Despite Gresham, the bullion from the Spanish ships remained in the Tower.

[88] Cecil on behalf of Privy Council to Merchants Adventurers, 10 September 1569, Lansd. 12/10, f. 20.

[89] Despes to Philip II, 1 July 1569, *CSPSp. 1568–79*, 169–71; La Mothe Fénélon to Charles IX, 5 August 1569, MF, II, 142.

[90] La Mothe Fénélon to Charles IX, 15 August 1569, MF, II, 153–4.

[91] Despes to Philip II, 5 and 27 August 1569, *CSPSp. 1568–79*, 185–6 and 189.

[92] Indicated by the figures of cloths re-directed from Hamburg, printed by Ehrenberg, *EH*, 329. There was a sudden jump in the dispatch of kerseys in October.

[93] *Ante*, 9–10; also the essay by W. Brulez, 'Les routes commerciales', there cited.

[94] Gresham to Cecil, 14 August 1569, Lansd. 12/8, pr. Ellis, *Original Letters*, sec. ser., II, 315–19.

[95] Custom was charged on 100,457 short cloths, of which Englishmen and

Hansards shipped 88,251, other foreigners the rest. To these figures one ninth must be added, to represent the duty-free 'wrappers'. A few 'cottons' were also exported. 'An account of the woollen commodities exported', undated, SP 12/58/ 26.

[96] Ehrenberg, *EH*, 112.

[97] Cf. *ante*, 282–3.

[98] Despes to Philip II, 25 and 30 July 1569, *CSPSp. 1568–79*, 181–2; La Mothe Fénélon to Charles IX and Catherine de Médicis, 1 September 1569, MF, II, 199.

[99] Summary of letters complaining of piracies by the English, September 1570, SP 70/114/840; Loddington to Burghley, 17 August 1571, SP 70/119/1273.

[100] Hamburg newsletters, 4 November 1569, KL, V, 501–2; 5 January 1570, SP 70/110/491; 30 June 1571, KL, VI, 147.

[101] *Ib.*, 5 December 1570, 1 August 1571, 3 November 1571 and 27 March 1572, KL, VI, 20, 159, 209 and 355.

[102] Ehrenberg, *EH*, 132.

[103] Hamburg to Queen, 4 October 1571, SP 70/120/1339; corn export licence for Peter Rentzell, 5 January 1572, *CPR 1569–72*, 376.

[104] Hamburg newsletter, 5 January 1570, SP 70/110/491.

[105] *Ib.*, 26 February 1572, KL, VI, 328.

[106] La Mothe Fénélon to Charles IX, 15 August 1569 and 27 April 1570, MF, II, 154 and III, 132; estimate of convoy costs, 12 March 1570, SP 12/67/18; Queen to Clinton, 23 March 1570, SP 12/67/32.

[107] Killegrew to Cecil, 6 April 1569, SP 70/106/182.

[108] Ehrenberg, *EH*, 118–20. A study of the market for English cloths at Nuremberg by Dr W. R. Baumann is due shortly for publication.

[109] Despes to Alva, *c.* 18 February 1569, KL, V, 297.

[110] La Mothe Fénélon to Charles IX and Catherine de Médicis, 20 April 1569, MF, I, 329.

[111] For cloth prices, see below, 163–4.

[112] Memorandum of Sir Walter Mildmay, 8 December 1570, NRO F. (M.) P. 171. Imports at London fell sharply to approximately the level of 1564 – 'Account of the customs and subsidies of London, Sandwich and Chichester', 20 June 1570, SP 12/71/20.

[113] Philip II to Governor &c. of the province of Holland, 31 March 1569, Smit, *Bronnen*, No. 1163. Presumably similar orders were sent to the other maritime provinces.

[114] The point was clearly made in Grey to Burghley, 31 July 1571, SP 15/20/63.

[115] Case of Martyn *v.* Folter, 25 November 1570, HCA 13/18, ff. 86v *et seq.*

[116] La Mothe Fénélon to Charles IX, 21 March 1569, MF, I, 270 *et passim*; Cecil to Norris, 3 July 1569, *Cabala*, 153.

[117] Listed, Grey to Cecil, 31 July 1569, SP 15/20/63.

[118] Despes to Philip II, 5 August 1569, *CSPSp. 1568–79*, 186.

[119] *Ib.* to *ib.*, 27 September 1569, *ib.*, 197.

[120] Port books, London, 1565 and 1566–7, E 190/2/1 and 4/2.

[121] Anglo-Barbary trade has been investigated by T.S. Willan, 'English trade with Morocco', *Studies*, 92–312. To his findings this and the following paragraphs are indebted.

[122] Despes to Philip II, 18 January 1570, *CSPSp. 1568–79*, 230; evidence in the case of Dowghty *v.* Wilkinson, 5 May 1573 and subsequent days, HCA 13/19, ff. 523 *et seq.*; 13/20, ff. 1 *et seq.*; Willan, *Studies*, 114 and 318.

[123] 'Reasons offered to the queen for the establishing of an exclusive trade with the Barbary States', undated *c.* 1574, TP, II, 48–9; Willan, *Studies*, 160–2.

[124] F. C. Lane, 'The Mediterranean Spice Trade: Its Revival in the Sixteenth Century', *Venice and History* (Baltimore, 1966), 25–34.

[125] This has been investigated by A. E. Sayous, 'Le commerce de Melchior Manlich et Cie d'Augsbourg à Marseille et dans toute la Mediterranée entre 1571 et 1574', *Revue Historique*, CLVI (1935), 389–411.

[126] M. Aymard, *Venise, Raguse et le commerce du blé pendant la seconde moitié du XVI^e siècle* (Paris, 1966), 138.

[127] *Ib.*, 90–2. See also the general account by J. Tadić, 'Le port de Raguse et sa flotte au XVI^e siècle', in *Le Navire et l'Economie Maritime du Moyen-Age au XVIII^e siècle*, ed. M. Mollat (Paris, 1958), 9–26. Also F. W. Carter, 'The commerce of the Dubrovnik republic, 1500–1700', *EcHR*, second ser., XXIV (1971), 370–94.

[128] *CPR 1563–6*, 357. On Ragusan merchants in England, see G. D. Ramsay, 'The City of London and the Republic of St. Blaise in the later sixteenth century', *Dubrovnik's relations with England*, ed. R. Filipović and M. Partridge (Zagreb, 1977), 31–46 and the sources there listed.

[129] Mediterranean traders to Council, undated *c.* 1575, Add. 48,020, f. 376. There is another copy of this document at Lansd. 112, No. 49.

[130] Queen to officers of navy, hand of Cecil, 24 January 1570, SP 12/66/23. The vessel was called both Venetian and 'the arragusyn ship'.

[131] Hastings to Cecil, undated *c.* June 1569, SP 12/60/79; papers on the staple of spices, 29 June 1569, SP 12/51/18 and 19; 'Considerations ... that the staple of spices ... be kept in England', same date, Cotton Nero B I, No. 64; account of customs and subsidies for merchandise shipped in England for Portugal and Barbary, September 1568, SP 12/47/90.

[132] Silva to Philip II, 26 June 1568, *CSPSp. 1568–79*, 44; Bannister and Geoffrey Duckett to Muscovy Company, 12 August 1568, printed in *Early Voyages and Travels to Russia and Persia*, ed. E. D. Morgan and C. H. Coote, II, Hakluyt Society, LXXIII (1886), 258–61; in general, Willan, *EHRC*, *passim*.

[133] 'A short declaration of the merchants' answer to the ambassador of Portugal', *c.* 1555, printed in *Europeans in West Africa, 1450–1560*, ed. J. W. Blake, Hakluyt Society, sec. ser., LXXXVII (1942), 355–8.

[134] The rapid survey of Anglo-Portuguese political relations in the later sixteenth century by E. Prestage, 'The Anglo-Portuguese Alliance', *TRHS*, fourth ser., XVII (1934), 81–8, needs to be interpreted in the light of the discoveries by T. S. Willan, *Studies, ut supra*. On the importance of Portugal for the English in 1569, see also Williamson, *Hawkins*, 230–2.

[135] Admiralty judges to Cecil, 16 January 1569, SP 12/49/26; *CPR 1566–9*, 331.

[136] Queen to King Sebastian of Portugal, 2 January 1569, SP 701015/7.

[137] Portuguese ambassador to Cecil, 5 January 1569, Cecil Papers, 4/65. The date was incorrectly stated in *HMC Salisbury*, XIII, 91.

[138] Cecil to Norris, 18 June 1569, *Cabala*, 152.

[139] Despes to Philip II, 14 June 1569, *CSPSp. 1568–79*, 164–5; La Mothe Fénélon to Charles IX, 21 June 1569, MF, II, 38; *cf.* the evidence of Robert Oldborough and others in the case of George Downe, 6 August 1573, HCA 13/20, ff. 26v *et seq.*

[140] Despes to Philip II, 17 September 1569, *CSPSp. 1568–79*, 192–3.

[141] Evidence of Laurence Coxon and others, from 5 August 1570 onwards, HCA 13/17, ff. 416 *et seq.* Much colourful detail was supplied in these depositions.

[142] *APC 1558–70*, 378–9; Privy Council to Christmas, 25 September 1570, Cotton Nero B I, No. 71.

[143] Council to Admiralty judges, 25 September 1570, SP 12/73/69.

[144] *APC 1571–5*, 4–6.

[145] Declaration of the merchants trading to Portugal, 29 December 1571, with postscript in the hand of Marsh, SP 12/83/37. The Londoners included Christopher Hoddesdon, John Rivers and Thomas Altham. There is a copy of this document at Cotton Nero, B I, No. 79. A portion of it was printed by J. Vanes in

her edition of *Documents illustrating the overseas trade of Bristol in the sixteenth century* (Bristol, 1979), 156–7.

[146] Evidence of Thomas Pope, 18 September 1572, HCA 13/19, ff. 220 *et seq.*

[147] Evidence of William Kelinge, 10 October 1572, HCA 13/19, ff. 263 *et seq.*

[148] *APC 1571–5*, 20–1; evidence of Hector Nunez, 1 March 1571, HCA 13/18, ff. 217–217v.

[149] Information about the London Marranos is contained in two pioneering essays by L. Wolf, 'Jews in Elizabethan England', *Transactions of the Jewish Historical Society of England*, XI (1924–7), 1–91, and 'Jews in Tudor England', *Essays in Jewish History*, ed. C. Roth (London, 1934), 73–90. There is a short general account in C. Roth, *History of the Jews in England*, third ed. (Oxford, 1964), 139–43. The paper on the staple of spices, 29 June 1569, SP 12/51/18, was endorsed by Cecil 'Reasons from a portyngale to move the trade in to England'.

[150] Alva to Philip II, 8 August 1569, *CSPSp. 1568–79*, 186–7.

[151] Evidence of Hector Nunez, 5 June 1570, HCA 13/17, ff. 388v–9.

[152] Evidence of Robert Byrde, 24 May 1569, HCA 13/17, ff. 54v–58v. See also the remarks of T. S. Willan, *Studies*, 110 and 112.

[153] London Port Book, 1565, E 190/1/4, entries for 10 and 12 May, 2 and 23 June &c. Cochineal at this time was a novelty in north-western Europe.

[154] Evidence of Robert Byrde, *ut supra*; of George Barrie, 25 January 1570, HCA 13/17, f. 227.

[155] On this outbreak of lawlessness, *cf. supra*, 85–6.

[156] *Supra*, 90–1.

[157] Evidence of John Smith, 7 July 1569, HCA 13/17, ff. 134v *et seq*. For Bowes, see *Isham*, xli–xlv.

[158] Evidence of Fernando Alvarez and Nicholas Culverwell, 4 June 1569, HCA 13/17, ff. 72v–106 *passim*.

[159] Evidence of Walter Russell, John Gullick and Stephen Cobb, from 22 July 1571 onwards, HCA 13/18, ff. 283–5; and of Phylypp van Asselyers of Antwerp, 15 October 1571, *ib.*, 378 *et seq. Cf. APC 1571–5*, 45–6. Hawkins in 1573 appeared in a somewhat dubious role as the intermediary between the pirates and the underwriters of a cargo of Barbary sugar – Williamson, *Hawkins*, 290–1.

[160] This topic has been clarified by K. R. Andrews, *Elizabethan Privateering* (Cambridge, 1964).

[161] *Supra*, 135.

[162] Petition of Steelyard merchants, undated, probably early 70s, SP 12/106/4.

[163] 13 Eliz., caps. 5, 6, 8, 11, 13 and 15.

[164] 13 Eliz. *c.* 25, sec. viii.

[165] Draft bill, undated but probably May or June 1572, SP 12/91/66; objections to the bill, SP 12/86/60 I.

[166] *Commons' Journals*, I, 101. A similar bill actually reached the statute-book in 1576 – 18 Eliz., *c.* 16.

[167] Duckett to Burghley, 6 August 1573, Ellis, *Original Letters*, sec. ser., III, 37–8.

[168] L. Stone, *The Crisis of the Aristocracy 1558–1641* (Oxford, 1965), 629.

# Chapter VII

## Elizabeth, Alva and the merchants

With the unauthorized and unwelcome return of Assonleville to Brussels from London in mid March 1569, Alva felt at a loss for his next move. The Duke was already weary of his tasks as viceroy of the Netherlands and pining for a speedy recall; as his secretary reported, he was ageing greatly, weak in health, and very tired.[1] Although he had recently quelled an open rebellion, he had not quenched the general discontent. He was gravely short of finance and making preparations to gather the tax known as the hundredth penny, despite the small co-operation on the part of the restive Estates of the various provinces.[2] On top of these problems, he was now faced with a commercial crisis springing from the rupture with England. He regularly received news of English preparations to dispatch the cloth fleet to Hamburg; but to the repeated exhortations from Despes that he should intercept it, possibly by sending warships to lie in wait for it at the mouth of the Elbe, he remained deaf.[3] It was his conviction that any worsening of relations with the Queen of England should be avoided, and he so advised his master.[4] Meanwhile the trade of Antwerp, and indeed of all the ports of the Netherlands, was being strangled. It was estimated early in April at Antwerp that there must be over 120 ships, with a treasure of unknown size in money and merchandise, interned in English harbours.[5] To prevent further losses, traffic with England was forbidden, and the order was issued that all vessels leaving the Netherlands should be armed.[6] Assonleville in June was glumly commenting on the decay of trade. It was whispered that Alva's visit to Antwerp in that month, ostensibly to inspect the fortifications, was in reality to forestall riots.[7] Only Italian and other neutral merchants kept the port alive, by shipping their goods on French or Breton ships.[8]

At Madrid, King Philip II was taken aback to learn early in 1569 the extraordinary news from northern Europe. For him, the moment was anything but propitious for further commitments, since he had on his hands a rebellion of the Moors of

Granada – not until the next year were they to be crushed – and there were fears of a Turkish naval offensive in the Mediterranean. So when confronted by dissonant counsel from Alva and Despes (not to mention the views of the Queen of England conveyed through his Paris embassy), he made up his mind with unusual speed. He found 'the English proceedings very strange and very incompatible with the ancient friendship of the House of Burgundy and the English crown'.[9] He naturally ordered the arrest of English shipping in Spanish ports. But he refused to believe that Elizabeth Tudor could dare to become his enemy, and in mid February he firmly endorsed the temporizing policy advocated by Alva.[10] His resolution was strengthened by the information that reached him in subsequent weeks. In April, he received a petition from his merchants at the seaports, eloquently depicting how the wool export traffic of Spain had come to a standstill – to the loss not only of the traders but of the crown, which could collect no customs.[11] By July, Philip was informing Alva that many of the Spanish merchants in trade with the Netherlands were utterly ruined, and that their activities must be re-started.[12] Earlier, he had followed hopefully the progress of Assonleville's mission, and on learning of its failure had instructed Alva to dispatch another envoy to England – not Assonleville, but someone of more ability and standing, who would be better esteemed at London.[13]

Alva's choice for this assignment was astute. He selected neither a Netherlander nor a Spaniard, but a Florentine soldier of fortune, by name Ciappino Vitelli, who had been created Marquess of Cetona by Philip II for his military services in Italy. Vitelli was now in employment in the Netherlands, where he had recently been superintending the erection of the new fortifications at Antwerp. He was a highly cultivated man, supple and crafty in his ways, unencumbered by any prejudices or – as some said – by any beliefs.[14] His instructions were to approach the Queen in sorrow rather than anger. He was not himself to put forward the merchants' plan for a restitution of goods, but if it was mentioned to him he was to enquire how far it might be taken, and explain how Philip II was anxious to resume the old friendship – with the return of the merchants to Antwerp and the revocation of all the arrangements and innovations at Hamburg, Emden and elsewhere. If at this point he met a blank wall, he was to take the opportunity to point out privately to the Queen that the least prince in the world could not fail to resent her behaviour to the King. He was to caution her against self-seeking councillors and remind her of the ancient proverb that *conseillers ne sont point payeurs*.[15] Such an approach might early in the year have had some prospect of success. But by the autumn of 1569 the chances of a reconciliation had receded far. Most important of all, the English had now received confirmation that the Antwerp mart was not indispensable. Hamburg might not be so satisfactory, but it served. On the plane of international politics, Elizabeth from the summer onwards had been seeking to insure herself against any sudden withering of the ancient Anglo-Burgundian amity by the characteristic device of reviving negotiations for her marriage to a prince of the French royal family. The French ambassador transmitted home her advances somewhat sceptically, but at the court of the French King they met with a cordial response.[16] Elizabeth accordingly was enabled to contemplate with less trepidation a *renversement des alliances* and the loss of the friendship of Philip II.

Vitelli cannot have been aware that the cards were so heavily stacked against him when in early October he started on his journey to London. Even before crossing the Channel, he was held up by doubts about the validity of his passport.[17] He arrived at Dover with a suite of forty-four persons, among whom was Secretary de la Torre, who had himself conducted a mission to England some seven years previously; but permission to proceed further was given only on condition that he left behind most of his entourage.[18] At the court of the Queen he was offered meagre lodgings at an inconvenient distance. Elizabeth consented to receive him in audience, but she raised difficulties about the scope of his authority and insisted upon humiliating conditions before practical negotiations might be opened.[19] Vitelli was evidently a man of some personal charm, which Alva expected him to deploy.[20] Unlike the touchy Assonleville, he refused to be either daunted or provoked by rebuffs. He managed to strike up a friendship with Leicester, with whom he discussed art, as one connoisseur with another. Even the Queen seems ultimately to have taken a fancy to him. If Vitelli is to be believed, he was able at one audience to fulfil his instructions and privately to urge her not to be misled by those who had brought her to the present pass, to which she retorted that neither Cecil nor the Lord Keeper Bacon had counselled her to lay hands on Netherlands shipping.[21] During most of November, it looked as if Vitelli might make some real progress, if only because he was personally such a success. Doors shut to Despes were opened to him. Then, quite suddenly, the atmosphere lost its cordiality. Before the end of the year, Vitelli was on his way home, with little more than some empty praise from the Queen and the gift of a pair of geldings from Leicester to show for his pains.[22]

The explanation of this brusque reversal lay in the outbreak of an open rebellion in the north of England, led by the Earls of Northumberland and Westmorland, late in November. The whole year 1569 had been marked by growing political tension, springing in part from the breach with Spain and the Netherlands. The English government was aware that Despes maintained touch with the agents of both the Queen of Scots and the northern earls, and what it did not know it suspected. Although the restraints imposed on Despes in January had been greatly relaxed six months later, he remained under surveillance. His maladroit financial agent, the Florentine merchant Roberto Ridolfi, was arrested at London in October and held in custody for a few weeks.[23] If the threads of conspiracy passed through the hands of Despes, a natural though mistaken deduction was that they were pulled by Alva, in English eyes the tyrant of the Netherlands and the enemy of their country. Why had Alva dispatched so suave and beguiling an agent as Vitelli to England at such a moment? Suspicion was soon transmuted into allegation. Near the end of November, Vitelli received a private warning sent by Leicester, to the effect that he was said to be forwarding financial aid to the rebels; a day or so later, this was reinforced by an equally private and courteous message from the Queen, with the advice that for the moment at least he had better return home in the interest of his own personal safety.[24] When he delayed so as to secure the consent of Alva to his return – Alva being anxious as ever to continue negotiations – a further rumour gained currency, that so renowned a military leader could only be lingering until the rebels had won control of a port to admit foreign troops – whose command he would then assume.[25]

In fact, there persisted on the English side an enormous ignorance of political realities in countries other than France, where there was a resident English ambassador to supply information. Secretary Cecil, as well-informed and shrewd a politician as there was in England, still believed that Despes was 'the Duke of Alva's creature'.[26] He would assuredly have been astonished to learn the truth – that Alva and Despes were completely at loggerheads. Alva, like his old master the Emperor Charles V, still believed that a friendly England provided the essential strategic and political link between Spain and the Netherlands, besides being a vital component of the foreign trade by which the prosperity of Antwerp and the Netherlands was maintained. In the daring but impracticable schemes of Despes he saw only disaster ahead. He repeatedly requested Despes not to become involved in any dealings directed against the Queen or her councillors, never to listen to any proposals about Ireland, and to be very cautious in his relations with the Queen of Scotland: in short, to do nothing that might give offence to Elizabeth.[27] He surmised, correctly enough, that Despes was disregarding his wishes and poisoning relations with the English.[28] He strove to keep him out of the negotiations in the autumn of 1569, which was not in fact too difficult, since the Queen no longer allowed Despes access to her presence. Alva's complaints were met somewhat tardily by Philip II, who in November assured him that royal authority in northern Europe was delegated to him, and that he was instructing Despes to carry out Alva's orders.[29] Philip remained eager for the success of the Anglo-Netherlands negotiations since, as he put it, the embargo was causing a great loss to his revenue and grave damage to his subjects.[30] But he was slow in speaking his mind.

Negotiations in the world of princes thus petered out before the end of 1569. But among the merchants, contacts were maintained and even developed. Soon after the return of Assonleville to the Netherlands, the neutral Italians had reappeared in their role of international conciliators, their first approach to Secretary Cecil being made at least as early as May 1569.[31] Earliest in the field were the merchant bankers of Florence, the brothers Guido and Stiata Cavalcanti and Roberto Ridolfi, all with heavy personal interests in the London–Antwerp traffic. The English response was cool, but nevertheless Cecil took part in confidential discussions with one of the Cavalcanti brothers.[32] Alva clutched at the opportunity presented by the Florentines. He also consulted some Genoese merchants, and he sent Tommaso Fiesco, a Genoese resident at Antwerp who was personally interested in the confiscated treasure, to confer with his friend and compatriot Benedetto Spinola at London.[33] When these dealings were divulged to Philp II, he gave his approval to their continuance. But as the King distrusted the pro-French

Florentines, Alva for the future restricted his confidence to the Genoese.[34] Alva seems to have thought that if Spinola had indeed been the first instigator of Elizabeth's actions, he was all the more suited as a conciliator.[35] The Genoese were certainly realists. One of their first proposals was that Cecil and Leicester should be gratified by handsome presents to favour their negotiations.[36] Cecil when approached named the sum of 10,000 ducats – about £3,000 – as his price.[37] Alva subsequently fell in with this course and the King gave it his sanction.[38] Cecil and Leicester may well have pocketed the fees, but it need not be assumed that their actions were thereby influenced.

The aim of the merchants was for the time being limited to a simple restitution of the wares seized on either side of the sea. It was hoped that a resumption of traffic might subsequently ensue. The application of ordinary commercial practice solved the problem of the bullion aboard the treasure ships that had sought refuge in English harbours in November 1568, a concern for which had led Despes into precipitating the whole crisis. This was now laid up in the Tower of London and treated by Elizabeth as her own loan from the Genoese. She does not seem to have offered interest but she completed the return of the capital in 1574.[39] The restitution of merchandise proved a more prickly matter. The English government had in principle no objection to it, and in the City it must have been popular. Fiesco was at London on a first visit with the backing of Alva in June 1569, and thenceforward the talks between the merchants on either side edged forward.[40] During the summer months, hopes were raised in business circles that some sort of realistic compromise might be arranged without becoming entangled in politics.[41] Tension between England and the Netherlands appeared to be on the wane. The English merchants held at Antwerp had been allowed to leave for home in March on giving bond; at an early stage a number seem to have slipped quietly away with the connivance of the guard.[42] The Spanish sailors interned in England at the outset of the quarrel were released in June, when news was received that Alva had not detained some English mariners and fishermen taken on the coast of Zeeland.[43] The Queen in August issued a stern proclamation against harbourers of pirates, in the hope of diminishing lawlessness at sea.[44] But she refused the assurance sought by Vitelli, that ships of the subjects of Philip II might again ply between Spain and the Netherlands without fear of arrest. This must, she repeated more than once, await the arrival of another envoy with fuller powers.[45]

Despite the assiduity of Fiesco and his fellow-mediators the mutual restitution of merchandise proved slow to get going. At London, where an official inventory of the seized property had been compiled at an early stage, there were complex problems of ownership to be settled. On both sides of the sea, it became urgent to dispose at least of the perishable goods before they became worthless. Because cloths could not be stored un-damaged by moths for ever, Alva in December 1569 had the English merchants' warehouses at Antwerp unsealed and the contents removed, in the face of protests from the seven English factors still in residence at the English House. In the course of the next year, these cloths were sold, at good prices.[46] Mean-while, the Merchants Adventurers had formally requested per-mission from the Privy Council to follow up on their side the proposals of the Italian intermediaries. They were warned to be on their guard.[47] However, in late March 1570 Governor Marsh together with the Londoners Thomas Aldersey and Richard Saltonstall made their way, with official English approbation, to Brussels. Here they were received without delay by Alva and given 'a very courteous welcome and entertainment'. He no-minated commissioners to treat with them, and before long gave his assent to the ten requests they put forward.[48]

It might have been thought that the mutual restitution of goods could now be arranged and concluded within a matter of weeks. But this was to reckon without the Queen of England. There were, it must be remembered, four parties to be satisfied before any settlement could be achieved. On the Netherlands side, Fiesco and his friends were eager for an accommodation, and were whole-heartedly supported by Alva. On the other hand, the English merchants, while hopeful of agreement in varying degrees, were on the whole growing less keen. Some – we do not know how many – were like Governor Marsh and his associate Aldersey, strong protestants who detested Alva and all that he stood for, prepared to suffer some material loss if he could be worsted.[49] Behind them, and in ultimate control of events, Elizabeth Tudor considered herself the victim of shabby treatment of which the most malevolent act had been the arrest of her merchants at Antwerp in December 1568. But from the end of 1569 onwards her resentment towards Alva was greatly heightened by the way in which the rebel northern earls, condemned traitors, together with other enemies were now receiving not merely shelter but – as it might seem – encouragement in the Netherlands. Despes was using the freedom he had once more been permitted since July 1569 to intrigue with the agents of the Queen of Scots.[50] It is not surprising that these were the years in which the great Spanish bogey was taking shape in English imagination: it was to be given further substance in 1571 by the papal excommunication of Elizabeth in 1570, followed by the Ridolfi plot. Its nearest and most dangerous tentacle was represented by Alva. Elizabeth allowed the negotiations for the restitution of goods to proceed. There were commissions, conferences and further dispatches of envoys which need not be followed in these pages. But for the present she had every intention of keeping Alva at arm's length.

When Governor Marsh visited the Netherlands in the spring of 1570 he had tasks beyond the negotiation for mutual restitution of seized goods to pursue. He also collected information about the activities of English traitors on Netherlands soil, and sent home a warning that Secretary Cecil and the Lord Keeper Bacon were in danger of assassination. The man to hold in his hand the threads of conspiracy he reported to be Dr John Story, an outstanding civil lawyer held in execration by Londoners for his prominent part in the persecution of protestants during the reign of Mary Tudor, when he had been chancellor to Bishop Bonner and Queen's Proctor at the trial of Archbishop Cranmer. Story was now being maintained by the Netherlands government and as 'a preferrer of all the English traitors' business and causes' enjoyed, as Marsh averred, 'continual access' to Alva.[51] Acting on a nudge from Cecil, Marsh arranged to have him kidnapped. The cloth fleet of the Merchants Adventurers had not anchored at Barrow since 1563, but in the disused English House there an English concierge with local knowledge still dwelt. Marsh was able to recruit some young English merchants to help the concierge in the exploit. Dr Story was lured to the English House at Barrow. Here he was further persuaded to step aboard a ship, and stowed below the hatches while it sailed for England. He was brought forthwith to London and – a deliberate touch – lodged in the Lollards' Tower. He was subsequently tried, condemned as a traitor and executed.[52] The French ambassador reported the abduction with wry pleasure, pointing out that Alva could hardly pass over such a slight to the integrity of the Netherlands.[53] In fact, Alva was in no position to take up the matter with the English government, so overriding a consideration was the re-opening of trade with England.

Whether or not Dr Story had a hand in murder plots is for present purposes beside the point. He was removed because he was suspected of it, and because he was able, and dangerous. In another age, diplomatic channels would have been used to put a stop to his designs. But there was no longer an English ambassador resident at either Madrid or Brussels. Worse, the official emissary of Philip II at London was Despes, whose influence was used to heighten rather than lessen international tension. It is arguable that the English government tolerated for far too long the presence of Despes: it was near the end of 1571 before the Queen finally informed Philip II that she was expelling him.[54] Alva, who from time to time tried to restrain him, would doubtless have been glad to see him go in 1570 or 1569. More than once, Alva explicitly instructed Despes to keep his busybody friend Ridolfi out of Netherlands business.[55] The Duke in August 1571 alleged to Philip II that Despes had conceived such a hatred for the Queen and all the rest of the English that his judgment was impaired.[56] There is no reason to doubt the sincerity of Alva when a few years later, in a more tranquil environment, he told an English envoy at Madrid that if Despes had not died on his way home in 1572 he ought for his misbehaviour to have lost his head or at least suffered continual imprisonment.[57]

A further result of the intrigues of Despes was to distort the picture of the world of princes as seen at London, and so to speed the realignments in trade and politics that took shape during the years of his embassy, 1568–72. It was difficult for the Queen and her councillors to rectify this distortion because of the paucity of information available to them. For alternative sources of honest news they were still limited to the dispatches of the English ambassador to France and the naive and one-sided reports of merchants and other politically unsophisticated agents.[58] The English misconception of the outlook and aims of Alva sprang only in part from an irrelevant religious prejudice: it was also the fruit of sheer ignorance. The depth of this ignorance was tragi-comically illustrated in the summer and autumn of 1570, when the Austrian archduchess who was to become the fourth wife of Philip II was making her way via the Netherlands to Spain. Given the lawless conditions prevailing in the waters off north-west Europe, it was necessary that she should be well escorted during her voyage. But the English government refused to believe that the warships being assembled by Alva were intended merely to serve this purpose. Espionage was set afoot in the Netherlands, the royal navy was mobilized to watch the Channel, and the southern coast put on the alert – all to fend off a danger that could have been proved imaginary by some effective diplomatic representation at Brussels.[59]

However, some three and a half years after the rupture occasioned by Alva's arrest of the Merchants Adventurers, the Queen of England softened in her attitude towards the government of the Netherlands. Valid political reasons to explain this may be suggested. The conspiracies centring on the Queen of Scots, now half-captive in England, had for the moment been snuffed out. Despes, protesting to the last, had quitted the shores of England in March 1572, and with him a hub of misunderstanding had been removed. Zweveghem, who was liked at the royal court, returned as Netherlands envoy in March 1571 and remained for over a year; he undoubtedly helped to smooth away differences.[60] Besides, the alliance with France was losing some of its attractions. France was no substitute for the Netherlands as a commercial gateway to the continent: the Merchants Adventurers had fully explained why under no foreseeable circumstances would they ever establish their mart at a French port.[61] Elizabeth was alarmed by the Huguenot incursion into the Netherlands in the spring of 1572; it was followed by the massacre of French protestants on St Bartholomew's Day, which seemed to put an end once and for all to any hope of a lasting Anglo-French collaboration. Although Catherine de Médicis hastened to explain away the bloodshed and to assure Elizabeth that friendly relations were unchanged, the effect of the episode could not be completely erased.[62] All in all, there were good political grounds for a reconsideration of the English attitude to Spain and the Netherlands. But there were also fiscal and economic reasons for veering back towards the seaway to Antwerp.

The reform of rates imposed by Lord Treasurer Winchester in May 1558 had restored the customs to their place as a major regular source of crown revenue – indeed, the only resilient one.[63] It remained to ensure that the customs officers received and handed over to the exchequer every penny due to them. During the next ten years, it was evident that various perplexing administrative problems were involved in this. The government

was well informed about them, from the reports of its
officials, the complaints of the merchants, and the many pro
presented by hopeful third parties, often with remarks that
reflected on the honesty of men at the ports. There were, as it
seemed, two devices by which the yield of the customs could be
maintained at a maximum. Neither was without flaws. One, to
which old Winchester always demurred, was to farm out this or
that branch for a fixed income for a term of years. This was
nevertheless adopted for wine from 1567 onwards, and for
imports at London from 1570. The other was to intensify the
already existing system of check and supervision. A convenient
way of doing this was to issue a commission granting powers of
inspection, which the commissioner or his deputy might use to
unearth defaulters, with a reward comprising a share of the
goods on which customs had not been paid. Especially from
1567, this also was being done. As a result, the merchant might
find that persons outside the regular customs sytem were
pouncing upon his goods in the Custom House or even at sea,
citing royal authority to demand that the ship be searched to see
if customs had been paid in full. In the discussions about ways
and means of ensuring that merchants paid their customs
duties, the centre of interest was naturally provided by the most
lucrative source of tax, the cloth exports from London. The
limelight inevitably fell upon William Byrde, the collector of the
petty custom outwards there, who was responsible for its yield.[64]

Byrde was a well-off man, experienced as a merchant. His task
brought him into contact with all sorts and conditions, from the
great personages of the City or the courtier with a pension on
the London customs to the porters, lightermen and seafarers at
the riverside. Although the level of duties established in 1558
might by standards of later centuries appear modest – indeed,
hardly worth the trouble of evading – this was not an opinion
shared by contemporaries.[65] The English or Hanse merchant
paid on each pack of ten undressed 'short cloths' £3: i.e., 6s. 8d.
per cloth, with a duty-free 'wrapper'. He might have laid out
perhaps £50 at Blackwell Hall for the lot, so that the effective
rate was a mere 6 per cent. The addition of licence money and
port charges might raise this to 8 per cent.[66] But to dismiss these
export levies as negligible would be to disregard the hunger of
the sixteenth-century merchant adventurer for ready money of
any sort. Much of his business, as we have seen, was conducted
on credit.[67] The £12 or £15 required for duty on four or five

packs often enough could not be found until the cloths had been
sold at Antwerp and part at least of the purchase price repatri-
ated. Byrde looked at this situation as a merchant might, and
was prepared to accept a 'bill of debt', i.e., to give some credit,
probably short-term, perhaps with some concealed interest for
himself.[68] The customs requirements were thereby eased for
many a merchant, but at the cost of making more complex the
accounts kept by Byrde's staff of clerks. Further, since the exchequer, to which he had to render his account twice a year,
required money not bills, how did he make sure that his debtors
had all completed payment by the day of reckoning? It would
seem that he got round this problem by adjusting, when pressed,
the dates of export in his ledger, so that payment might appear
to belong to a later period for settlement of the account at the
exchequer. This was disingenuous even if not dishonest.

  Byrde's easing of the procedures of payment did not put a
stop to outright evasion of customs. The government in the
1560s was more dependent than earlier in the century upon
customs revenue and therefore more sensitive to fears that
smugglers were at work.[69] Merchants, particularly foreigners,
continued to be prosecuted in the exchequer for customs
offences. After the first interruption of trade with Antwerp in
1563–4, the rules for shipment of cloths from London were
revised. The choice of quays allowed in 1559 by Winchester was
now curtailed, so as to allow for a closer customs supervision.
The Merchants Adventurers henceforth were compelled to concentrate their loading operations at the Custom House Quay
and the adjacent 'Old Wool Quay'.[70] This doubtless made for
congestion. It also had the inconvenience of making the merchants more dependent upon lighters to convey their cloths to
the sea-going ships. Altogether, a stricter customs regime seems
to have prevailed in the years 1565–8 inclusive, involving the use
of the new uniform port-books to be kept and duly returned to
the exchequer. By the summer of 1568, the Merchants Adventurers were complaining of the 'great grief and loss' being inflicted upon them by 'the searchers and new-appointed officers
at the waterside', who insisted upon examining their cloths to see
if any entered as 'short cloths' were in fact over the prescribed 28
yards in length and seizing them if they were – by ever so little –
without taking into consideration either the weight or any com-
pensating shortfall in width.[71] Governor Marsh informed Secretary Cecil how the cloth-ships had been held up by the fiat of

the recently-appointed commissioners, to the damage of the market. He pleaded that 'such are the hindrances of the Company many other ways as it is a great pity to hinder them by such vexation', and asked that the Merchants Adventurers might be exempted from these extra searches.[72]

With the closure of Antwerp from 1569 onwards the situation acquired new dimensions, political and economic. The long royal proclamation of 6 January included a formal interdiction of trade by subjects of the Queen with any countries subject to Philip II.[73] Two days later, the Merchants Adventurers were reminding the Privy Council how the experiment of the Emden mart in 1564 had shown that if an alternative mart outside the Netherlands were to be successfully established, no leakages of traffic to or from the Netherlands, by either English or foreign merchants, could be tolerated.[74] During the mission of Assonle-ville in January–March 1569 we may imagine much consultation between Governor Marsh, Secretary Cecil and other interested parties. At the beginning of March, the wishes of the Merchants Adventurers were presented in detail to the Privy Council. They asked that 'no commodities of the realm be transported into any of the Low Countries by any person of any nation whatsoever, either directly or indirectly, by licence, safe-conduct, letters, favour of officers, passing through France, or otherwise howso-ever'. The Italians as a concession might be allowed to ship to Hamburg with the Englishmen, but no cloths should be permitted to go to French ports east of Rouen.[75] The Londoners thus were reiterating the lessons of the Emden mart.[76] No doubt they were scarcely displeased when at the end of the month Alva forbade any trade with England or Englishmen, whether by natural subjects of King Philip or by others residing in his dominions.[77] At a general court of the Merchants Adventurers held in London on April 26, regulations to enforce the canalization of trade to Hamburg were enacted.[78] At or before this time, the Privy Council set up its own committee of members to supervise the enforcement of the trade restrictions. It worked in close collaboration with the Merchants Adventurers.[79]

But if the Netherlands market was craving for English cloths and the English reciprocally felt a grievous need of the manu-factures usually got from the Netherlands, and insufficiently available at Hamburg, for how long could the two parties be held asunder by mere administrative means? From the start, Alva was defied by a trickle of English cloths entering his vice-

royalty from Hamburg or Emden, for which the frontier town
of Nijmegen provided a staging-post. Other consignments of
English cloths were sent direct on ships ostensibly bound for
Hamburg but actually making for Antwerp or elsewhere in the
Netherlands and returning to England with forbidden wares.[80]
Two of Alva's chief officials, including his own secretary Albornoz, were in 1570 believed to be involved in smuggling English goods into the country, escaping conviction by committing a
murder.[81] Alva in June that year was sufficiently concerned to
issue a proclamation in the name of his master in which it was
sorrowfully admitted that English wares were being brought
into the Netherlands by indirect ways and means, and Netherlands goods shipped to England. He therefore ordered that an
inventory should be made of all undyed English textiles. Only
when their source had been satisfactorily explained might cloth-
finishers and dyers work on them, and merchants re-export
them. A particular warning was given to the Governor and
Council of the maritime province of Holland.[82] Nevertheless,
the prohibited English products continued to be brought to light
in Antwerp and doubtless elsewhere.[83] An English observer
writing from Hamburg in the summer of 1571 notes how the
merchants of the Netherlands in the town were doing a great
trade with England, concealing their identity by using the names
of Hamburg citizens.[84] Thus unwittingly he was confirming the
fears of the Netherlands government.

On the English side also, the fences were not quite high
enough. The question naturally arose whether the customs
officers were doing their duty. The English ambassador in
France – a personage whose words were always intently heard –
reported home in February 1570 that they were reputed to be
'marvellously corrupted' and ready to pass goods 'for little
money'.[85] Doubts at the court of the Queen were thereby fortified. At the all-important port of London, import duties other
than on wine were from 1570 being farmed out to the veteran
Mr Customer Smythe. He was naturally concerned by the drastic
shortfall in the revenue collected from his branch of the customs: it had dropped from £12,984 in 1567–8 to £7,771 in
1568–9, a decline that he attributed in particular to the harsh-
ness of the special commissioners and their deputies in their
dealings with the merchants and mariners. Smythe alleged that
they were especially severe at London, where they were established within the Custom House. Owners and transporters of

goods that could be proved Netherlands or Spanish by origin were fined and otherwise punished. As a result, goods were much more often than hitherto being landed stealthily further down the river, at Barking or elsewhere; they were then concealed in beer drays or colliers' carts and so brought into the City. Few were caught.[86] It was also said that some ships put in at Southampton and other southcoast ports in order to avoid the privateers of the Prince of Orange at the mouth of the Thames, as well as the royal police ship at Gravesend and the vessels of the crown and its commissioners lurking in the Downs or off the North Foreland.[87] Altogether, there was evidence to suggest that the unpleasantness of using the Custom House Quay at London was frightening the merchants into evasion.

Much more important than that of Customer Smythe's import duties was the yield of the cloth export tax at London. It too was falling year by year – from £31,552 in 1567–8 and £32,596 in 1568–9 to £30,714 in 1569–70, £26,894 in 1570–1 and £22,967 in 1571–2.[88] The uneasiness of the English government was presumably reflected in the issue of a grant, dated 21 August 1570, to Oliver Dawbenye of London and his deputies, giving them power to examine, search and try out all concealments of customs, subsidies and other duties. Dawbenye as a reward was to receive a half of all the sums he might recover for the crown. He was instructed to act under the supervision of Secretary Cecil, doubtless because the Lord Treasurer Winchester was no longer very active – he was near the end of his long life.[89] Less than three months later, another commission delegated far-reaching powers to fifteen persons, almost all being well-known London Merchants Adventurers, to search out irregularities in the seaborne trade of the Kentish coast. Three of the merchants provided a quorum, so that the commission was enabled to operate simultaneously in several places.[90] The purpose of this body was to close the side door into the Netherlands by putting a stop to clandestine traffic through Calais and other French ports nearby. Government and Merchants Adventurers between them were thus imposing an emergency control upon the trade of the south-east coast, identical in object though not in administrative method with that improvized in the summer of 1564.[91]

Dawbenye at London was inevitably drawn to concentrate his attention upon the hapless Byrde and his accommodating methods. Initial disclosures provided sufficient material to justify the issue of yet another commission in June 1571, this

time to investigate the ominously narrow topic of financial malver-
sation.[92] It was addressed to thirteen individuals headed by the
veteran diplomat Sir Thomas Chamberlain, five of them being
merchants and most of the rest lawyers. The quorum was four.
With the aid of the clues supplied by Dawbenye, these further
commissioners were able to bring to light various alterations in
the customs registers for which Byrde and his staff of clerks were
responsible. Their report was confined to statements of fact, with
the supporting evidence. They did not explicitly accuse Byrde of
dishonesty, but neither did they explain what had led him to tam-
per with his accounts. Their words were irrefutable though for the
purposes of the government not very helpful – Secretary Cecil and
his fellow privy councillors could hardly have been unaware that
the entries in the London customs books had been erased or
omitted because they were for 'the cloths of divers merchants to
whom the customer at the latter end of the year gave credit', to
quote a contemporary memorandum that may have emanated
from the commissioners.[93] But given the dependence of City business upon credit, what could usefully be done about it?

The government in seeking to make its customs controls effective had in fact stubbed its toes upon an essential part of the
financial structure of the City. The Chamberlain commission
was evidently very much disliked by the merchants. It was implemented almost entirely by its lawyer members. Its report was
subscribed by only five names, four of them being gentlemen
from the Inns of Court, including the elder Richard Hakluyt:
the solitary merchant to sign was not a personage of consequence in the City. Among the other commissioners, Chamberlain
himself does not seem to have taken any part; the Recorder of
London, William Fleetwood, also stood aside, as did the prominent Merchants Adventurers Richard Milles and James
Harvye, the latter of whom near the end of the year took his seat
upon the bench of aldermen.[94] When the commissioners sought
to take a sworn statement from Alderman James Hawes, shortly
to be Lord Mayor, he gave them the rough edge of his tongue,
and in general they seem to have met with a good deal of
obstruction and ill-feeling.[95] Hakluyt privately pointed out in
November 1571 to Cecil (now ennobled as Lord Burghley) how
'the honest virtuous gentleman Mr. Dawbenye' would be broken
unless he were further supported against 'the mighty bulls of
Basan that, propped up with spoil and wealth and great friends,
would seem to overlook all men and make the world believe that

the moon is made of green cheese'.[96] A little later, Dawbenye more prosaically enquired of Burghley if 'the concealments found against Mr. Byrde' were to 'be presented by order of law or otherwise determined by composition'.[97] Burghley, soon to be Lord Treasurer on the demise of Winchester, seems to have opted for the first course. A verdict was obtained against Byrde in the Court of King's Bench, but the matter was not further pursued, and he continued to hold his office.[98]

Indeed, in the face of continuously falling receipts from the London customs, the need was for leniency rather than severity at the Custom House there. It might have been advantageous to encourage rather than discourage the grant of credit. The merchants were being driven elsewhere — to ship their cloths clandestinely, out of reach of customs officials and special commissioners alike. And one misdeed shaded into another. Not only, it seemed, were the owners of smuggled cloths robbing the Queen of her revenue, but unpatriotically trying to circumvent the trade embargo with the Netherlands. The great men who dominated the Company of Merchants Adventurers became thoroughly alarmed in the course of 1571 at the way in which trade was threatening to seep back into its former channels, with the ruin of the Hamburg mart in prospect. When suspicion was aroused that some of the Netherlands refugees at London were involved in the illegal traffic with their homeland, a solemn warning was delivered in November to the ministers and elders of their churches, both French- and Dutch-speaking, through the mouth of Governor Marsh himself.[99] But during 1572 the situation failed to improve. In an outspoken letter to Burghley after his appointment to the office of Lord Treasurer in July, the Company of Merchants Adventurers pointed out that the future of the Hamburg mart was in jeopardy.[100] The Queen of England thus had further reason to consider more sympathetically the possibility of ending the breach with the Netherlands. As in 1564, her revenue was endangered.[101] And the organization of foreign trade was being undermined.

## NOTES TO CHAPTER VII

[1] Albornoz to Çayas, 11 March 1569, Gachard, *Correspondance de Philippe II*, II, 70–1; *ib.* to *ib.*, 4 April, *ib.*, 78–9; Alva to Cayas, 31 October, *ib.*, 111.

[2] For the problems involved in this fiscal levy see W. Brulez, 'La portée fiscale et politique du centième denier du duc d'Albe', *Acta Historica Bruxellensia*, I (1967), esp. 373.

[3] Despes to Philip II, 9 May 1569, *CSPSp. 1568–79*, 144–8; *ib.* to Philip II and Alva, 31 May and 1 June, *ib.*, 157–8.

[4] Alva to Philip II, 10 March and 10 May 1569, *ib.*, 132–3 and 149.

[5] Curiel to anon., 6 April 1569, Gachard, *Correspondance de Philippe II*, II, 82.

[6] Proclamation in name of Philip II, 31 March 1569, Smit, *Bronnen*, No. 1163.

[7] Assonleville to anon., 21 June 1569, KL, V, 407–8n; Norris to Cecil, 7 June 1569, SP 70/107/257.

[8] Antwerp newsletter, 17 September 1569, KL, V, 459.

[9] Philip II to Despes, 18 February 1569, *CSPSp. 1568–79*, 108–9.

[10] *Ib.* to *ib.*, *ut supra*; *ib.* to Alva, same date, *ib.*, 109–10.

[11] Spanish merchants to Philip II, 28 April 1569, *ib.*, 143–4.

[12] Philip II to Alva, 19 July 1569, *ib.*, 177–8.

[13] *Ib.* to *ib.*, 15 May 1569, *ib.*, 150 and also Gachard, *Correspondance de Philippe II*, II, 91. *Supra*, 110–1.

[14] On Vitelli see entry in *Biographie Nationale*; also Poullet, *Granvelle*, III, 259n.

[15] Alva's instructions to Vitelli, *c.* 28 September 1569, KL, V, 466–73.

[16] La Mothe Fénélon to Charles IX and Catherine de Médicis, 27 July 1569, MF, II, 115–19.

[17] Vitelli to Alva, 10 October 1569, KL, V, 477–8.

[18] *Ib.* to 16 October, *ib.*, 483–4; for Secretary de la Torre *vide ante*, 199–201.

[19] *Ib.* to *ib.*, 23 and 31 October, *ib.*, 489–93.

[20] E.g., Alva to Vitelli, 4 December 1569, *ib.*, 533–6.

[21] Vitelli to Alva, 18 November 1569, *ib.*, 513–21, and 19 do., *ib.*, 522–3.

[22] For the geldings, La Mothe Fénélon to Charles IX, 27 December 1569, MF, II, 412–13.

[23] Leicester and Cecil to Walsingham, 7 October 1569, SP 12/59/3; Cecil to Rowe and Walsingham, 26 January 1570, SP 12/66/30.

[24] Vitelli to Alva, 6 December 1569, KL, V, 541–3; Despes to Alva, 1 December 1569, *CSPSp. 1568–79*, 213.

[25] La Mothe Fénélon to Charles IX, 10 December 1569, MF, II, 389.

[26] Memorial of the state of the realm by Cecil, *c.* 1569, Haynes, 584. The English delusions were of course encouraged by the French envoy – see his dispatch of 6 April 1569, MF, I, 295–6.

[27] Alva to Despes, 2 and 14 July 1569, *CSPSp. 1568–79*, 171–2 and 175.

[28] Alva to Philip II, 8 August 1569, *ib.*, 186.

[29] Philip II to Alva, 18 November 1569, *ib.*, 210.

[30] *Ib.* to *ib.*, same date, *ib.*, 209–10.

[31] Cecil to Norris, 15 May and 4 June 1569, *Cabala*, 151–2, presumably refers to this; see also La Mothe Fénélon to Charles IX and Catherine de Médicis, 20 April 1569, MF, I, 324.

[32] Draft reply to Cavalcanti in hand of Cecil, 24 May 1569, SP 70/107/238; La Mothe Fénélon to Charles IX, 28 May and 21 June 1569, MF, I, 41i and II, 50–54.

[33] Alva to Philip II, 13 June 1569, *CSPSp. 1568–79*, 162–4; *ib.* to Despes, 2 July, *ib.*, 171–2. For the personal interest of Fiesco, Curiel to Philip II, 16 August 1568, Simancas MS kindly communicated by Dr J. Retamal Faverau.

[34] Philip II to Alva, 19 July 1569, *ib.*, 177–8.

[35] Alva to Philip II, 13 June 1569, *ib.*, 162–4. *Supra*, 91–2.

[36] Alva to Despes, 2 July 1569, *ib.*, 171–2.

[37] Despes to Philip II, 17 July 1569, *ib.*, 176.

[38] Alva to Philip II, 31 October 1569, Gachard, *Correspondance de Philippe II*, II, 112; Philip II to Alva, 18 November 1569, *CSPSp. 1568–79*, 209–10. For a recent discussion of the pensions granted in the 1550s by Philip II to prominent Englishmen, see the introduction to 'The Count of Feria's Dispatch to Philip II

of 14 November 1558', ed. M. J. Rodriguez-Salgado and Simon Adams, Camden Miscellany XXVIII (1984), 315–17.

[39] Established by C. Read, 'Queen Elizabeth's seizure of the Duke of Alva's pay-ships', *Journal of Modern History*, v (1933), 464. See also *supra*,?.

[40] Alva to Despes, 2 July 1569, *CSPSp. 1568–79*, 171.

[41] La Mothe Fénélon to Catherine de Médicis, 5 July 1569, MF, II, 77.

[42] Grantz de Pommar to Leicester, undated c. 1569, *HMC Pepys*, 172–3; anon. to Merchants Adventurers, 16 October 1569, KL, v, 485; newsletter, 7 December 1570, KL, VI, 21–2.

[43] La Mothe Fénélon to Charles IX, 10 June 1569, MF, II, 14–15.

[44] Royal proclamation, 3 August 1569, HL, II, No. 563.

[45] Vitelli to Alva, 19 December 1569, KL, v, 555–9; Elizabeth to Philip II, 20 December 1569, *ib.*, 555–8n. and *CSPSp. 1568–79*, 221–3.

[46] Measures taken at Antwerp, 29 December 1569, KL, v, 561–3; Alva to Philip II, 15 January 1570, Gachard, *Correspondance de Philippe II*, II, 121. The English valued their cloths seized at Antwerp at £46,252 Flemish – Smit, *Bronnen*, No. 1259.

[47] Merchants Adventurers to Privy Council, undated c. 1570, SP 12/66/32; 'Things to be considered upon the demand of the merchants', hand of Cecil, 24 February 1570, SP 70/110/560.

[48] Englefield to Duchess of Feria, 30 April 1570, KL, v, 628–30n.; Alva to Philip II, same date, Gachard, *Correspondance de Philippe II*, II, 130; Marsh *et al.* to Alva, with his comments, 4 May 1570, KL, v, 646–50.

[49] The lukewarm feeling of the Merchants Adventurers in favour of agreement with the Netherlands and Spain was expressed in their letter to Burghley, undated c. 1572–3, KL, x, 547–8 (where it is unconvincingly ascribed to 1578).

[50] On the release of Despes, see La Mothe Fénélon to Catherine de Médicis, 11 July 1569, MF, II, 86.

[51] Marsh to anon., 11 April 1570, KL, v, 624–5.

[52] Story is noticed in the *DNB*. Much information about the abduction survives. For present purposes the most relevant documents are the letters of the concierge Bradleye to Leicester, undated c. 1571, Dudley Papers, III, f. 109; Marsh to Cecil, 27 August 1570, SP 12/73/32; *ib.* to Leicester and Cecil, 11 September 1570, KL, VI, 2–4n.; *ib.* to *ib.*, 14 September 1570, SP 12/73/62.

[53] La Mothe Fénélon to Charles IX, 26 August 1570, MF, III, 288.

[54] Elizabeth to Philip II, 17 December 1571, Gachard, *Correspondance de Philippe II*, II, 212–13.

[55] Thus Alva to Despes, 3 and 25 May 1570, KL, v, 643 and 657. Later, Alva was to remind the King how correct his assessment of Ridolfi had been – Alva to Philip II, 18 March 1573, Gachard, *Correspondance de Philippe II*, II, 320–1. See also *supra*, 156.

[56] Alva to Philip II, 27 August 1571, *ib.*, 193–4.

[57] Smith to Walsingham, 5 February 1577, SP 12/143/1072. The sense is not exactly reproduced in the calendared version, *CSPF 1575–7*, No. 1236. See also the Spanish evidence cited by G. Parker, *The Dutch Revolt* (London, 1977), 124–5.

[58] A good example of honest but highly misleading foreign intelligence from a merchant is Hogan to Norris, 12 August 1570, *CSPF 1568–70*, No. 1173.

[59] The scare may be followed in *APC 1558–70*, 379–80; list of ships in the royal navy, 30 July 1570, SP 12/71/70; Queen to Lord Admiral, 1 August, SP 12/73/1; instructions to Cobham, August, KL, v, 689–91; Cobham to Cecil, 18 August, *ib.*, 689n.; *ib.* to *ib.*, 28 August, *ib.*, 689–90n.; Queen to Lord Admiral, 29 August, SP 12/73/36 and 37; Cobham to Cecil, 4 September, KL, v, 706–8. For an example of invasion rumour, newsletter of 3 August, *ib.*, 683–4. A comparable incident had marred Anglo-Netherlands relations in February 1539, when

Henry VIII misread the news that Charles V was accumulating a war-fleet for action against the Turks: Smit, *Bronnen*, No. 613.

[60] Instructions of Alva to Zweveghem, 28 February 1571, KL, VI, 72–80; farewell letter of Zweveghem to Cecil, 25 April 1572, *ib.*, 399–400. For Zweveghem's earlier mission to England, *ante*, 278–9.

[61] Answer of Merchants Adventurers to French King's offer, July 1572, SP 70/124/264 – signed by Governor Marsh and two others.

[62] La Mothe Fénélon to Charles IX, 14 September 1572, MF, V, 122, and *passim*; also his intercepted letter of 7 October 1572, SP 70/125/318.

[63] *Supra*, 10–11.

[64] For Byrde, *ante*, 154–5 &c.

[65] Cf. Willan, *TBR*, xlviii.

[66] *Ante*, 151.

[67] *Ib.*, 57–9.

[68] The merchants trading to Emden were specially permitted to pay their export duties in 1565 after a period of grace – Queen to Winchester, 4 January 1565, Lansd. 9/10.

[69] A whole repertoire of devices to escape payment of customs duties was submitted to it in an unsigned report dating probably from the early sixties, Lansd. 41/9.

[70] Burghley and Mildmay to London customers, 19 May 1582, Lansd. 171, f. 468; customs officers to Burghley, 9 July 1582, *ib.*, 35/35; opinion and report of Mr Smith and Mr Yonge, undated *c.* 1584, E 178/7075. For the regulations of 1565, see 'Orders for the Custome howse in the Porte of London', undated 1565, SP 15/21/118, f. 258.

[71] Merchants Adventurers to Privy Council, undated *c.* August 1568, SP 12/185/56.

[72] Marsh to Cecil, 8 August 1568, KL, V, 141–2.

[73] HL, II, No. 556; *supra*, 99.

[74] Merchants Adventurers to Privy Council, 8 January 1569, SP 12/49/15.

[75] *Ib.* to *ib.*, 1 March 1569, Cotton Faustina C II, No. 19.

[76] Cf. *ante*, 266–71.

[77] Proclamation by Alva, 31 March 1569, KL, V, 354–5n.

[78] An act for keeping the mart at Hamburg, 26 April 1569, Sellers, *York Mercers*, 184–5.

[79] The acts of the Council for this period do not survive; but there are references to the committee in 'Reasons to move the forbearinge of trafique with Flanders', undated *c.* March 1572, SP 15/20/64, and in the Merchants Adventurers' letter to Burghley, undated late 1572, SP 12/120/67.

[80] Examples for 1569–70, Smit, *Bronnen*, No. 1163 *et seq.* A long list of English cloths unearthed at Nijmegen in 1570 is at No. 1182.

[81] G. Parker, 'Francesco de Lixalde and the Spanish Netherlands (1567–1577)', *Tijdschrift voor Geschiedenis*, LXXXIX (1976), 2.

[82] Proclamation, Brussels, 13 June 1570, SP 70/112/719; Philip II to Governor and Council of Holland, 3 June 1570, Smit, *Bronnen*, No. 1177.

[83] Instances in *Bulletin des Archives d'Anvers*, I (1864), 298, 304, 308.

[84] Grey to Burghley, 31 July 1571, SP 15/20/63. The London port book for 1571–2, covering imports, supplies corroborative evidence, E 190/5/5.

[85] Norris to Cecil, 25 February 1570, SP 70/110/565.

[86] Customer Smythe to Leicester, undated *c.* 1571, Dudley Papers, III, f. 49; London customs inwards 1558–69, Lansd. 14/50.

[87] 'Cawses of decaye', anon. memorandum undated *c.* 1570, Lansd. 110/56.

[88] 'A note of the particular sums', undated, SP 12/157/59.

[89] *CPR 1569–72*, 21.

[90] *Ib.*, 31.

[91] *Ante*, 268–9.

[92] The documents connected with the commission, including its report, are at E 178/1348. There is further information scattered among the state papers.

[93] 'The answer which the officers of the custom house did make', undated *c.* June 1571, Lansd. 14/55.

[94] Fleetwood seems at the outset to have participated – he signed the letter of the commissioners to Fanshaw, 22 June 1570, SP 46/29, f. 52.

[95] Commissioners to Hawes, enclosed with Byrde to Burghley, 21 July 1571, SP 12/80/7.

[96] Hakluyt to Burghley, 7 November 1571, *The Original Writings and Correspondence of the two Richard Hakluyts*, ed. E. G. R. Taylor. Hakluyt Society, second series, LXXVI (1935), I, 93–5.

[97] Dawbenye to Burghley, 27 February 1572, SP 12/85/53.

[98] Minutes of the information entered against Byrde in the King's Bench are at SP 12/88/32 and Lansd. 14/40. Why Byrde was taken to court there and not in the Exchequer is not clear.

[99] Minutes of the consistory of the French church, 14 November 1571, *Actes du consistoire de l'église française de Threadneedle Street, Londres*, II, *1571–77*, ed. A. M. Oakley. Huguenot Society of London, quarto series, XLVIII (London, 1969), 34.

[100] Merchants Adventurers to Burghley, undated *c.* August 1572, SP 12/120/67. Another copy at Cotton Galba C I, No. 41.

[101] *Ante*, 282.

# Chapter VIII

## *The agony of the Antwerp mart*

In the course of 1572, Elizabeth was thus gradually being induced to consider some amelioration of her relations with Alva.
Her stance in the world of international politics was one of
power and assurance rather than of weakness; but she could not
afford to see the legitimate traffic of her merchants to their new
mart at Hamburg crumble away bit by bit, and with it the main
prop of her customs revenue. And now, she initially contributed
to a far more speedy rapprochement with the government at
Brussels than might have been expected since the rupture of
trade in January 1569, by some actions that at the time must
have appeared of small political significance. By the spring of
1573, she was able coolly to reach a working agreement with
Alva, and Antwerp seemingly lay once more open to her merchants. But the agreement had been overtaken by events. It was
too late to restore old times. Alva had indeed crushed the first
open rebellion of the Prince of Orange and his brother in 1568,
but he lacked the resources to put an end to the privateers who
ranged the northern seas in the name of the rebels. Worse, from
the spring of 1572 the revolt was once more to spread to dry
land, and this time not to be quenched. The well-frequented
waterway up the Scheldt to Antwerp, essential to the Merchants
Adventurers and other neutral traders, soon became a central
theatre of conflict. Neither contestant paid more respect to
neutrals' safety than was required by a narrow sense of political
advantage, and the commerce of Antwerp was throttled.

The fatal train of events had been set in motion by the un-
witting Queen of England. In retaliation for the grant of asylum
in the Netherlands to the Earl of Westmorland and other English rebels, she had tolerated in her ports, and especially at
Dover, the presence of sea-rovers carrying letters of marque
issued by the Prince of Orange, i.e., the 'sea-beggars', *Gueux de
Mer*.[1] In the Channel they mingled with the Huguenot and
other members of the international fraternity, three-quarters
pirate one-quarter traders, who since 1568 had been making the

seas unsafe for honest merchantmen. But the depredations of the Netherlanders, led by the ruffian Count de la Marck, grew so indiscriminate that from 1571 complaints against them were being lodged by neutrals of differing nationality – including the City of Hamburg, which the Queen could not afford to ignore.[2] La Marck and his men had become an intolerable nuisance, and in October she privately ordered the arrest of his malefactors, though for the moment sparing the man himself.[3] But when he was ordered by the Privy Council to make restitution of plundered goods, he prevaricated.[4] So in February 1572 a message was sent to him through the Mayor of Dover, that he must depart.[5] Soon afterwards, a royal proclamation expelling all freebooters was issued.[6] La Marck sailed away most unwillingly – after all, where was he to find a new base for his operations?[7] With a last-ditch audacity he decided to defy Alva and make a bid for one of the water-girt strongholds on the coast of the Netherlands. He descended upon the remote haven of Brielle at the south-west extremity of Holland and established himself there. His luck was extraordinary. For it was just at this moment that a Spanish garrison was to be sent to the port of Flushing on the nearby island of Walcheren. The townspeople, heartened by the advent of the *Gueux*, refused to admit them. Within a few days, the whole island had cast off the authority of Alva save for a small Spanish garrison at Middelburg. Large areas of Holland and Zeeland were soon in revolt.

Flushing thenceforth became the headquarters of the *Gueux*, eclipsing Dover or even La Rochelle as a nest of freebooters. La Marck's handful of vessels was soon reinforced by scores of ships from all over the Netherlands, drawn in varying degrees by a desire to fight Alva or by an appetite for plunder. Alva had no naval force adequate to contain them. For mercantile activity at Antwerp the upshot could hardly be other than catastrophic, since Flushing, at the mouth of the Scheldt, lay athwart the route to the sea. The patronage of the Prince of Orange lent to the *Gueux* some formal legality in their practices, though their actual deference to him in point of fact was limited. Their profession that they were in revolt against Alva only and not against King Philip signified little. Dramatic illustration of the damage they might wreak was soon forthcoming. On June 10 a convoy of some 57 merchantmen arrived from Spain at the mouth of the Scheldt. With it there travelled the Duke of Medina Celi, who was being groomed as successor to Alva in the viceroyalty of the

Netherlands. It was intercepted by a sortie of fly-boats from Flushing, three great ships of the Spaniards being burnt and two more captured. Others grounded on the southern bank of the estuary, and Medina Celi himself made an undignified scramble to safety at Bruges.[8] An even more drastic fate awaited the spice fleet from Portugal that appeared three days later: 24 indubitably neutral ships with a consignment of tropical produce believed to be worth over 200,000 ducats, i.e. £66,000 or so. All save three were seized and taken to Flushing, where the cargoes were promptly unloaded.[9] The days of peaceful traffic along the Scheldt were demonstrably over.[10]

The political and economic repercussions of these events were manifold. The *Gueux* at Flushing speedily attracted an afflux of volunteers, English and French, fired by an enthusiasm worthy of a less rapacious cause; the several hundred English sympathizers who crossed the sea to fight with them included Sir Humphrey Gilbert the navigator and politician. Munitions of various sorts, including cast-iron cannon, were soon being shipped from England to help them. Such imports, it was said, were being financed by bills given to the Flushingers by wealthy supporters among the merchants of Antwerp, which at Hamburg were taken up by friends among the Merchants Adventurers, Governor Marsh being named as one.[11] They in turn were remunerated by funds raised from churches at London or, probably much more, by the sale of the illicitly seized goods in England. The Portuguese agent in England was naturally stung to indignation when he learnt that the merchandise seized at Flushing was being auctioned in England with, as he believed, the deliberate backing of Lord Treasurer Burghley.[12] But the English government in fact was far from certain how to approach the problems raised by the establishment of the *Gueux* on Netherlands soil. In the eyes of the Queen, they were rebels, marauders, undeserving. There was ground for alarm at the number of French volunteers reported to have arrived at Flushing: to have French soldiers in the Netherlands was even less desirable than to have Spanish. If it came to the disagreeable choice between French and Spanish control there, then it might become advisable to let Alva know secretly that the Queen was disposed to assist the King his master – on conditions, of course.[13] This was a train of thought that, especially after St Bartholomew's Day, pointed towards the resumption of normal relations with the government of the Netherlands.

At Brussels, however sharp the initial anger at the English share of responsibility for the fresh outbreak of trouble, it seemed on reflection preferable to propitiate the Queen. The reasons that since 1569 had led Alva to seek to appease her remained valid. In his eyes, an agreement now would further serve to prevent a full Tudor–Orange alliance – a nightmare haunting him – and also cut off the *Gueux* from any overt help from England.[14] Alva assured his master that he had no subject who desired the ruin of Elizabeth more than he, but that the first task was to drive a wedge between her and the Prince of Orange.[15] There being no longer either a Spanish or a Netherlands envoy at London, the Spanish merchant Antonio Guarras acted as go-between in further negotiations with the English government in the winter of 1572–3. He had a well-filled purse at his command – indeed, he boasted to the French ambassador that he had handed over 10,000 ducats for the favour of one single person of authority – perhaps Leicester or Burghley.[16] The Intercourse was reactivated, and with it a provisional agreement was patched up to cover a resumption of trade for two years pending a full conference.

The agreement was based on the two principles that the merchants on either side should receive compensation, and that neither prince might shelter rebels against the other nor protect freebooters at sea.[17] The Queen herself did not sign it; instead, signatures were exchanged by Burghley and Guaras at London in March 1573. The rapprochement elicited some grumbles from old Viglius in his retirement, and there was also a murmur from Assonleville and his protectionist friends at Antwerp.[11] But Alva could afford to disregard these. The provisional agreement ultimately blossomed forth into a definitive treaty signed at Bristol on 21 August 1574. Its terms covered chiefly the details of the reciprocal restoration of property seized since January 1569.[19] The Netherlands objection to the English customs tariff of 1558, prime cause of the breakdown of the Bruges colloquy eight years earlier, was among the issues silently waived.[20] The Queen thus won at Bristol in 1574 – hands down, but too late – what she had failed to secure at Bruges in 1566.

Only with difficulty did Alva manage to extract from King Philip a ratification of the agreement of March 1573. Philip characteristically felt small concern on the score of English cloths, but he was sensitive to the reproach that he was deserting the cause of the English papists and the Queen of Scots and – as he put it – he was afraid that the Pope and all Christendom would cry shame.[21] His consent, tardy and grudging, was elicited with the aid of various Netherlands notabilities, doubtless prompted by Alva. The finance specialist Berlayment assured the King how urgent it was to restore the traffic with England, which afforded so many thousands of his subjects their livelihood, and how his heart would melt with pity were he to see the desolation and poverty to which its interruption had led.[22] The Secretary of State Prats, the Bishops of Arras and Ypres and the Abbot of Anchin in turn depicted the misery of the whole countryside because of the excesses of the Spanish soldiery and the dislocation of trade. The disorders, violences and extortions of the troops had led to the flight of whole families, lawlessness was rife, and in both town and country an infinity of houses and properties lay empty.[23] There is no reason to doubt the substantial truth of this dismal picture, which in the following year was confirmed by the English envoy Thomas Wilson.[24] Six years of military tyranny, enforced by a foreign soldiery and interspersed by outbreaks of civil strife, had dragged the richest country of Europe far down into misery. At Antwerp, the cessation of traffic with England had led to the emigration of many well-to-do merchants. There had also been an exodus of artificers, some no doubt for the sake of religion, but others to follow the English cloth mart to Hamburg or elsewhere in Germany.[25] The value of house property at Antwerp had been falling since 1567, and the rents payable on commercial buildings – a fair index of business activity – had dropped by a third and more.[26]

But now, hopes of better times were suddenly encouraged. News of the agreement with the English was greeted throughout the Netherlands with 'incredible joy', as Alva put it.[27] The lords of Antwerp feasted 'with great honour' the English in their city – it is unlikely that they were numerous.[28] Memories of what had happened in January 1565, at the end of the Emden venture, must have been in many minds. But in fact the fate of the Antwerp mart was passing beyond international agreement. The diplomatic world of the princes might seem to function much as before, but that of the merchants had been distorted and transformed. When a proclamation in the name of Elizabeth I invited her subjects from the beginning of May 1573 to 'use the lawful intercourse of merchandise, as before the late restraint was by them used' in the dominions of the King of

Spain, the Merchants Adventurers were not thereby assured of a resumption of their traffic under the old conditions.[29] There was not to be any sudden afflux of English cloths to Antwerp. The Merchants Adventurers continued to trade chiefly at Hamburg. They were soon to discover that they had no other choice, for the *Gueux* from their base at Flushing held the traffic of the Scheldt at their mercy. However, for another nine years the Company continued its efforts to resuscitate the Antwerp mart, with what measure of success it remains to enquire.

The Merchants Adventurers were no longer led by John Marsh, sturdy protestant, who was doubtless as cool about any return to Antwerp in 1573 as he had been in 1564.[30] In his place there was a new Governor, Thomas Heton, who, as events were to show, was ready to take up his residence there. The merchants had foreseen and feared that the presence of the *Gueux* on Walcheren was going to complicate the situation and had consulted the Privy Council as to how a safe passage might be assured along the river to Antwerp.[31] It was doubtless on the prompting of the Council that the Company in April 1573 wrote to the Prince of Orange to request free passage for its ships and those of the Staplers. It accredited to Orange with this letter two of its members, Richard Goddard and George Southwick, whose business was to ensure that orders should be given at Flushing to this end, and be obeyed by the Flushingers.[32] The response cannot have been satisfactory, for at the beginning of May the Company sent another letter, addressed this time to the Governor, Burgomaster and Aldermen of Flushing, couched in minatory terms and warning them of the wrath of the Queen of England and the King of Spain.[33] This missive was duly debated by the Town Council of Flushing and in the end referred to Orange for a decision. Orange viewed the situation as the wily politician that he was. He expressed dismay to learn that the Queen had come to an agreement with 'the common enemy'. He would have preferred it otherwise. But as a special concession the Merchants Adventurers might be allowed to dispatch no more than four ships at a time to Antwerp, to be laden with English produce only, and excluding any 'new draperies' which might compete with the products of the looms of Holland. The ships must proceed to Flushing, where they would be searched and disarmed before being permitted to proceed upstream. In return, Orange stipulated that his Hollanders and Zeelanders might traffic freely in England and that the Company of

Merchants Adventurers should lend him 50,000 florins (about £8,000).[34]

With this far from satisfactory answer, Goddard and Southwick made their way home.[35] The cloth fleet in the Thames was awaiting their news. When it was learnt, almost all the ships set sail not for the Netherlands but for Hamburg, as the Alderman of the Steelyard observed.[36] Indeed, the Merchants Adventurers had done prudently to wait, for a little earlier the Staplers had dispatched to Bruges their five small wool ships, and three of them had been seized by the Flushingers near their destination.[37] The perils of navigation in the Scheldt were now clear, as also the further danger of dragging the trade of the Merchants Adventurers, and with it the economic well-being of England, into the violent politics of the Netherlands. As far as Antwerp was concerned, the last word seemed to lie with Orange, within the limits of his control over the Flushingers. Orange wanted to deprive the provinces still obedient to Alva of their maritime links with the outer world. He told one English envoy 'that if he could but hinder that in a year's space there came no salt into Flanders (i.e. from the western coast of France), he should win such a peace as he wished for'.[38] In particular, he was not prepared to tolerate the supply of English wool for the looms of Flanders – the Staplers were 'the chiefest which nourished his enemies', as he argued on another occasion.[39] But England was for him a potential ally, a source of recruits, munitions of war and other provisions, and a market where goods might be sold as well as bought. He could not afford to antagonize its Queen. Hence his readiness to offer smooth assurances, to come to terms with the Merchants Adventurers, and to permit them some small traffic at Antwerp. A limited revival of their trade there carried the additional advantage of giving them something to lose, and providing him with hostages. In April 1574, he found it advisable to improve the conditions previously offered to the Merchants Adventurers, increasing to six the number of ships they might send at one time, and promising that they should not be detained for search at Flushing for more than one tide.[40]

Elizabeth Tudor, much as she disapproved of rebels, did not on her side wish to see Orange completely crushed by Spanish military might, nor driven in desperation to seek French protection. She was therefore willing to give him some encouragement and to negotiate, though not at the expense of her merchants.

But the suave exchanges of princes' diplomacy were related only in a curious ethereal way to the brutal conditions now prevalent in Netherlands waters, and especially in the Scheldt estuary. The ships of the Merchants Adventurers were bound to call at Flushing if making for Antwerp. But they might wait long for clearance, and if the Flushingers wanted to raise money their cargoes might be impounded.[41] The Flushingers also levied the customs and other dues payable in the province of Zeeland, but at enhanced rates.[42] It was possible to buy licences to trade in goods not covered by the agreement of the Company with Orange; but as Southwick found, their use was fraught with trouble and disaster.[43] There was an admiralty court at Flushing where justice was dispensed – usually, as the English thought, to the detriment of the foreigner. The English envoy Daniel Rogers, believed by the merchants to be unduly partial to the *Gueux*, after trying in vain to secure restitution of English goods unfairly seized, confessed how 'I never thought before to have found such iniquity and barbarousness as I find daily among the Flushingers'.[44] Outside the Scheldt, marauders based on Flushing ranged far afield, with or without letters of marque from Orange, laying hands on ships even off the English coast, so that Elizabeth had to authorize special measures to grapple with them. One problem that had vexed her the *Gueux* did however help to solve – the fall in the yield of the cloth export tax. Organized clandestine shipments of cloth to the Netherlands were no longer worth while. The cloth export tax recovered, yielding to the exchequer £26,901 in 1572–3, £31,036 in 1573–4 and £33,411 in 1574–5.[45] In April 1575, the patents of Dawbenye and other informers were withdrawn.[46]

The concern with which the exchanges between Merchants Adventurers and *Gueux* were followed at Antwerp and still more at Brussels may be imagined.[47] Alva's prime object was naturally to prevent the rebels from receiving any aid from England; as a corollary to this, he sought to put a stop to any trade with the areas in revolt.[48] In December 1573 he laid down his office and left the Netherlands, his successor being a Castilian nobleman, Luis de Requescens. A new personality had arrived; but there was no change in the system or objectives of government. Requescens made it clear that ships arriving at Antwerp after paying any sort of levy to the rebels downstream were unwelcome, though like Alva he deemed it prudent to temporise with the Queen of England.[49] After the relaxation of the controls at Flushing conceded by Orange to the English in April 1574, there seems to have been some faint revival of traffic along the Scheldt. Near the end of May, Requescens observed that Antwerp was full of Englishmen.[50] Some of them, it may be assumed, were connected with the business of the Merchants Adventurers. He evidently felt that the time had come to put his foot down on their trade, tainted as it was by payments at Flushing. So when the next couple of cloth ships anchored at Antwerp they were promptly arrested. Despite the intervention of Elizabeth herself, Requescens stuck to his guns.[51] As Orange and the Flushingers also stuck to theirs, an impasse was reached.[52] The revival of trade along the Scheldt, adumbrated in the spring of 1573, thus petered out after little more than a year.

It was, of course, no wish of Requescens that trade between England and Antwerp should cease. If the Scheldt was impassable, why should not the Merchants Adventurers travel as the King's subjects had to, through one of the Flemish ports still under his control?[53] A new line of approach to Antwerp was therefore opened, along which English cloths from late 1574 were being dispatched – through Gravelines, Dunkirk, Ostend, Nieuwpoort and Sluys. Certainly during the winter of 1574–5 no ships from Antwerp arrived in the Thames at London, though imports from the Netherlands were coming both from Flemish ports and from places north of the Scheldt, including the rebel stronghold of Flushing.[54] This new Netherlands route gave no great satisfaction to English cloth merchants. Their wares were always in danger of capture by the Flushingers at sea, and on land were subject to the local taxes and restrictions enforced in Flanders, more onerous than those to which they were accustomed in Zeeland or Brabant. Merchandise was also liable to seizure at the whim of the captain of the Spanish garrison at Ghent.[55] The presence of Dr Thomas Wilson as English envoy at Brussels from November 1574 to March 1575 did only a little to ameliorate the situation.[56] The bulk of the traffic of the Merchants Adventurers continued to pass to Hamburg. A mere score of merchants or mercantile agents sufficed to man the English House at Antwerp in December 1574.[57] No doubt this failure to revive the old trade at Antwerp more than slightly provided a stimulus to some of the London merchants to press ahead in these years with a direct trade to Italy and the Mediterranean.[58]

Requescens was in a tight corner, chronically short of funds to maintain his government, pay his troops or even support the envoys he sent from time to time to England. No mariners could be recruited in the Netherlands, for nobody was prepared to fight the *Gueux*, whose ships swept the Scheldt virtually unchallenged.[59] He was often in residence at the castle of Antwerp, which for practical purposes was the headquarters of the forces fighting the rebels in Holland and Zeeland. He feared a sudden rising of the inhabitants of the city, with the support of the *Gueux*. On the afternoon of 12 December 1574, some eighty rebel ships, some of them large, appeared only a league off, and exchanged fire with the castle. Members of the Spanish and Italian merchant communities joined the garrison in patrolling the city. On the following morning, the rebels drew close. But there was no sympathetic response from land. The revolutionary ardour of 1566 had been cowed, and the conspiracy resulted only in some arrests and executions, the departure of some timorous merchants and a setback to trade.[60] No less damaging to the business life of Antwerp was the presence of the Spanish and other foreign troops. In April 1574 there occurred a serious mutiny of unpaid Spanish soldiery: the mutineers moved into Antwerp and took possession of the Town Hall. After dark they ran among the streets, terrifying the inhabitants, shooting their weapons, shouting *arma, arma pagate cives*, and threatening to enter the houses and pillage them. Requescens believed that they were restrained from plunder only by his own presence. The lords of Antwerp and the merchants, according to his story, besought him to remain with them. The Bourse stood empty and credit had vanished, so that there was much difficulty in scraping up enough money to assuage the mutineers and in cajoling them to depart.[61]

When Requescens unexpectedly died in March 1576, the situation markedly deteriorated. His troops completed his plans by their capture of the rebel stronghold of Zierickzee in the summer; but there was no political authority to enforce further decisions. Power passed nominally to the Council of State pending the arrival of the next viceroy, but in fact the Spanish soldiery acknowledged no superior. Unpaid, cynical and mutinous, the foreign troops moved south in the autumn, out of the combat area. The unoffending towns of Aalst and Maastricht were plundered by them with much carnage, arson and rapine. They then moved upon Antwerp, the greatest prize of all even in its decline. The sack of Antwerp that occupied three days in early November has gone down in history as 'the Spanish Fury', but it was a coldly-planned and methodical as well as a brutal operation. For months, the city had been gripped by alarm, and many merchants had taken their departure.[62] Trade was dead. But much remained to destroy and loot. Some six hundred houses were estimated to have been burnt, and the new Town Hall – *edificio bellissimo et superbissimo*, as the Florentine envoy lamented – also went up in flames with all its pictures and ornaments as well as its commercial archives.[63] The number of persons slaughtered or drowned in the Scheldt reached five figures. The Englishman George Gascoyne who witnessed the proceedings estimated that 5,000 persons 'or few less' were killed in cold blood for failing to produce money sufficient to ransom themselves. In the final phase, the soldiery, clad in velvets and satins looted from merchants' wardrobes, paraded the streets and played with each other at the dicing tables that now desecrated the Bourse.[64]

The mutineers were not merely veterans hardened in the field, but were also sophisticated in screwing money from civilians and ready if need be to accept bills where cash was not available. They had no respect for age, cloth nor nationality. Some of them forced their way into the English House, where the 'comely aged man' Governor Heton was in residence; they threatened him 'with naked swords and daggers', laid hands on such money, plate and jewels as were in the House, and compelled him to agree to pay a ransom, partly perforce in bills. Some Englishmen elsewhere lost their lives. But the sack, momentous as it was in the history of Antwerp and of Europe, did not provide a turning-point in the trade of the Merchants Adventurers. It is unlikely that more than a handful of them was present in Antwerp at the time, or that the broadcloths and kerseys in their warehouses were plentiful. As we have seen, they did not like the overland route through Flanders, and although the Company had earlier in the year made financial concessions to secure the re-opening of the river to the cloth-ships the Queen had refused to ratify the agreement. This was partly because of the payments the Company by its terms was to make to the rebels. It was also partly owing to the persistent piracies of the Flushingers, which had provoked her into the expensive course of dispatching units of her fleet to police the Narrow Seas and seizing in retaliation some of Orange's warships. As far as the evidence goes, no ships of the Merchants Adventurers had sailed up the Scheldt since 1574.[65]

An envoy, the experienced Wilson, was dispatched with speed by Queen Elizabeth to extricate Governor Heton and the other merchants from the ruined city and to press for compensation. Wilson's protests met with evasive replies at both Antwerp and Brussels, though he managed to secure the cancellation of the bills given in ransom to the Spanish soldiers.[66] Then in December came information that the new viceroy, the King's half-brother Don John of Austria, was arriving in the Netherlands. The Queen accordingly accredited Sir Edward Horsey to him, with instructions to seek further assurances for English merchants. Horsey upon audience shrewdly judged him to be no friend to his country.[67] However, after some delay Don John confirmed the order that the merchants' bills should be discharged and agreed that the 'writings and books of accounts' seized by the soldiers should be sought out and restored to their owners.[68] The few remaining English merchants were ultimately allowed to retire from Antwerp to Bruges. The situation was all the more serious because the ten-year agreement of the Merchants Adventurers with the city of Hamburg was now nearing its term. The Queen on behalf of her merchants applied in October 1576 to Burgomasters and Senate to request its renewal. She received no reply, and had to write again in more peremptory style the following February.[69] There was no satisfactory answer to this second letter; but ultimately in July 1577 the Hamburg Senate agreed to prolong the privileges of the Merchants Adventurers for one more year.[70]

The political convulsions of the Netherlands were meanwhile taking a new turn. Don John speedily learnt that he did not receive the unqualified respect accorded by dutiful subjects to his predecessors. The Estates were the incomplete masters of a country united in its detestation of the Spanish soldiers, who now drew together and marched southwards out of the Netherlands. In February 1577, a solemn civic ceremony was enacted at Antwerp in front of the burnt-out Town Hall. The scaffolding used in the happy days nearly sixteen years earlier for the Festival of Rhetoric was taken out of storage, re-erected and hung with tapestry. From this platform an official proclamation of peace was read out, 'with the greatest solemnity of singing, ringing and shooting of ordnance that hath been heard', as Wilson reported. Shortly afterwards, the Spaniards completed their evacuation of the castle.[71] An epoch of relatively mild and increasingly protestant civic government was now inaugurated. It lasted for almost eight years, until the siege and recapture of Antwerp by the next Spanish viceroy, the Prince of Parma. The inhabitants set to work to rebuild their city, restoring the Town Hall and dismantling in part the castle. The foreign merchants returned from Cologne and other places of refuge; the Merchants Adventurers were back for the Sinksen Mart at the end of May. They were assured that the payments to the Flushingers and others downstream would no longer be exacted. The Scheldt was apparently once more freely open, and hostilities over. In September the Prince of Orange, on his way to attend the Estates at Brussels, stopped for a day or two at Antwerp where, courteous as ever, he once more visited the English House.[72]

Whether any considerable quantity of English cloths was actually shipped up the Scheldt to Antwerp for the Sinksen Mart in 1577 there is no means of knowing. But it is certain that the bright prospects were soon clouded over and that hopes of a reversion to the good old days were again dashed. The government of the Estates at Brussels was in great financial difficulties, mainly because of the need to find money to maintain the troops whose loyalty protected them from the Spanish viceroy. This need could be met only by the levy of new taxes and imposts. The Merchants Adventurers were naturally enough quick to protest at these fresh exactions, which violated the Intercourse. The Council of State at Brussels was anxious not to offend the Queen of England, whose merchants were always buttressed by the diligent diplomacy of her envoys. But it could not afford to exempt the Englishmen from the new taxes as a special favour, for all the other foreign merchants would claim as much, and some would seek to evade payment by inducing English associates to 'colour' their goods.[73] In fact, the Merchants Adventurers attempting to open up trade along the Scheldt in the autumn of 1577 were disconcerted to find that not only were the new payments being required of them when ships passed through Zeeland waters, but that the 'double toll', from which they were specifically protected by the promises of the lords of Antwerp as well as by the terms of the Intercourse, was also being exacted.[74] There seemed no way of getting round these levies, which in their eyes were arbitrary as well as onerous. Ultimately, in June 1580 a General Court of the Company at

Antwerp ruled that a record should be kept of all such sums paid out 'contrary to the Intercourse', presumably in the hope that at some future date they might be reclaimed.[75] No more could be done.

Relations between the Merchants Adventurers and the Netherlands authorities were further complicated by the way in which the Queen of England adapted herself to the changing political situation. She had lacked sympathy for the *Gueux*. But the members of the Council of State at Brussels were men of a different stamp, highly respectable and in no way rebellious though tenacious of their local liberties. She perceived that their interests and hers closely overlapped.[76] Besides, while the fate of the Hamburg mart hung in the balance, as was the case in 1577–9, their good will was worth cultivating. She was willing therefore to lend them money, on stringent terms maybe, or encourage others to do so. Late in 1577 she agreed that they should contract a loan of £100,000, of which a portion was repayable directly to her agents the Genoese financiers Horatio Palavicino and Benedict Spinola. The transaction was more complex than need be expounded here. It produced friction rather than amity, despite repeated and obsequious assurances from the Council of State whose resources proved unequal to the burden of servicing the debts to the English crown and to its bankers.[77] As time passed and the interest mounted up, Elizabeth grew more menacing in her attitude. When in 1580 the Merchants Adventurers satisfactorily established a mart once more at Emden, one strong reason for tenderness towards Netherlands interests disappeared. Elizabeth believed, or affected to believe, that the Estates of the Netherlands were trifling with her. When the lords of Antwerp, anxious to placate her, tried to arrange for payments, she rounded upon them. They were, of course, the most vulnerable members of the defaulting Estates. On her instructions, Mr Secretary Walsingham reluctantly arranged to report to her the arrival of any worthwhile Antwerp ship at London, so that it might be held as security.[78] This would naturally have led to the arrest of any English ships at Antwerp. In May 1581 the Governor of the Merchants Adventurers – no longer old Heton but the more lively Christopher Hoddesdon – had actually suggested that to avoid such a disaster the Company should allege the weight of the taxes laid on trade there as an excuse for removing its mart to some safer town in Holland or Zeeland.[79]

How many English merchants actually traded at Antwerp and what quantity of goods they handled in the six years 1576–82 we cannot tell. It is unlikely that business was other than small, though it may momentarily have quickened in 1579, during the interval between the end of the Hamburg mart and the resettlement of the Merchants Adventurers at Emden in 1580. Hanse merchants, no longer enjoying any privileges in England, were in this year eagerly buying English cloths at Antwerp, where they were said to have forced the price of an ordinary pack of ten broadcloths up from £60 to £110 Flemish.[80] The yield of the cloth export tax at London continued to be satisfactory, with only minor fluctuations from 1577 onwards.[81] The cloths at first mostly went, it may be assumed, to Hamburg and subsequently to Emden. But there were various other openings more promising than submitting wares to the scrutiny of Netherlands tax-collectors. The Londoner could participate in the newly-developed direct trade to the Mediterranean and Levant, sending his kerseys, new draperies and tin through the Straits of Gibraltar. Or he might ship to the Baltic, where by order of the Privy Council the newly-chartered Eastland Company was compelled to admit to membership any merchant adventurer who paid the entry fine of £10.[82] In addition, the partial eclipse of Netherlands trade springing from the revolt had presented English merchants with opportunities to develop a transit traffic between northern and southern Europe. Thus in the summer of 1576 spices, sugar, fruits and other tropical or Mediterranean products were being re-exported in quantity from London to Emden, Hamburg, Danzig and elsewhere in the Baltic, while tar, wax, hollands and other northern merchandise was carried to Portugal, Spain and the Mediterranean.[83] There was also a carrying trade in English ships that by-passed English harbours, disliked by the regular Merchants Adventurers because it allegedly involved some initial sale of English cloths at cut-price rates, the profit being made up at a later stage by the carriage of goods direct from one foreign country to another.[84] Ventures of this sort contributed to the buoyancy of the City in the later 1570s.

Other foreign nations besides the English were turning their backs on Antwerp. The southerners were affronted by the protestant ascendancy, which from 1580 grew more marked. Protestant strangers were alarmed by the continued advance of the Spanish viceroy Parma, whose troops from 1579 were raiding to within a mile of the walls.[85] Even before the end of 1580,

Governor Hoddesdon was remarking how the trade of Antwerp was 'waxing daily less and less' and 'the danger thereof increasing by leaps', so that the mart of the Merchants Adventurers would have to be removed to some place in Holland.[86] Indeed, from the earliest years of the revolt, English cloths were being spirited across the North Sea to Holland and Zeeland: interlopers and 'stragglers' could not be deterred from making for Amsterdam, Dordrecht or elsewhere with their cloths.[87] It is likely enough that Company discipline had for some years been weakening because the merchants were keeping clear of Antwerp – this would help to explain why the Lord Treasurer Burghley intervened in the summer of 1580 with an order to the London customs officers to allow no ships to be freighted to north-west Europe save by members of the Company of Merchants Adventurers.[88] The welcoming attitude of towns in Holland and Zeeland towards the Merchants Adventurers need not be doubted. In the 1560s, Middelburg as well as Bruges had angled for their mart.[89] Subsequently Orange in the 1570s several times indicated that he would be glad to see them establish themselves in Holland or Zeeland – offers to which the Englishmen remained coy, in view of his attitude to their shipping in the Scheldt.[90] Then in August 1578 the Town Council of Rotterdam resolved to solicit the Merchants Adventurers to set up their mart there, with an offer of lodgings and pack-houses for the cloths: this was taken up three months later by the Estates of Holland, and again in October 1580.[91] At London, there had meanwhile been a rumour that the Company was planning a settlement at Middelburg and Dordrecht.[92]

When the successful negotiations with Middelburg were initiated is not known. But the final phase may be dated from the fall of Lier in August 1582, which provoked a further dispersal of the foreign mercantile community at Antwerp.[93] The Spanish troops seized this fortified town, no more than a dozen miles distant, through treachery. The news produced a great shock at Antwerp, where the sense of insecurity was heightened, many sought to sell their houses, and merchandise ceased to arrive.[94] To many German and Italian merchants it seemed prudent to retire to Cologne or Wesel, beyond the jurisdiction of the King of Spain. They or their agents could travel to bargain with the English vendors of cloths at some more northerly town where security was better.[95] On 5 October the municipality of Middelburg finally came to an agreement with the Merchants

Adventurers by which they were assured of extensive privileges, legal, fiscal and political: the Company was in effect recognized as a sort of half-independent authority responsible for the commercial life and demeanour of its members resident there.[96] Long before the end of the month, most of the Englishmen had migrated to Middelburg, where on an island within easy reach of home they could feel safe.[97]

The lords of Antwerp were greatly dismayed by the removal of the English merchants. They asked the Duke of Anjou, who with English encouragement and French troops was at the time championing the cause of the Estates, to write to Queen Elizabeth on their behalf, and they also demanded of the Merchants Adventurers the reasons for their departure. The Deputy Governor in residence had no difficulty in pointing out to them how 'we have here neither convenient sale of our goods, nor good wares to make return' – without any embarrassing reference to the political danger of a sudden seizure of Antwerp goods in England by royal order.[98] There were repercussions in high politics. The Prince of Orange was reported to be 'somewhat troubled' by the migration of the Merchants Adventurers, for the edifice presented to them as the new English House at Middelburg had been sold by him a little earlier to the municipality, and his popularity at Antwerp suffered because he was suspected of conniving at the move.[99] His habit of being all things to all men evidently brought some inconvenient moments. In mid October there was a last flicker of life at the English House at Antwerp when, with the merchants gone, the English military commander Norris entertained at 'a splendid banquet' within its walls the Princes of Orange and Chimay, the geusts including 'many of the nobility, and many noble matrons and maidens'. The company was entertained 'with good music and other honest recreation till 2 or 3 a.m.'.[100] The merchants had wound up their business, and with unconscious symbolism the high politicians and soldiers made merry in their place.

NOTES TO CHAPTER VIII

[1] This point was well put in Burghley's draft letter to Zweveghem, 22 February 1572, KL, vi, 321–5. The 'sea beggars' have been studied by J. C. A. de Meij, *De Watergeuzen en de Nederlanden 1568–72* (Amsterdam, 1971).

[2] *APC 1571–5*, 44, 45–6, 46–7, 49, 67, 69; Hamburg to Queen, 28 September 1571, Simson, No. 5998 (see also No. 6088); Horsey to Burghley, 20 October 1571, KL, vi, 184–5n.

[3] Copy of royal order, 3 October 1571, Brussels, AGR, 403, ff. 134–5.

[4] La Marck to Privy Council, 25 and 27 January 1572, SP 70/122/51 and 55.

[5] Queen to Mayor of Dover, 21 February 1572, Murdin, 210–11.

[6] Proclamation, 1 March 1572, HL, II, No. 585.

[7] La Marck to Queen, 1 March 1572, KL, VI, 330–2.

[8] On the mission of Medina Celi, see A. W. Lovell, 'Some Spanish attitudes to the Netherlands (1572–1578)', *Tijdschhrift voor Geschiedenis*, 85 (1972), 20.

[9] Morgan to Burghley, 16 June 1572, KL, VI, 425–7; Medina Celi to Alva, 10 to 17 June 1572, Gachard, *Correspondance de Philippe II*, II, 262–3. See also C. R. and W. D. Phillips, 'Spanish wool and Dutch rebels: the Middelburg incident of 1574', *American Historical Review*, LXXXII (1977), 312–30.

[10] Flushing to agents in England, 17 June 1572, KL, VI, 429; Alva to Philip II, 24 June and 21 August 1572, Gachard, *Correspondance de Philippe II*, II, 263 and 274.

[11] Fogaza to Ruy Gomez, 23 June 1572, CSPSp. *1568–79*, 395; *ib.* to Alva, 20 September 1572, *ib.*, 415. Useful as these letters are, they need to be taken with a pinch of salt. See also Fogaza to Alva, 26 October 1572, *ib.*, 427.

[12] Request of Giraldi, July 1572, *CSPF 1572–4*, No. 452; with answer, *ib.*, No. 454; Fogaza to Alva, 16 September 1572, CSPSp. *1568–79*, 414.

[13] 'Memorial for Flanders', 3 June 1572, KL, VI, 420–1.

[14] Anon. to Burghley, 24 June 1572, Murdin, 221–2; Alva to Philip II, 17 January 1573, Gachard, *Correspondance de Philippe II*, II, 307–8.

[15] *Ib.* to *ib.*, 16 April 1573, *ib.*, 340.

[16] La Mothe Fénélon to Charles IX, 9 November 1572, MF, V, 196–7.

[17] Text in KL, VI, 675–7; summary, *CSPF 1572–3*, No. 863. See also proclamation of 30 April 1573, HL, No. 595.

[18] Memorandum of Viglius, Tisnacq and Assonleville, 20 December 1572, KL, VI, 600–5; Alva to Viglius, 29 December 1572, *ib.*, 601–2n; Viglius to Alva, 7 January 1573, *ib.*, 618–22; Antwerp memorandum possibly addressed to Assonleville, December 1572, KL, VI, 592–3.

[19] Summary of text, *HMC Salisbury*, II, 81; also Gachard, *Correspondance de Philippe II*, III, 138–40, and Rymer, VI (4), 153–4.

[20] *Supra*, 29–30.

[21] Philip II to Alva, 24 February, 15 April and 8 July 1573, Gachard, *Correspondance de Philippe II*, II, 314, 332 and 383–4.

[22] Berlayment to Philip II, 15 April 1573, *ib.*, 332–3.

[23] Prats to Philip II, 29 April 1573, *ib.*, 351–2; the letters of the ecclesiastics, dated 13 May, are at 357–8.

[24] Wilson to Burghley, 11 December 1574, KL, VII, 382–4.

[25] Evidence collected by H. van der Wee, *Antwerp market*, II, 238.

[26] *Ib.*, I, 486; E. Scholliers, 'Un indice du loyer; les loyers anversois de 1500 à 1873', *Studi in honore di Amintore Fanfani* (Milan, 1962), V, 593–617; Castelyn to Burghley, 29 May 1575, KL, VII, 523–4.

[27] Alva to Philip II, 15 April 1573, Gachard, *Correspondance de Philippe II*, II, 332.

[28] Guarras to Alva, 13 May 1573, KL, VI, 733.

[29] Royal proclamation, 30 April 1573, HL, II, No. 595.

[30] *Supra*, 67.

[31] Merchants Adventurers to Privy Council, undated *c.* winter 1572–3, Cecil Papers, 141/275.

[32] Merchants Adventurers to Orange, 15 April 1573, *ib*, 7/99.

[33] Merchants Adventurers to Flushing, 2 May 1573, Smit, *Bronnen*, No. 1218.

[34] Orange to Goddard and Southwick, 25 May 1573, KL, VI, 740–1; *ib.*, to Merchants Adventurers, 26 May 1573, *ib.*, 745–6.

[35] See their discouraging views in their letter to Governor Heton, 12 May 1573, Lansd. 16/62.

[36] Zimmerman to Suderman, 26 June 1573, Höhlbaum, II, 41, No. 334.

[37] Newsletter from Bruges, 7 June 1573, KL, VI, 759; Guarras to Alva, 8 June 1573, ib., 761; Fogaza to Alva, 9 June 1573, CSPSp. 1568–79, 471.

[38] Rogers to Burghley, 9 October 1575, KL, VII, 561–4.

[39] Ib. to ib., 29 August 1575, KL, VII, 562–4.

[40] Treaty negotiated by Goddard and Southwick, 3 April 1574, Smit, Bronnen, No. 1251.

[41] List of forfeitures, 15 September 1573 to 30 April 1576, Smit, Bronnen, No. 1316; 'A reply made unto certain answers', 2 May 1575, KL, VII, 526–9.

[42] 'Certain complaints of Zeeland', June 1573, KL, VII, 529–30.

[43] Southwick to Burghley, 4 October 1575, KL, VII, 587–9. Other documents exist for his case.

[44] Rogers to Burghley, 14 September 1575, KL, VII, 575–8.

[45] 'A note of the particular sums', undated, SP 12/157/59.

[46] APC 1571–5, 370–1; Privy Council to Dawbenye, 27 April 1575, Lansd. 20/47.

[47] Langen to Prätor and Suderman, 12 June 1572, Höhlbaum, II, No. 131, pr. app. 352–4.

[48] Proclamation, 28 February 1573, SP 70/126/434 and 435.

[49] Thus Requescens to Zweveghem and Boisschot, 22 June 1574, KL, VII, 183–6; ib. to Philip II, 28 June 1574, Gachard, Correspondance de Philippe II, III, 115.

[50] Ib. to ib., 26 May 1574, ib., 91; anon. letter of 7 June 1574, KL, VII, 167.

[51] Elizabeth to Requescens, 8 August 1574, KL, VII, 289–90.

[52] Merchants Adventurers to Governor &c. of Flushing, 23 July 1574, Smit, Bronnen, No. 1262; Governor &c. of Zeeland to Merchants Adventurers, 15 August 1574, ib., No. 1265.

[53] Requescens to Zweveghem and Boisschot, 21 July 1574, KL, VII, 221; ib. to Elizabeth, 17 September 1574, ib., 333; ib. to Wilson, 11 December 1574, ib., 374–7.

[54] E 190/6/3 supplies entries of London imports for the six months from October to March 1575. A new revised agreement between the Merchants Adventurers and the Gueux made in December 1574 would appear to have been abortive – see text in Smit, Bronnen, No. 1279.

[55] Wilson to Requescens, 22 January 1575, KL, VII, 419–22, summarizes the grievances of the merchants.

[56] Wilson's instructions, c. 5 November 1574, KL, VII, 349–52.

[57] Wilson to Burghley, 20 December 1574, KL, VII, 389–93. For the efforts of the Merchants Adventurers to re-establish their trade with Antwerp in 1573–6, see the fuller narrative in Smedt, EN, I, 381–406.

[58] This development is discussed by G. D. Ramsay, 'The undoing of the Italian mercantile colony in sixteenth-century London', Textile History & Economic History', ed. N. B. Harte and K. G. Ponting (Manchester, 1973), 22–49.

[59] Alva to Philip II, 16 April 1573, Gachard, Correspondance de Philippe II, II, 340.

[60] Requescens to Philip II, 14 and 15 December 1574 and 9 January 1575, ib., 216, 217–20 and 235–40. Wilson in reporting the episode to Burghley gave the rebel ships as merely 'over 40 hoys' and played it down, 20 December 1574, KL, VII, 389–93.

[61] Requescens told his story in a series of letters to the King, 28 April to 15 May 1574, Gachard, Correspondance de Philippe II, III, 56–67. For a neutral account, Lafferden to Suderman, 4 May 1574, Höhlbaum, II, 53, No. 466, pr. app. 407–8.

[62] Champagny to Philip II, 10 August 1576, Gachard, Correspondance de Philippe II, IV, 291–4; Roda to ib., 29 September 1576, ib., 402–3.

[63] Guicciardini to Duke Francesco, 10 November 1576, Battistini, 364–70; Council of State to Philip II, 6 November 1576, Gachard, *Correspondance de Philippe II*, v, 8–11.

[64] G. Gascoyne, *The Spoil of Antwerp* (London, 1576) has been reprinted more than once in modern times and is readily accessible in *Tudor Tracts*, ed. A. F. Pollard (London, 1903), 419–49. It is a masterpiece of vivid reportage. The essential source is the collection of documents by M. P. Génard, *La furie espagnole. Documents pour servir à l'histoire du sac d'Anvers en 1576.* Annales de l'Académie d'Archéologie de Belgique, XXXII, i.e. 3ᵉ série, tom. II (Antwerp, 1876).

[65] *APC 1575–7*, 193; Villiers to Walsingham, 30 August 1576, KL, VIII, 442–6; Walsingham to Villiers, 6 September 1576, *ib.*, 452–4; instructions for J. Taffin, 13 October 1576, *ib.*, 466–7. See also account in Smedt, *EN*, I, 396–402. The London port book E 190/6/4 indicates that no ship during the summer months of 1576 gave Antwerp as its destination.

[66] Wilson to Council, 19 November 1576, KL, IX, 35–43; *ib.* to Leicester, 3 December 1576, *ib.*, 67–9.

[67] Instructions to Horsey, 14 December 1576, *ib.*, 85–90; memorandum of Horsey, same date, *ib.*, 90–1; Horsey to Burghley, 29 December 1576, *ib.*, 108–9.

[68] Effect of Don John's letter to Rodas, December 1576, *ib.*, 77–8.

[69] Queen to Hamburg, 8 October 1576 and 28 February 1577, Simson, Nos. 7119 and 7242.

[70] Hamburg to Queen, 19 July 1577, Höhlbaum, II, No. 1145, pr. in appendix, 478.

[71] P. Heyns to Ortelius, 27 February 1577, *Epistulae Ortelianae*, ed. J. H. Hessels (Cambridge, 1887), 161–3; Wilson to Walsingham, 1 March 1577, KL, IX, 229–32; *ib.* to *ib.*, 21 March 1577, *ib.*, 247–8.

[72] Narrative in Smedt, *EN*, I, 415–17.

[73] Wilson to Walsingham, 8 June 1577, KL, IX, 330–1; States-General to English ambassador, 10 June 1577, *ib.*, 333–4.

[74] English merchants to Orange, October 1577, Smit, II, No. 1343; Orange to Zeeland, 7 October 1577, *ib.*, No. 1339; Merchants Adventurers to English ambassador, October 1577, SP 83/3/79.

[75] Act passed 9 June 1580, Sellers, *York Mercers*, 227–8.

[76] See memorandum of Burghley, 8 December 1577, KL, X, 152–4.

[77] There are discussions by Smedt, *EN*, I, 430 *et seq.*, and by L. Stone, *An Elizabethan: Sir Horatio Palavicino* (Oxford, 1956), ch. ii.

[78] Walsingham to Gilpin, 19 May 1582, SP 83/16/20.

[79] Hoddesdon to Walsingham, 6 May 1581, SP 83/14/63.

[80] Laffarden to Suderman, 26 October 1579, Höhlbaum, II, 184, No. 1648.

[81] According to the list at SP 12/151/6, f. 1, the yield (to the nearest £) was: 1576, £35,069; 1577, £28,756; 1578, £30,704; 1579, £29,472; 1580, £31,111; 1581, £32,584. For preceding years, see *supra*, 167.

[82] Hoddesdon to York Merchants Adventurers, 17 August 1580, Sellers, *York Mercers*, 241. For the revival of direct English trade to the Mediterranean, see G. D. Ramsay, 'The undoing of the Italian mercantile colony in sixteenth-century London', *ut supra*.

[83] London port book, E 190/6/4.

[84] Marsh to Burghley, 25 October 1576, SP 15/24/94; act of Merchants Adventurers, 18 March 1580, Sellers, *York Mercers*, 226–31.

[85] Davison to Walsingham and Wilson, 1 March 1579, KL, XI, 306.

[86] Hoddesdon to Walsingham, 17 December 1580, SP 83/13/80.

[87] Goddard and Southwick to Company, 18 May 1573, KL, VI, 738–40; Hoddesdon to Walsingham, 27 May 1581, SP 83/14/76; see also Smit, *Bronnen*, No. 1389.

[88] Burghley to London customs officers, 18 August 1580, Höhlbaum, II, 207–8, No. 1804. But the prime target was Hanse.

[89] W. S. Unger, *Middelburg als Handelstad (XIIIe tot XVIe eeuw)* (Middelburg, 1935), 118; *supra*, 66.

[90] Hastings to Burghley, 2 December 1575, KL, VIII, 59–68; instructions to Rogers, *c.* 22 June 1577, KL, IX, 356–65; Rogers to Leicester, 20 July 1577, *ib.*, 399; Rogers to Walsingham, 24 July 1577, *ib.*, 423–4.

[91] Resolution of Rotterdam Town Council, 31 August 1578; also resolutions of Estates of Holland, 14 November 1578 and 15 January 1579, Smit, *Bronnen*, No. 1370 and p. 1239 n. 2.

[92] Zimmerman to Liseman, 25 July 1579, Höhlbaum, II, 171, No. 1548.

[93] Herle to Walsingham, 1 and 2 September 1582, *CSPF 1582*, No. 302 – a virtual transcript of SP 83/17/1.

[94] Doyley to Walsingham, 26 August 1582, SP 83/16/126; Longston to *ib.*, 28 September 1582, SP 83/17/24.

[95] On this general point, see TP, II, 61–2, and Smit, *Bronnen*, pp. 1239–40, n. 2.

[96] Agreement between Middelburg and Merchants Adventurers, 5 October 1582, Smit, *Bronnen*, no. 1448.

[97] Danett to Walsingham, 28 October 1582, SP 83/17/49.

[98] Longston to Walsingham, 13 October 1582, SP 83/17/34; Danett to *ib.*, 28 October 1582, SP 83/17/49.

[99] Danett to *ib.*, 7 October 1582, SP 83/17/31.

[100] Bizarri to *ib.*, 20 October 1582, SP 83/17/42.

# Chapter IX
## *Envoi*

The departure of the English merchants in October 1582 was only one of a series of misfortunes that now beset Antwerp, which three months later narrowly escaped occupation and sacking by the French troops in the pay of the Duke of Anjou. Then in the autumn of 1584 Parma at length was able to lay siege to the city, which in August 1585 capitulated. It was henceforth once more under the authority of the King of Spain. Parma had no wish to damage Antwerp as an international trading centre, but he was under orders to extirpate religious dissent. The heretics, for whose services the cathdral and other churches had recently been requisitioned, were given four years' grace to settle their affairs, pack up their belongings and depart. At the termination of this period, in 1589, the inhabitants of Antwerp are believed to have numbered 42,000, i.e. less than half of its population of twenty years earlier.[1] As in the years 1572–6, a battlefront lay across the Scheldt, the lower banks of which were firmly in the control of the rebels, now organized in a Dutch republic. In any case, England was at war with Spain from 1585 to 1604, during which period there could for the merchants be no question of any return to Antwerp. The membership of the cloth-finishers' gild, once so large and influential, diminished, partly by emigration to the new mart towns of the Merchants Adventurers. Survivors lamented the disappearance of the basis of their livelihood, the sign of which was the empty English House in the Prinsstraat.[2]

For many years the lords of Antwerp cherished the hope that when peace was restored the English would return to their old haunts. This did not happen. By the early seventeenth century the Merchants Adventurers had adapted themselves to a new pattern of trade. Their chief mart town, from 1569 onwards, lay usually in north-west Germany, while from 1582 there was a supplementary mart town in the Dutch republic. Traffic along the Scheldt continued to be impeded. Ultimately in 1608 the lords of Antwerp, despairing of the return of the English

merchants, turned over their former headquarters to the
Jesuits, who in consequence acquired locally the nickname of the
'English Fathers'. When the Jesuit Order was dissolved in 1773
the former English House was sold. It served various humdrum
purposes until in 1929 the Jesuits bought it back and restored it.
Within its walls they established a college of commerce which is
now absorbed into the university of Antwerp.[3] There is nothing
to remind the visitor that the building once housed a famous
company of English merchants. Indeed, so far in popular and
local memory has the connection of the Merchants Adventurers
with Antwerp receded that when in 1965 another Queen from
England, also called Elizabeth, paid an official visit to the city,
neither the former English House – nor indeed the sites of the
former English Quay and English Bourse – had a place in the
itinerary arranged for the royal traveller.

In general, all memory of the commercial world of sixteenth-
century western Europe soon faded, in contrast to the fame of
princes and the strife of ecclesiastics. There was a modest revival
of activity at Antwerp in the first half of the seventeenth century,
chiefly in the field of high finance, but the city failed to recover
anything like its dominant position in international commerce.
The Scheldt was barred to through traffic between Antwerp and
the sea, in the interests of Amsterdam and the other cities of
Holland. The Merchants Adventurers too declined from their
commercial eminence, losing for ever their privileges in the later
seventeenth century. Their Company came finally to an end
when the mart town of Hamburg was occupied by the French in
1809. Their records were lost and their activities forgotten in
England until William Cunningham and other historians drew
attention to them from the late nineteenth century onwards.
This was also a time when Georg Schanz, Richard Ehrenberg
and Henri Pirenne abroad were re-discovering the crucial importance of Antwerp in the European economy of the sixteenth
century.

From the Queen downwards, the participants in English
politics in the later sixteenth century had no doubts about the
vital importance of the Merchants Adventurers and their traffic
to the mart town on the continent. This attitude was reflected by
William Camden, who enjoyed the counsel of the aged Burghley
when he first set about compiling an account of the reign of
Elizabeth. At his disposal he had all the state papers – in embarrassing profusion, as he confessed.[4] He laid more stress, for

instance, on the episode of the Emden mart in 1564 than writers of text-books in mid twentieth century are wont to do. His narrative of the breach with the Netherlands in 1569 also stands comparison with that of subsequent historians.[5] It was in a later age, when historical writing was swayed by ecclesiastical part-isanship or moved by a romantic interest in feminine rulers, that the cloth traffic was allowed to sink into oblivion. For long it has been the conventional approach to the history of the reign of Elizabeth I to centre the political narrative down to 1585 upon the ecclesiastical settlement, Anglo-Scottish relations and the plots of the conspirators who sought to place the Queen of Scots upon the throne of England.[6] This is not to argue that the history of Elizabethan England ought to be written around the ups and downs of the Merchants Adventurers, though it would be a perfectly legitimate enterprise to attempt it. But even in a so-called 'political history' do not the merchants of the City deserve as much if not more mention as the successive schemes of conspirators to unseat Elizabeth Tudor and the measures of her government to foil them?

Without any commitment to a determinist interpretation of history, it is not fanciful to argue that certain courses apparently open on the political plane were for other reasons impracticable for any English government to pursue. If, *per impossibile*, Eliza-beth Tudor in the 1560s had yielded to the demands from Brussels and dismantled the 1558 customs tariff and curtailed the jurisdiction of the high court of admiralty, her government would have found itself in much severer straits for money and its control over the seas much reduced. If, further, Granvelle had successfully bridled the free-trade lords of Antwerp, hind-ered any recourse to Emden or Hamburg and thereby caused a contraction in English cloth exports to the continent, a reduction of output would have been forced upon the cloth-producing regions. The two setbacks taken together would have meant a regression in political, social and economic terms to conditions that had prevailed a hundred or more years ealier, with benefit to nobody in England save perhaps the Company of Merchants of the Staple. There is thus some truth in the argument that the smooth maintenance of the Hispano-Burgundian alliance im-plied for England a reversion to conditions more characteristic of the fifteenth than the sixteenth century. But in actual fact, the twin phenomena of a rapid rise in population and the industrial-ization of particular regions, as we may in retrospect observe them, had raised ramparts which the government was firm to defend in 1563–4 and again from 1569. And the Queen was aware of the stakes for which she was playing.[7] A running-down of the textile industry and a withering-away of monarchic power, as happened in contemporary Poland, might just conceivably have been possible, but only if a very incompetent or prejudiced ruler sat on the English throne, and at the cost of an incalculable upheaval.

If then there were limits to political action set by social and economic developments, does not the attempt in the foregoing pages to explain how the Merchants Adventurers came to detach themselves from their mart at Antwerp seem unduly political in its colouring? It would no doubt be possible to excuse this by pointing to the nature of the evidence that survives, in which the dispatches of ambassadors and other mainly political papers have a preponderant place. But it is more important to grasp that – as Richard Ehrenberg so clearly saw in the last century – trade ran in channels that were politically predetermined. Cloths were made in England and consumed chiefly in Germany: this was an economic phenomenon. But who should be allowed to engage in the international cloth traffic, who should reap most financial gain by taxing it, where the cloths should change hands, and even how tolerable life should be for the merchants who financed the traffic – these were matters of political consequence. The business of the merchant was deeply affected by international political alignments and agreements – witness the implementation of the Intercourse and of the treaty of Cateau-Cambresis, and the abortive conferences at Bruges in 1565 and 1566. It was for reasons of high politics that the Duke of Alva on that fatal day in December 1568 was moved to effect the arrest of the English merchants at Antwerp and so to bring to an end for most purposes an association that for both Merchants Adventurers and their customers at Antwerp was basically satisfactory. As we have seen, the Antwerp mart thereafter was never much more than a ghost of its former self.

If we try to fathom the reason for this action, we find that Alva was following – reluctantly – some urgent but misguided advice from his master's ambassador in England, Don Guerau Despes. But why did King Philip select this devoted Aragonese, so resilient and so imaginative but so lacking in judgment, to represent him at the court of a vital though difficult ally? Here, in our zigzag course from political to social and economic history and back again, the imaginary line must once more be crossed. The availability of suitable diplomatic representatives is one of many indications of the social maturity of a state, and not the least revealing. It may be, that in view of the dearth of men both willing and competent to accept so burdensome a post as the London embassy, he had little choice. For reasons that deserve investigation by the social historian, only the republic of Venice at this time was able to man a far-reaching and effective diplomatic service. The Queen of England certainly found it difficult to recruit gentlemen of ability to represent her abroad. Her ablest and best trained subjects were needed to serve at home, where there were all too few of them.[8] Professional diplomacy was as yet a very new sort of career, for which the universities had hardly started to offer any real preparation.

As well as some sort of social, political and intellectual training, an unusual hardihood of both body and mind was required to serve as a permanent envoy in sixteenth-century Europe. An ambassador might be starved of money and news, cold-shouldered at the court to which he was accredited, moving dangerously in a world of strangers, and yet however severe the tensions afflicting him, obliged to maintain a dignified and affable exterior whenever he emerged from his lodgings. The strain on health was marked: Bishop Quadra died at his post, while Chaloner, Man and Despes survived their departure by only a few months. Upon these harrassed individuals the supreme issues of peace or war might hinge, whether through the terms of their dispatches or their demeanour towards the foreign personalities whom they had to cultivate. A royal audience was sometimes a special event in their lives. From the envoys that Elizabeth I and Philip II exchanged in the 1560s, both in general derived a variable service: Chaloner and Silva at least were reasonably effective. Both these men purveyed shrewd advice, likely to promote the maintenance of peace. Ambassadors who were wilful or blind wreaked positive damage – rather than such, it was more advantageous and certainly cheaper to pay an adventurous amateur, a Herle or a Gascoigne, or even to rely on some friendly foreigner such as Utenhove or Cavalcanti. It was at least in part through the lack of efficient intermediaries that the mind-pictures on either side grew more and more distorted as the years passed, offences and menaces being seen where none were intended, and bogeys far removed from reality taking fearsome shape. Of the various failures of English intelligence, perhaps the most striking was the persistent inability to perceive that Alva in the late 1560s need not be written off as an enemy, but was an adaptable realist.

The development of prejudice may to some extent be surveyed in the mind of Secretary Cecil – a shrewd, unbiased and humanist *politique*, as well-informed and intelligent as anyone serving the Queen. He had some acquaintance with Spanish literature and language, and was no vulgar xenophobe; in religion, he had conformed under Mary Tudor and was not a fanatic. But when pondering upon the course of events, probably in the midst of the turmoil and dangers of the year 1569, he could only deduce an ingrained malevolence on the part of the Spanish monarchy. He perceived the same hand in the misfortunes that led up to the loss of Calais and the failure to recover it at the peace negotiations in 1559, in the Netherlands trade embargo of 1563–4 and in the treatment meted out to English envoys in Spain culminating in the expulsion of Dr Man. And now these deeds were capped by the 'audacious arrest' of the English merchants in the Netherlands by Alva, an ungrateful return for the refusal of the Queen to give any support to Netherlands rebels although she had been 'solicited to have given aid to the Prince of Orange'.[9] Ten years later, the colours had deepened. The intrigues and deceptions of Despes, with their ramifications reaching out to the Duke of Norfolk, the Queen of Scots and the northern rebels, could be added to the list. Then came the attempted invasion of Ireland mounted from a Spanish port, and the activities of the Spanish envoy Mendoza, 'very many, manifest and malicious'.[10] When even Cecil felt obliged to think along these lines, it is scarcely surprising that less well-informed Englishmen followed. The Queen for long was less sure, because she had a personal acquaintance with Philip that had not been available to her servants. But even she could not stomach the arrest of the English merchants at their mart town in December 1568, which marked the effective termination alike of the ancient Burgundian alliance and the Antwerp mart.

On the other side, the signposts direct us to the personality of Philip II himself. He was a man of mediocre intelligence and little imagination, suffused by an overmastering sense of duty inculcated at an early age. He had a less independent mind than Elizabeth, and he was probably less ready to discount the prejudices and short-sightedness of his agents and courtiers. Power had been thrust into his hands by a series of family marriages which had been planned by earlier generations, and a sequence of unexpected deaths. His education had left him ignorant of the speech, not to mention the outlook, of his northern subjects. His father had tried to govern many peoples by moving from one realm to another, wearing down his health in the process; Philip himself is not to be censured for choosing to settle in the part of his dominions where he felt most at home. In any case, he had made a genuine effort to maintain the union of England and the Netherlands by offering his hand to Elizabeth Tudor immediately upon her accession: had she accepted, he could hardly have withdrawn for long to central Castile. What he compelled himself to attempt was something untried, save perhaps by the Emperor Frederick II in the thirteenth century, since the fall of the Roman Empire – to wit, the government of a part of northern Europe from the south. And Frederick had commanded direct unhampered access by land to his empire north of the Alps, while the southern civilization that he represented was in most respects more advanced than that of the north. Neither was true of Philip II in his relations with the Netherlands.

Philip was also at a disadvantage in his relations with the money-dealers of his time. They were men of ability, sophisticated in their ways and hard in their methods. He had little or no notion of the complex structure of the Antwerp cosmopolis and its Bourse. His ignorance of the merchants who furnished him with ready money was evidently mingled with some disdain – otherwise he would not have defaulted three times on his debts, to the horror of all the financial exchanges of Europe. Elizabeth Tudor, who may have felt no more liking for merchants as such, showed herself more adroit in her treatment of them. She understood the need to keep their confidence and with it her credit. Not only did she hold sufficiently to the rules to maintain her credit and borrow money at a comparatively reasonable rate of interest, but she perceived the tight connection between politics and the state of the commercial market. This was not evident to Philip.[11] It may be that Elizabeth cared for trade merely because of the revenue she drew from it in her customs, and because it supplied the livelihood of thousands of her subjects in the industrial areas of England, where trouble was certain if it failed. But it is also possible that she had some inkling of the manner in which commercial and financial techniques were in her day outpacing the methods of government.

Yet before pinning responsibility for the end of the English mart at Antwerp upon Philip II, it is important to notice some significant maritime and economic trends lying outside the control of any one man. Antwerp during the last phase of its epoch of greatness in the 1560s was pre-eminently a centre where wares of any sort might be bought and sold. It was the universal bazaar of Christendom. It was also firmly established in its function as a financial clearing-house, and the headquarters shared by the directors of the European economy. At Antwerp, their polyglot clerks totted up their sums in arabic numerals – in counting-houses that lay conveniently within a few yards of each other. Such propinquity had its advantages. But where space was needed, Antwerp was less suitable. Anchorage facilities in the Scheldt were limited, so that most ocean-going ships tended to unload and take on their cargoes at Arnemuiden or other ports at the mouth of the river.[12] Only the Merchants Adventurers of England enjoyed the privilege of being able to count upon immediate access to a particular landing-place – the English Quay – where their cloth-ships could anchor on arrival.[13] The river was always crowded, and with the irresistible growth of traffic throughout the sixteenth century the congestion and the inconvenience could not but increase. Saturation-point lay not far ahead. Antwerp was approaching the end of its mission as the central power-house of economic activity, and the time was nearing when other ports were bound to participate in its primacy.

Signs were accumulating during the years 1560–85 that whatever the events in the world of princes, the lords of Antwerp might have to alter their attitude to freedom of trade. As we have seen, the rise of their city owed much to the liberal welcome accorded to merchants from other countries. But as the years passed, many foreigners acclimatised themselves to permanent residence at Antwerp. Some at least of these residents began to resent the passive attitude of their adopted city towards more recent newcomers, many of them transient visitors. At the time of the Bruges colloquy in 1565–6 Giles Hooftman, cloth-merchant and banker, had expressed his hostility to the grant of unilateral concessions to his English rivals. He and his friends found patrons and allies in old Viglius (before his death in 1577) and in the anglophobe Dr d'Assonleville.[14] Although Hooftman momentarily revealed himself as a Calvinist in 1567, he was subsequently protected from trouble by Assonleville.[15] The interests represented by Hooftman reappeared after the interruption of trade in 1569–73. In 1574, Governor Heton writing from Antwerp told Secretary Walsingham of how Viglius and Assonleville were 'marvellous enemies' to the English and were spurred on by Antwerp merchants 'that have gotten great wealth in England', Hooftman being the first on his list.[16] The English merchants were inclined to see the hand of these rivals in the troubles they experienced while trading in the Netherlands, which no doubt helps to explain the deliberate harrassment of the foreign merchants at London in the 1570s.

The large-scale traders resident at Antwerp were as wealthy and numerous as their brethren in other European cities of the first rank. Their resources entitled them to plan an independent part in international commerce. They could hardly fail to observe the advantages derived by their rivals from organization and protection. Their ambitions were ultimately expressed by the foundation of trading companies on the English model. To serve these bodies, the city had its own modest but not inconsiderable merchant marine: the city gild of mariners was perhaps the one municipal organization that the lords of Antwerp were willing to sustain in the face of foreign competition.[17] The idea that the Antwerp merchants who traded to England should combine for their mutual support seems first to have been broached by Pensionary Wesenbeke when he was at London in the summer of 1564 as the envoy of the lords of Antwerp. But although the Antwerpians were responsive to the suggestion it did not bear fruit until the late date 1580, when a Netherlands 'Company of Merchants Trading to England' with its seat at Antwerp was founded. It was supported by big merchants of the city, Jacques della Faille being the second governor. In organization it followed the model of the Merchants Adventurers, with a governor and a court of assistants. But the stormy politics and the civil war then being pursued gave it little chance to function, and after around 1582 little or nothing has been discovered about its activities. A similar fate befell another Antwerp trading company founded at about the same time, for the merchants trading 'to the west', i.e. to the Atlantic coast of Europe.[18]

The demise of these two companies ended no more than a prologue, for they were to have famous successors – in a transplanted setting. Although Philip II and his emissaries might

seem to have toppled Antwerp down from an epoch-making sum-
mit of prosperity in the space of a couple of decades, this should
not be taken to indicate that the princes could ultimately get the
better of the merchants. Exactly the opposite was the case. Antwerp
itself was indeed ruined, but only the immovable property of its
merchants lay at the mercy of the King of Spain. Their movable
capital, their stock-in-trade, was dispersed among the warehouses
of cities beyond his control. It was thus not only the foreign firms
that were able to withdraw and continue their business in a safer
and more tolerant environment. Native Netherlands merchants
scattered in various directions and in the course of a generation
enlivened Hamburg, Frankfurt, Nuremberg and other places of
refuge. Above all, they provided the towns of Holland and
Zeeland with a stimulus whose results were to be seen in the rise of
the Dutch republic to world-wide commercial importance in the
early seventeenth century. For the men who provided the capital
and the driving force behind the East and West India Companies
of the free Netherlands included a number of merchants who
themselves or whose fathers had begun their careers at Antwerp
in the last years of its prosperity.[19] But they were firmly opposed
to any revival of maritime traffic on the Scheldt.[20]

For the Netherlands, the suppression of the Antwerp entrepôt
marks the end of a chapter of history only in a limited and
local sense. It led to a new concentration of capital and enterprise at Amsterdam and other towns, where trade was less cosmopolitan and in its conduct markedly more nationalist and
protectionist. In England, the impact went deeper. For the merchants of London, the closure of Antwerp was both a rebuff and
a stimulus. It meant that they had to approach the overseas
markets where cloths might be sold or tropical goods acquired –
the two were far from identical – directly. Long-range trade
replaced the short sea-route to the Scheldt. If the Englishmen
had been able to continue buying and selling happily at Antwerp, much of the stimulus to sail to the Mediterranean and to
the East and West Indies would have been absent, and events
would have taken a very different course.

NOTES TO CHAPTER IX

[1] W. Brulez, *Anvers de 1585 à 1650*, VSWG, LIV (1967), 75–99.
[2] Prims, *Antwerpen*, VIII (2), 18.
[3] Smedt, *EN*, I, 440–1 and II, 132–3. Also the works by Amand de Lattin and
P. Genard *ut ante*, 30, n. 40.

[4] W. Camden, *The history of the most renowned and victorious princess Elizabeth, late queen of England* (third ed., London, 1675), 71–2.

[5] *Ib.*, 122–3.

[6] An honourable exception is J. A. Williamson, *The Tudor Age* (London, 1953).

[7] They are well stated in the anonymous 'Collection of certain reasons...', undated *c.* late 1564, Cotton Galba C II, No. 2.

[8] *Ante*, 103–4.

[9] Memorandum by Cecil, *c.* 1569, Haynes, 584–5. See also the undated fragment at SP 70/146/8, not in the hand of Cecil, which belongs to approximately the same date.

[10] Memorandum by Cecil, *c.* 1580, Cotton Vespasian C XIII, No. 125, f. 414.

[11] *Supra*, 30.

[12] This point is well illustrated in the documents printed by B. Dietz, *Port and Trade of Elizabethan London, passim.*

[13] *Ante*, 22.

[14] Fitzwilliams to Cecil, 18 January and 23 February 1565, KL, IV, 159–61 and 183–5.

[15] *Supra*, 51.

[16] Heton to Walsingham, 19 June 1574, KL, VII, 181–2.

[17] *Ante*, 190.

[18] The information in this paragraph is derived from two articles by O. de Smedt, 'Het College der Nederlandsche Kooplieden op Engeland', *Antwerpsche Archievenblad*, I (1926), 113–20 and 341–8; 'Een Antwerpsche plan tot organisatie van den Nederlandsche zeehandel op het Westen' (1583); *ib.*, II (1927), 14–30.

[19] There is a crisp statement of the evidence in W. Brulez, 'De Diaspora der Antwerpse kooplui op het einde van de 16e eeuw', *Bijdragen voor de Geschiedenis der Nederlanden*, XV (1960), 279–306.

[20] J. I. Israel, *The Dutch Republic and the Hispanic World 1606–1661* (Oxford, 1982), 15.

# Appendix

## Royal instructions to the commissioners sent to Bruges, 1565.[1]

### Elizabeth R.

A memorial of the matters to be entreated at the colloquy to be holden at Bruges betwixt the commissioners of Her Majesty that is, the Viscount Montague, Mr. Dr. Wotton one of Her Majesty's privy council, and Mr. Haddon master of requests of the one part: and the commissioners of the King of Spain of the other. Made at Westminster the 11th of March 1564, in the seventh year of Her Majesty's reign.

First, the commissioners for Her Majesty shall have in remembrance, both at their entry and in all the rest of their treaty, to show and make plain that whatsoever hath passed to and fro in these matters of merchandises or in any other controversies, suits or complaints raised and made by any the subjects of either party for their particular respects: yet Her Majesty hath always remained in all her intentions and certainly resolved and determined to keep firm and inviolable the ancient amity, as the same hath been now of long time betwixt the progenitors of Her Majesty and the said king. And with the same intention and full purpose, Her Majesty hath now at this present time sent you, her commissioners, to treat upon all matters passed that may appear to have tended to the impairing or any manner of diminution of the said amity. And thereupon, to remove all such impediments, and to establish the said amity according to the alliances and leagues of amity made betwixt Their Majesties' most noble fathers Charles the Emperor and king Henry VIII.

Secondly, you the said ambassadors shall call to your remembrance as many of the consultations and conferences as you may attain unto, which have been as well heretofore made in former colloquies held for the matters of the Intercourse, as now in Council by Her Majesty's appointment, whereunto specially you Mr. Wotton and Mr. Haddon have been from the beginning privy; as also you the said Viscount Montague have been since you were assigned by Her Majesty to be the principal minister of this colloquy.

And because the matters concerning the intercourse of merchandise are very many and almost infinite; although the same are for the most part to be referred to a Treaty of Intercourse made between Henry VII and Duke Philip of Burgundy in the year of our Lord God 1495: of which Treaty and of the controversies risen and moved by the subjects of either party, you the commissioners are informed as much as the time could serve, what hath been heretofore thought upon. Yet because it is meet that you be also instructed what Her Majesty shall direct you to answer thereunto, hereafter followeth a memorial of the matters that are supposed will be by the commissioners on the one side moved and objected, with such answers thereunto as in reason for the time seem good and justifiable. To the maintenance whereof, Her Majesty doubteth not but you will employ your best endeavours with your knowledge and understanding.

First, it is to be considered that when Monsieur d'Assonleville was last here, he did propound as many things as could be then collected and imagined to be done on the part of England against the Treaty. And because at the same time the said d'Assonleville was by deliberate advice answered to the most and principal parts of his objections or demands, whereunto you the commissioners are made privy, Her Majesty remitteth you to be informed thereby and to follow the same manner of answer, saving in certain such points hereafter following, as wherein Her Majesty hath caused some further advice to be had and some other manner of answer to be devised than was before.

*Poundage.* The first matter that hath required a further answer is the maintenance of the right and duty called Poundage, whereof d'Assonleville having, as it should seem, known no more of the antiquity and continuance thereof than by perusing the common printed books of the statutes in the times of king Richard II, Henry IV, V and VI, hath argued the same poundage not to have continuance before the time limited by the Treaty for tolls and taxes, but at sundry times to have ceased. Where in very truth, it is to be proved by the ancient records of this realm that the payment of 12d. upon the pound, which is the duty called poundage, did never cease: but was yearly paid to every king from the 10th. of king Richard II, which was in the year of our lord God 1386, and so successively during the reigns of king Henry IV, Henry V, Henry VI and king Edward IV, and so from thence unto this present day without interruption of one year, containing in the whole hitherto 178 years, whereof is to be accounted from the 10th. of king Richard II to the year of our lord God 1493 which also was the 11th. year of king Henry VII, being the time of the making of the Treaty 109 years; or else from the said 10th. year of king Richard II until the 24th. year of king Henry VI (being 50 years before the date of the treaty), 61 years. So as it may plainly appear, that this manner of payment to pay 12d. upon the pound called Poundage is ancient and not new nor against the Treaty of this Intercourse.

*Books of Rates.* And where it is objected that the payments at this day be greater in sums of money for the same than they have been: the former answers made heretofore to Monsieur d'Assonleville may be maintained, in that the Queen's Majesty hath but 12d. upon the pound in value upon a favourable rate made thereof, under the common value of the which the same may be bought and sold here within the realm. Wherein Her Majesty might by reason and good justice (taking but 12d. upon the pound of all manner of wares coming into this realm as they be sold and are worth) advance the same kind of payment called Poundage to a far greater yearly sum than now she doth, by making the rates of the values under the prices for the which they are sold: as yourself may well conceive and be able to prove, if you take with you and consider the Books of Rates which were made in the time of Her Majesty's dear sister queen Mary.

*Employments.* 2. The next matter of moment that seemeth meet to be considered in the answer, is the offence that is found in the execution of the Statute of Employments, in which matter there is a collection made of certain statutes concerning Employments in the times of king Henry IV, king Edward IV and the third year of king Henry VII: all which laws were made before the date of the Treaty of the Intercourse and so are not now contrary to the same. But because it seemeth the manner of the execution of the said statutes should more offend the stranger than the law itself, it hath been thought meet to moderate the same: to be taken of favour and not by force of the Treaty. That is, where the merchandise or victuals be not above the value of £9, there the officers to take no bond nor surety for Employment against the will of the party. And from £10 to £20, to take bond of the parties alone, without surety; and with sureties also, of any stranger being denizen as well as of English. And to avoid all controversies upon the value of the said wares, it is thought that the same should be ruled always by the common books of the rates publicly appointed in the Custom House for poundage.

*Anchorage, buoyage, scavage, balliage, package, lighterage, carriage.*

3. Thirdly, where amongst former complaints there appeareth that the strangers be grieved with sundry taxes taken in the river of Thames, as anchorage and buoyage; and in the city of London, scavage, balliage, package, lighterage and carriage. Although heretofore answers have been made that whatsoever hath been augmented in any of those since the time limited in the Treaty should be reformed: where indeed it cannot be understood that anything hath been augmented, saving in a certain payment called buoyage, raised of late upon probable reason as shall be manifested unto you. Yet because it may be doubted what will be objected in all these charges, there hath been conference used with the several officers having to do therein, who have delivered several writings concerning the same matters to maintain the ancient and lawful usage thereof. Which writings shall be delivered unto you for your instruction. *A writing for buoyage & anchorage* (in margin).

And touching the payments belonging to the City, there shall attend upon you at the Diet certain persons ready to inform you as much as in reason and good order is to be required; and therefore you are to be remitted in those cases to their information.

*A writing containing the cause of levying more money for buoyage.* And as to the money demanded of vessels coming to the Thames for that which is called buoyage: there shall appear unto you by writing that shall be delivered herewith, the cause why more money is now of late years levied for that purpose than heretofore was. And nothing is required therin, but that may appear to tend to the benefit of them which own the vessels and pay the charges. And in this point, you are to receive our general advice that in all causes of complaints which shall be presented unto you concerning any exactions or demands made by the City of London, or by any other persons other than to the use of Her Majesty. In these causes, you shall give charge to such as shall be attendant for the merchants of England, to take care therof how to provide reasonable answers thereunto. And if they shall not therein satisfy you, then to advertise us or our Council thereof.

*A writing of Customers' demands.* And because complaint hath also been made of divers molestations and vexations by reason of greater demands made by the Customers, Comptrollers and other officers of the ports, it is fully intended (as reason is) that no greater sums be demanded than of ancient allowed by the treaties hath been used. And for that purpose there is provided to be delivered to you a writing containing the particular sums of all manner of payments demanded and usually received: and for proof therof, that which in reason can be demanded us offered to be done. (Having not any ancient record kept thereof, as be of duties to the crown or to societies; for that the said payments be but to private men for attending upon their offices).

*Custom for cloths.* 4. Fourthly, it is to be considered, which also appertaineth to the matters of Customs, wherein strangers complain to pay greater sums of money for the custom of woollen cloths going out of the realm than they were wont. For answer whereunto, because the matter is of great weight and consequence to Her Majesty and the crown of this realm, the same hath been newly considered. And thereupon is found that although the sums of money now demanded of strangers for custom and subsidy of cloths be greater than heretofore hath been, yet Her Majesty hath not thereby so much advantage by the said cloths as her progenitors have had by the quantity of wool which is therein contained: but receiveth less a great deal, as may be made plain and evident by comparing the custom of cloths now demanded and the ancient custom received more than two hundred years past for the quantity of wools contained in the said cloths. So as the matter being inwardly considered, although the diversity seem great at the first sight, yet neither hath Her Majesty any inordinate or greater gain than her progenitors had before the Treaty of the Intercourse, nor yet the merchant any loss or burden therein other than hath been borne by the like, the space of two hundred years past for the like quantity of the wool contained in the said cloths. Yet is also to be considered in this matter, that howsoever the custom now seem great, yet the merchants of the Low Countries and the Dukedom of Burgundy (which be the only persons for whom the Treaty requireth answer) have either none or very small cause to complain hereof. For all other nations that have presently or heretofore had companies haunting this realm by way of merchandise, there be and always hath been fewest of the said Low Countries that have and do use the trade of carrying woollen cloths of this realm.

Also it is evident that by the laws of the realm made before the time of the Treaty and being now in force at this time, it was lawful for no person of that country or other stranger to carry out any manner of cloths being not fulled, as appeareth by the statute of *anno* 7 Edward IV, nor any cloth unrowed, unbarbed and unshorn, as by the statute of 3 Henry VII appeareth. So as considering how small a number of cloths they be that are fulled, rowed, barbed and shorn in respect of the great quantity of unwrought, it will easily come to fall to a small reckoning whereupon to ground any complaint.

And therefore this matter would be well weighed and opened in a friendly manner: to declare that seeing there is a small matter or none whereupon the merchants of those Low Countries have cause to complain, and that Her Majesty hath no greater profit thereby than her progenitors have had in that cause, comparing the cloth to the wool. And that it is evident how all other princes in all countries have and do, for the maintenance of the great charges which daily do increase in this age, devise to set new taxes upon their subjects and people, as well of their victuals as of wares being merchandise; whereby all other persons resorting to those countries are forced to pay both for victuals and for wares far greater prices than of ancient time hath been used. Therefore if these things be considered by the King of Spain's ambassadors, as persons acquainted with government and with things requisite thereunto, adding also the expectation that the Queen's Majesty maketh of the sincere friendship of the said king towards her: it is not to be doubted but they will forbear to press this particular matter of the custom of the cloth. Which, if it were brought to the former price should little benefit the king's subjects, especially if Her Majesty would narrowly cause the ancient laws, having their force before and at the time of the Treaty, to be observed. And yet, if Her Majesty's customs hereby of her own subjects should by this intention be sought to be diminished, the same might at the first, percase, breed some lack of appearance. But yet, true it is that Her Majesty lacketh no power and good ordinary and lawful means by other devices to provide remedy therefore, in such sort as no stranger should have profit thereby. Which speech you may use to them, if they shall by their arguments press you thereunto. Otherwise, not.

And if complaint be made of the greatness of the custom of the cloth, for that the strangers pay now 14s. 6d. for a cloth, for the which in times past they paid but 6s. 3d: it may be well said that the same custom is not so great as they ought to pay for the wool by the value of 51s. 8d. in four cloths, as more plainly shall appear unto you if you will consider that which is added to the end of the Book of Rates. And thereto may be added, as some help of an argument, that the increase of the English custom is far greater in respect of the old than is the strangers'.

*Laws made against the Intercourse.* 5. Fifthly, where complaints are made that divers laws have been made in this realm, both contrary and since the time of the Treaty of the Intercourse, by the which the benefit of the same Intercourse is taken away from the subjects of the Low Countries, consideration hath been had what laws have been made since the year of Our Lord 1495 (which was in the 11th. year of king Henry VII) that might seem to contain any matter prejudicial to the articles of the Treaty. And thereupon, this difference is found – that some of the said laws, made since the Intercourse, contain prohibitions which were by former laws in force before the time of the said Treaty. And in that respect those prohibitions are not new.

*Memorial of certain statutes since the Treaty.* But in some of the said laws there be added to the said prohibitions greater pains than were before, as shall appear by a memorial of the statutes made since the Treaty, and by certain quotations in the margins thereof. Which pains cannot well be denied to be new. And therein it may be said generally, that alteration is to be used for the execution of those great pains being new, until by Parliament some provision may be made for the reformation therof. The other point of the difference also is that some things (but not many) are indeed newly prohibited which have an appearance to be against the Intercourse; so, as for anything presently otherwise known, can not be well denied to be made newly since the Intercourse.

And for good order of proceeding in these matters by them complained to be newly made against the Treaty, the best way seemeth to be to hear of them which laws they took to be new and made contrary to the Intercourse. And to answer to the same only and severally, and to no more. For it seemeth by consideration of the former complaints that they are not aggrieved with all the new laws being of this nature, but with some certain: and of them, with some more than with other. And to bring in question any other than such whereof they complain, were not wisdom. Therefore consideration hath been had particularly of every of them, and such answers devised to the same hereafter following, as for the present could be imagined, until it shall appear what they will reply to the said answers. Whereupon, if need shall be, a further consultation may be had.

(1) *Henry VIII, 22. Oxen, bullocks &c.* First, the prohibition of

carrying out of oxen, steers, bullocks, calves, kine and sheep was the 22nd. year of king Henry VIII, cap. 6; of which, no complaint hath been of late made. But if they shall, it may be answered that all the same things above-mentioned are victual, and that such liberties shall be given both for those and other victual as is agreeable with the words of the Treaty: that is, when no necessary nor reasonable cause shall constrain the same to be kept within the realm, liberty shall be given to any of the king's subjects of the Low Countries to carry them out. And if they shall not like of that answer, without accord that the very laws made for the restraint should be revoked; if otherwise they will not be satisfied, you may give them hope that therein shall be done which the Treaty requireth.

(2) *Brass, copper. 33 Henry VIII*. Secondly, the prohibition of carrying forth of the realm of brass, copper, latten, bellmetal, gunmetal, panmetal, shrovemetal, was made *anno* 33 Henry VIII; and thereof also no complaint hath been made, neither is it to be thought that any now will be. For indeed, none of these said things do naturally grow in any abundance here, but are and have been usually brought through those Low Countries into this realm. And in this behalf it were meet to press them, that the prohibitions made in those Low Countries of the same, contrary to the Intercourse, were at liberty. And in so doing, like liberty shall be of this side as of theirs, as far forth as concerneth any laws newly made since the Intercourse.

(3) *2 & 3 Edward VI*. Thirdly, the transporting of white ashes hath been forbidden *2 & 3 Edwardi sexti cap. 26*; whereof, if request and complaint be made to have the same at liberty you shall not much stay thereupon, but yield that the same shall be ordered according to the Treaty.

(4) *Beer &c. 2 Mary*. Fourthly, the transporting over the beer, herring and wood hath been prohibited by *primo et secundo Philippi et Mariae, cap. 5*. And as to the beer being required to be at liberty, you may answer it to be a very necessary kind of victual; and that so much passeth out of this realm for allowance of beverage for mariners, that thereby both the price is augmented, and the provision of cask is grown also so hard to be made that it cannot be spared out of the realm. And herein you shall use such kind of speech as may either cause the argument thereof to cease with satisfaction, or else let remain in suspense until you may advertise.

*Herring*. And so to herring, the like answer may be made, if it be demanded, which is not much likely. For that the herring which this realm occupieth are, for the greatest part, brought from the Low Countries and other parts beyond the seas: so as they are not merchandise to be carried out but rather to be brought into the realm.

*Wood.* And as to the carrying out of wood, it is not likely that complaint shall be made thereof, for that no word hath been uttered thereof at d'Assonleville's being here. Neither is it properly a kind of merchandise but rather a kind of munition, and properly also within the compass of victual. And therefore, if they shall make mention thereof, either the answer would be in this sort, or else passed over in silence.

5. *Salt hides. 1 Elizabeth.* Fifthly, the transportation of salt hides, backs and tallow hath been prohibited *primo* of the Queen's Majesty: whereof was necessary cause, for the scarcity and dearth of those things in the realm. But if complaint shall be made thereof, you shall do the best that you may to move them with the reason of the scarcity for the use of the realm, to forbear to press you therein. And if that cannot be obtained, then you may yield to have the same reformed according to the Treaty.

*Sheep skins, pelts &c. 5 Elizabeth.* The prohibition of carrying out of sheepskins, shorlings, morlings or the skins of any stag, buck, doe, goat, fawn or kid, or the pelts of them, was made *anno quinto* of the Queen's Majesty, upon urgent consideration for the relief of divers artificers of this realm working leather. In the which statute are two things to be considered: the one prohibiting the pulling or taking away the wool of any sheepskins which indeed, in Staple ware having the wool upon it, are called by the name of woolfells, which is prohibited to be carried to any place but to Calais, by the statutes of 2, 10 and 15 of Henry VI. So as there is reasonable cause why the prohibition was made that the wool should not be pulled off the said woolfells, of purpose to make them pelts. But if they were of their own nature become pelts, by losing of their wool, then it is not to be said that the same might have been carried out of the realm before the last statute. The other point in the same statute is the prohibition of carrying over of the same sheepskins, woolfells, or the skins or pelts of any of the things above mentioned. Whereunto is to be answered for the woolfells as is after mentioned, that they be Staple ware. For the rest, other answer cannot be made but that the same shall be ordered according to the Treaty.

Thus far is particularly recited all things prohibited to be carried out by any law since the Treaty. And now shall follow a like recital of the things prohibited to be brought into the realm of like nature by law, since the Treaty.

*Things brought into the realm. Fresh fish. 33 Henry VIII.* First, the buying of fresh fish of any stranger, upon the sea or beyond the sea, was forbidden *anno* 33 Henry VIII. And likewise, the buying of any herring not being sufficiently salted, packed or casked, of any stranger, was prohibited in *anno quinto* of the Queen's Majesty. Which two things, if they be pressed unto you to be set at liberty, are to be left as they were before the said two statutes, according to the Treaty.

*Cod and ling in cask.* Item, the bringing in of cods or ling in cask was prohibited by *anno quinto* of the Queen's Majesty's reign upon necessary reason; for that the same was found to be very deceitfully used in packing of the same fish: untruly laid, in the uppermost part of the vessel good and seasonable, and in the middle part evil and unwholesome. Wherefore, if it be required to have this act at liberty, there may be apparent argument made to defend the same; for that the bringing in of the same is not prohibited, but only the manner which is deceitful. And so nothing is intended by that law but to avoid deceit, which you may well defend to be agreeable to the Treaty. And yet, if such reason shall not content them, it may be answered that the same shall be used according to the order of the Treaty, and the deceit to be by other means provided and reformed.

There be also some other new laws that have appearance to contain matter prejudicial to the Treaty, as followeth:-

*Broad white cloths. 1 Henry VIII.* There is a prohibition in 15 Henry VIII that no broad white cloth should be sold to any stranger for the space of eight days: within which time, if it were not sold by the clothier to an Englishman for money to be paid within a month, then it might be sold to any stranger. This law remaineth in force, but hath not been put in execution of late years. And therefore, if complaint be made thereof, as it is not likely, it may so be answered and accorded, that it shall remain at liberty according to the Treaty.

*1 Elizabeth. Lading in strangers' bottoms: law touching the same lading in strangers' bottoms.* Secondly, there hath been a law made in the first of the Queen's Majesty, by which is provided that if any Englishman shall lade any wares in a stranger's bottom, the same Englishman shall pay strangers' custom. Which law if you do peruse, you shall perceive by the preamble thereof that the same tendeth rather to the benefit of the subject of the Low Country, than otherwise. For before that time, that is to say in *Quinto* of Richard II, and 3 of Edward IV and 4 of Henry VII, it was specially provided that no merchandise of this realm might be laden by Englishmen but in English bottoms; which laws remained in force at the time of the Treaty. So as the execution of the same laws should much more grieve the subjects of the Low Countries than this which hath been made in the Queen's time, being none other than upon Her Majesty's own subjects, for forbearing the lading in an English bottom, to lade in a stranger's bottom. And yet, the pain is no more than to pay like custom as strangers do. And therefore, the complaints have not herein so much wrong as they pretend: for it is permitted to the strangers to lade in their own bottoms, and the law no wise extendeth upon them, but upon the Queen's Majesty's subjects, which by special clause contained in the said Treaty is lawful for either prince to do towards their own subjects.

*5 Elizabeth. Carrying victual from port to port.* There is one other clause in an Act of Parliament of *anno quinto* of the Queen's Majesty, prohibiting the carrying of any vitual or wares in any stranger's bottom from port to port. Whereof, if complaint be made, you may allege the usage to be very new for strangers to carry with their vessels either victuals or wares from one port to another. But if they shall much press the release thereof, you may yield that the same shall be used according to the Treaty.

These prohibitions last remembered are the substance of all laws made since the Treaty, having appearance of any contradiction to the Treaty. Of the which, complaint hath been made of some of d'Assonleville's being here, but not of all. Wherefore, it is thought good that in these causes and in all other like, ye do observe this rule: not to bring in question by your answers, or rather treating anything but such only as whereof they shall make complaints particularly. And considering all the complaints that can be made by them are but of two kinds, that is: first, of things ordained by law, or otherwise used that were not lawful and used at the time of the making of the Treaty. The second, of things pretended by complaint to be against the Treaty or innovated since the time of the Treaty, although in very deed and truth they were lawful or used at or before the time of the Treaty.

Therefore, whensoever the complaints shall conceive any

particular thing that hath been ordained and innovated by the law since the time of the Treaty, the answers thereunto are to be considered and directed according to the memorial of things here before particularly recited. And if these kind of answers shall not satisfy them, you shall do well to suspend thereupon, and to advertise your manner of proceeding with them in the same. And as to the second kind of matters whereof they shall complain, which you shall perceive to have been lawful or used at the time, or before the Treaty (as you shall judge the same to be if they be none of the special cases here last remembered in this memorial, as innovated since the Treaty): in these cases, you shall generally answer them that you do not take any of them to be innovated since the Treaty by any order or usage. But if they have (whereof you may allege ignorance), then all such ordinances and new usages made or begun since the time of the Treaty concerning those causes shall cease and be suspended. And it is to be wished that such a general answer might satisfy them in those kind of causes, without entering into any further argument what was lawful or used before the Treaty, and what not. For it seemeth a sufficient proof that things be not against the Treaty, which cannot be proved by the complaints to have been ordered or innovated since the Treaty.

*Collection of ancient statutes and laws.* Nevertheless, if they shall mislike of that general kind of answer and that they will not otherwise be content, you shall then consider upon a sufficient memorial and collection made, which you shall have, to prove the most number of things pretended by them to be innovated, to have indeed been lawful at the time of the Treaty by ancient laws and statutes of the realm; which as need shall require you may allege unto them according to their several natures and quotations, if otherwise you see they cannot be satisfied. And if they shall make any doubt of the validity of any of those laws, you shall offer to them for the proof showed to the King's ambassador here, upon their motion and signification to be made to Her Majesty of their doubt: which kind of offer you shall in like manner make to them for the showing of any other record whereof they there shall make any doubt upon your allegations.

And thus much shall suffice for your instructions how to proceed upon their complaints, for laws and orders made against the Treaty; foreseeing that in no wise you yield to them to raze or suspend any laws made before the Treaty. And for the laws made since the Treaty, you shall do well to notify to them the manner of our policy: how the same laws are made in this realm by assent of three estates and are not to be made void but with their assent. And therefore a moderate kind of speech is to be used on Her Majesty's behalf, that the execution of them may be suspended by Her Majesty: as already she hath done, to continue so during the Treaty and Colloquy. But yet, the laws cannot be utterly abrogated without the like authority wherewith they were made; wherein they may be assured that Her Majesty both will and can do as much with her estates as any her progenitors, kings of this realm, have done.

*Doleances exhibited heretofore by the English.* Finally, like as you shall be fully occupied with the hearing of their complaints, so is it meet that they also should be informed and occupied with the hearing of yours on the part of the subjects of this realm. For the better instruction whereof to be given you, you shall consider as many of the former doleances as you can attain unto, which have been exhibited in other colloquies on the behalf of this realm, which were not either then sufficiently answered or not reformed. And besides the same, you shall take information of such persons as shall attend for the Company of the Merchants of the Staple and Adventurers, or of any other whom you shall think meet to inform you, with probability of any things innovated either by ordinance, edict or usage contrary to the tenor of the Treaty. And of them you shall receive the same complaints in writing; and thereupon you shall use discretion in the ordering and opening the same from time to time: and therewith to counterpease, as you see causes, their complaints by applying as many of the same doleances as you shall find on the part of England to be like or correspondent unto theirs, and thereby procure the like answers and satisfaction to your complaints as they shall seek to obtain of you to theirs. And not otherwise to condescend to any reformation for their part, than you shall have answered for them on the part of England.

*A book of the acts and judgments passed in the Admiralty and before the Commissioners.* Because it is likely that you shall have sundry grievous complaints made of depredations done upon the King of Spain's subjects, to the which it is hard by way of instructions to give you any particular information, you shall have delivered to you by the Judge of the Admiralty a book containing all the acts and judgements passed both in the ordinary Court of the Admiralty, and before him and other the commissioners joined with him in a Special Commission granted by Her Majesty two years past, only for the hearing and determining of all complaints made by the subjects of the Low Countries concerning matters of depredations.

After which book perused, you shall consider if any of the complaints made to you are the same, whereof by the said book you shall perceive answer may well be made: then, you shall give the same answer. And if the complaints be other, whereof no answer can be made by consideration of that book: then you may, as truth is, allege ignorance thereof and offer to send knowledge of the complaint hither. And so, it shall be meet that you do. And generally in those cases of depredations you shall so use your answers as in no wise any of the subjects of this realm be compelled to come thither to answer the same; but that justice be promised, with assurance to be ministered to them. And you, Mr. Wotton and Master Haddon, can very well of your own knowledge declare with what charge Special Commission was given to Dr. Lewys, Dr. Weston and others to hear and determine all those kind of complaints, which was altogether extraordinary, and prejudicial to ordinary justice and privately very chargeable to the Queen's Majesty, who hath by the space of fifteen months given special wages and daily salaries to four judges to attend the speedy relief of those causes.

Finally ye shall, as soon as ye may perceive what the intention of the commissioners of the other part shall be in the prosecution of this Diet, advertise, that thereafter consideration may be had what shall be meet to do. For that it is covenanted that the liberty of the Intercourse shall continue until the end of this treaty or only three weeks longer. Which is a very short time for the merchants of this nation to provide for alteration of their trade, if so it should fall out. But as ye shall see cause, you may let it appear by indirect speeches that if the merchants of England may not be received with goodwill in these Low Countries, there is small doubt but they may have trade in other countries with their merchandises, with no small favour. And you may use your terms as they may stand in doubt whether ye mean France or Emden. For indeed, both places may serve this purpose if those Low Countries should not be granted.

NOTE TO APPENDIX

[1] Of this revealing state paper, at least eight manuscript copies are known to exist. Its documentary origins may well spring from the notes made by Secretary Cecil, now at Cotton Galba C II, No. 1, perhaps jotted down by him after an

audience with his royal taskmistress. In the actual formulation of the instructions a number of people, from the Queen downwards, doubtless took a hand. There exist two early drafts, one with copious emendations and additions by Secretary Cecil, now at Cotton Galba C II, No. 3; and another among the Cecil Papers at CP 247/164. Two authenticated copies are in the Public Record Office at SP 70/ 77/864 and 865. There are at least four further copies in the British Library, Department of Manuscripts: one among the Yelverton papers, at Add. 48,007, f. 86; another at Lansdowne 155, No. 51, f. 113v; a third at Egerton 2,790, f. 165; and a fourth at Harl. 36, No. 16, f. 81. Yet another copy is among the Neville of Holt papers, II, 97, now in the custody of the Leicestershire Record Office. The copies not in official custody seem for the most part to have been made for preservation in volumes of selected instructions compiled and gathered together to serve as authorities for reference. Their very number lends weight to the supposition that the instructions here printed were regarded as authentic guidelines to the understanding of English commercial policy in the age when they were formulated.

There are printed summaries, in order of increasing brevity, at *CSPF 1564–5*, No. 1036; Smit, *Bronnen*, No. 1061; *HMC Salisbury*, XIII, 67.

The version here printed follows generally the text of SP 70/77/864, but in the interests of easier understanding certain liberties have been taken in presentation. Spelling has been transliterated into contemporary practice, roman numerals replaced by arabic, and punctuation and capital letters added or removed. Paragraphing has been inserted where this might seem helpful. Finally, the marginal notes in the original, though not in the same hand as the text, have been put into italics and incorporated in it as sub-headings.

The 'Treaty' of which there is frequent mention in the text, is always the *Intercursus* of February 1496: *supra*, 3. The law of *primo Eliz.* (section 5, p. 214) is stat. 1 Eliz., C. 10; the 'backs' to which allusion is there made are defined in its text as 'sole leather'.

# A postscript on sources
## and list of abbreviations used in the notes

Notes have a limited but essential purpose. They make possible the verification of statements of fact not found in text-books and well-known historical writings, and for this purpose have accordingly been supplied. It is hoped that no critic will find any difficulty in putting his finger on the whereabouts of the information used for building up the argument in the different chapters of this historical enquiry. Since the records of the Merchants Adventurers have been lost, what may be learnt of their Company is derived chiefly from the state papers of the governments at London and Brussels, together with such administrative and legal documents of the age as have been preserved. On the English side, with which the book is chiefly concerned, most are located in the Public Record Office, though there is also much valuable evidence scattered among the several collections at the British Library, Department of Manuscripts, and elsewhere. Indeed, there is virtually no limit to the documentation unprinted, un-calendared and unindexed, though the further the net is cast the more a law of diminishing returns operates.

Some records have been printed *in extenso*, notably in the great volumes of Kervyn de Lettenhove, and a short cut to the use of others has been provided by calendars and indexes drawn up by scholars of past generations. In this, pride of place goes to the achievements of L. P. Gachard for the Netherlands, of K. Höhlbaum for the Hanse records, and of the editors employed by the Public Record Office for the English archives. Much reliance has been placed on their work, though for certain classes of document, notably the state papers domestic at the Public Record Office, it has been necessary to go back to the originals.

*List of abbreviations used in notes*

| | |
|---|---|
| ACMC | London, Mercers' Hall, Acts of Court of the Mercers' Company |
| Add. | BL, Additional MSS |
| AGR | Brussels, Archives générales du Royaume |
| *Ante* | G. D. Ramsay, *The City of London in international politics at the accession of Elizabeth Tudor* (Manchester, 1975) |
| *APC* | *Acts of the Privy Council* |
| Baelde | M. Baelde, *De collaterale raden onder Karel V en Filips II (1531–1578)*, Brussels, 1965 |
| Battistini | M. Battistini, *Lettere di Giovanni Battista Guicciardini a Cosimo e Francesco de Medici scritte dal Belgio dal 1557 al 1577*, Brussels and Rome, 1950 |
| BL | London, British Library |
| Burgon, *Gresham* | J. W. Burgon, *The life and times of Sir Thomas Gresham*, two vols, London, 1839 |
| *Cabala* | *Cabala, sive scrinia sacra: ... letters of illustrious persons ...* Editor unknown, London, 1654 |

| | |
|---|---|
| Cecil Papers | Cecil Papers at Hatfield House, Herts. |
| Cotton | BL, Cotton MSS |
| *CPR* | *Calendar of Patent Rolls* |
| *CSPD* | *Calendar of State Papers Domestic* |
| *CSPF* | *Calendar of State Papers Foreign* |
| *CSPSp* | *Calendar of State Papers Spanish* |
| *DNB* | *Dictionary of National Biography* |
| Dudley Papers | Dudley Papers at Longleat House, Warminster, Wilts. |
| E 122 | PRO, Exchequer, Customs Accounts |
| E 178 | PRO, Exchequer, Special Commissions of Enquiry |
| E 190 | PRO, Exchequer, Port Books |
| E 356 | PRO, Exchequer, Customs Accounts (Pipe Office) |
| *EcHR* | *Economic History Review* |
| Egerton | BL, Egerton MSS |
| *EHR* | *English Historical Review* |
| Ehrenberg, *EH* | R. Ehrenberg, *England und Hamburg im Zeitalter der Königin Elisabeth*, Jena, 1896 |
| Ellis, *Original Letters* | *Original Letters illustrative of English History*, ed. H. Ellis, eleven vols, in three series. London, 1824–46 |
| Gachard, *Correspondance de Philippe II* | *Correspondance de Philippe II sur les affaires des Pays-Bas*, ed. L. P. Gachard, five vols, Brussels, 1848–79 |
| Gachard, *MP* | *Correspondance de Marguerite d'Autriche, duchesse de Parme, avec Philippe II*, ed. L. P. Gachard, three vols, Brussels, 1867–81 |
| Gelder, *MP* | *Correspondance française de Marguerite d'Autriche, duchesse de Parme, avec Philippe II. Supplément, 1566–8*, ed. H. A. Enno van Gelder, Utrecht, 1942 |
| Gras, *EECS* | N. S. B. Gras, *The Early English Customs System*, Cambridge, Mass., 1918 |
| HCA | PRO, High Court of Admiralty records |
| Harl. | BL, Harleian MSS |
| Haynes | S. Haynes, *A collection of State Papers Left by William Cecil, Lord Burghley*, London, 1740 |
| HL | *Tudor Royal Proclamations*, ed. P. L. Hughes and J. F. Larkin, three vols, New Haven, Mass., and London, 1964–69 |
| *HMC* | *Historical Manuscripts Commission* |
| Höhlbaum | *Kölner Inventar. Inventare hansischer Archive des sechszehnten Jahrhunderts*, ed. K. Höhlbaum and H. Keussen, two vols, Leipzig, 1896–1903 |
| *Isham* | *John Isham, Mercer and Merchant Adventurer. Two Account Books of a London Merchant in the Reign of Elizabeth I*, ed. G. D. Ramsay, Northamptonshire Record Society, XXI, 1962 |
| Journals | City of London Records Office, Journals of the Court of Common Council |
| KL | J. M. B. C. Baron Kervyn de Lettenhove and L. Gilliots van Severen, *Relations politiques des Pays-Bas et de l'Angleterre sous le règne de Philippe II*, eleven vols, Brussels, 1882–1900 |
| Lansd. | BL, Lansdowne MSS |
| Letter Books | City of London Records Office, Letter Books |
| *LPH* | *Letters and Papers, Foreign and Domestic, of the reign of Henry VIII*, ed. J. S. Brewer *et al*, 21 vols, London, 1862–1910 |

| | |
|---|---|
| MF | B. de S. de La Mothe–Fénélon, *Correspondance diplomatique*, ed. A. Teulet, seven vols, Paris and London, 1838–40 |
| Murdin, W. | W. Murdin, *A collection of state papers left by William Cecil, Lord Burghley*, London, 1759 |
| NRO | Northampton, Delapré Abbey, Northamptonshire Record Office |
| Pepys Papers | Pepys Papers at Magdalene College, Cambridge |
| Poullet, *Granvelle* | *Correspondance du cardinal de Granvelle*, ed. E. Poullet and C. Piot, twelve vols, Brussels, 1878–96 |
| Prims, *Antwerpen* | F. Prims, *Geschiedenis van Antwerpen*, eight vols, Antwerp, 1927–49 |
| PRO | London, Public Record Office |
| Rachfahl, *Wilhelm von Oranien* | F. Rachfahl, *Wilhelm von Oranien und der Niederländische Aufstand*, three vols, Halle and The Hague, 1906–24 |
| RBPH | *Revue belge de philologie et d'histoire* |
| Rep. | City of London Record Office, Repertories of the Court of Aldermen |
| Rich, *Ordinance Book* | *The Ordinance Book of the Merchants of the Staple*, ed. E. E. Rich, Cambridge, 1937 |
| Rogers | *The letters of Sir John Hackett, 1526–1534*, ed. E. F. Rogers, Morgantown, West Virginia, 1971 |
| Royal | BL, Royal MSS |
| Rymer | T. Rymer, *Foedera*, third ed., ten vols, The Hague, 1739–45 |
| Schanz | G. Schanz, *Englische Handelspolitik gegen Ende des Mittelalters*, two vols, Leipzig, 1881 |
| Sellers, *York Mercers* | M. Sellers, *The York Mercers and Merchant Adventurers*, Surtees Society, cxxix, 1917 |
| Simson | *Danziger Inventar: Inventare Hansischer Archive des 16. Jahrhunderts*, ed. P. Simson, Leipzig, 1913 |
| Sloane | BL, Sloane MSS |
| Smedt, *EN* | O. de Smedt, *De Engelse Natië te Antwerpen in de 16e Eeuw*, two vols, Antwerp, 1950–54 |
| Smit, *Bronnen* | *Bronnen tot de geschiedenis van den handel met Engeland, Schotland en Ierland 1485–1585*, ed. H. J. Smit, two vols, 'S-Gravenhage, 1942–50 |
| SP 10 | PRO, State Papers Domestic, Edward VI |
| SP 11 | PRO, State Papers Domestic, Mary I |
| SP 12 | PRO, State Papers Domestic, Elizabeth I |
| SP 15 | PRO, State Papers Domestic, Addenda, Edward VI to James I |
| SP 46 | PRO, State Papers Domestic, Supplementary |
| SP 63 | PRO, State Papers, Ireland |
| SP 68 | PRO, State Papers Foreign, Edward VI |
| SP 69 | PRO, State Papers Foreign, Mary I |
| SP 70 | PRO, State Papers Foreign, Elizabeth I |
| SP 83 | PRO, State Papers Foreign, Holland and Flanders |
| Stow | J. Stow, *A survey of London*, ed. C. L. Kingsford, two vols, Oxford, 1908 |
| Theissen, *MP* | *Correspondence française de Marguerite d'Autriche, duchesse de Parme, avec Philippe II. Supplément, 1565–6*, ed. J. S. Theissen, two vols, Utrecht, 1925–42 |
| TP | *Tudor Economic Documents*, ed. R. H. Tawney and E. Power, three vols, London, 1924 |

| | |
|---|---|
| *TRHS* | Transactions of the Royal Historical Society |
| *VSWG* | *Vierteljahrschrift für Sozial- und Wirtschaftsgeschichte* |
| Weiss | *Papiers d'état du cardinal de Granvelle*, ed. C. Weiss, nine vols, Paris, 1841–52 |
| Willan, *EHRC* | T. S. Willan, *Early History of the Russia Company*, Manchester, 1956 |
| Willan, *Studies* | T. S. Willan, *Studies in Elizabethan Foreign Trade*, Manchester, 1959 |
| Willan, *TBR* | T. S. Willan, *A Tudor Book of Rates*, Manchester, 1962 |
| Williamson, *Hawkins* | J. A. Williamson, *Sir John Hawkins, the Times and the Man*, Oxford, 1927 |
| Wright | T. Wright, *Queen Elizabeth and Her Times*, two vols, London, 1838 |

Numerical references, save when otherwise indicated, are to pages.

# Index

Aalst, 183
Admiralty Court, High Court of
    Admiralty, 7, 18, 23, 140, 218
Affaitadi of Lucca, family of, 43
Africa, 63, 139
Aldersey, Thomas, 106, 117, 159
Alexandria, 137
Alicante, 137
almonds, 136
Alps, the, 62
alum, alum farm, alum staple, 77–9,
    136
Alva, Duke of, 2, 48, 52–7, 65, 73, 78,
    85–9, 95–100, 102–4, 108–10, 116
    121, 126, 130, 138, 142–3, 153–62,
    165–6, 174–8, 180–1, 200
Ames, Dunstan, 143
Amsterdam, 98, 122, 189, 196
Anabaptists, 34, 40, 44, 54
Anchin, Abbot of, 178
anchorage dues, 7, 208–9
Andalusia, 138
Anjou, Duke of, 190, 195
Antwerp
    arrests at, 8, 9, 13
    Bourse, 34, 42–3, 55, 78–9, 196, 201
    Castle, 54, 183, 186
    company for trade organised at, 23,
        203
    English Quay, 196, 202
    foreign merchants at, 42–8, 50, 54
    lords of, patricians, 7, 21, 24, 26, 35–
        48, 54, 65–6, 71, 97, 178, 183, 187,
        190, 195, 202–3
    Margrave of, 48
    money market, 5, 49–51, 55, 201
    smothering of, 204
    Town Hall, 43, 45, 55, 66, 183–6
Aragon, Katherine of, 3
Arctic navigation, 62
argosies, 138; see also Ragusa
armour, 138
Arras, Bishop of, 178

Artois, 21, 129
Arundell, Sir John, 94
Ascham, Roger, Latin secretary, 125
Assincourt, Sieur d', 27
Assonleville, Dr Christophe d', 13, 19–
    21, 24, 26–7, 30, 51, 66, 74, 76, 88,
    90, 105–10, 125, 128, 153–5, 157,
    165, 177, 202–3, 207–8
Atlantic islands, 136
Austria, 2
Augsburg, 50, 137

Bacon, Sir Nicholas, Lord Keeper of
    the Great Seal, 89, 102, 107, 160
Balbani, Giovanni, 50
balliage, 7, 208–9
Baltic, Baltic lands, 41, 62–3, 77–8,
    135–6, 139, 188
bankrupts, bankruptcies, 5, 72–3, 127,
    145
Barnstaple, 141
Barbary, 67, 78, 135, 137, 139, 143
Barrow, Bergen-op-Zoom, 7–8, 48,
    73–7, 123, 160
Basel, 51
Basque iron, 136
Basques, 141
beer transportation, 213
Benison, Francis, 124
Bergen-op-Zoom; see Barrow
Berlayment, Count of, 179
Bilbao, 95
bills of credit; see credit
Bond, Alderman William, 106–7, 109
Bonner, Bishop, 160
Book of Rates; see customs
Bordeaux, 90, 136
Boulogne, 116
Bourbourg, 6, 8
Bowes, Sir Martin, 144
Bowes, Thomas, 144
Brabant, 10, 20, 35, 38, 67, 75, 182
    fairs of, 3

Breda, 51
Brederode, Count, 37, 39, 49
Breton ships, Breton traders, 141, 153
Bribes; *see* corruption
Brielle, 175
brimstone, 138
Bristol, 141
  Treaty of, 177
Brouage, 136
Bruges, 6, 11, 14, 17, 20, 24, 26–30, 42, 66, 69–71, 74, 77, 98, 102, 105, 108, 124, 176–7, 180, 185, 189, 198, 202
Brussels, 8–10, 21–3, 29, 39, 41, 52, 54, 56, 76–7, 105–6, 109, 136, 159, 161, 174, 177, 182, 185–7, 197
buoyage, 19, 209
Burghley, Lord; *see* Cecil, William
Burgundy, Dukes of, House of, 2, 12, 69, 154
  Dowager Duchess of, 2
Byrde, William, 163–4, 167–8

Calais, 1, 6, 10–11, 67, 105, 167, 200
  cloth mart at, 2–4, 10–11
Calshot Castle, 93
Calvin, Calvinists, Calvinism, 22, 34, 36, 39–40, 43–9, 51, 73–4, 86, 127, 130
Camden, William, 196
Canterbury, 17
carriage (port charge), 208
carrying trade, 188
Castile, Council of, 12–13, 87, 201
Cateau-Cambresis, Le, 17, 198
Cathay, 79
Catholic Kings, 3
Cavalcanti brothers, Guido and Stiata, 157, 199
Cecil, William, Secretary Cecil, Lord Burghley, 14, 21, 23, 26–7, 35, 45, 49–50, 53–4, 68–71, 78, 87–8, 91, 93–6, 98–9, 102–4, 107–8, 117, 123, 133, 140, 155–8, 160, 164–5, 167–9, 176–7, 189, 196, 200
Chaloner, Sir Thomas, 199
Chamberlain, Sir Thomas, 8–9, 168
Champernowne, Sir Arthur, 94
Channel, English, 87–90, 92–3, 116, 174
Chapuys, Eustace, 6, 8, 13
Charles V, Holy Roman Emperor, King of Spain, etc., 4, 6, 8, 13, 157, 206

Charles IX, King of France, 53, 89, 95, 102
Chester, Alderman Sir William, 22
Chimay, Prince of, 190
Church of England services, 134
Civitavecchia, 136
Cinque Ports, Lord Warden of, 105
Cleves, 47
Clinton, Lord, Lord High Admiral, 101, 103–4, 107–8
cloth export licences, 23, 70, 129, 135
cloth fleet discontinued, 76, 126
cloth shipments, 1, 7, 11, 13–14, 63–4, 79
cloth smuggling, 166–7
cloth taxes, compared with wool, 210–11
Clough, Richard, employee of Sir Thomas Gresham, 39, 48–9, 55, 67, 131
cochineal, 143
Cologne, 51, 122, 124, 145, 186, 189
commercial debts, 72–3
commercial legislation, 72–3, 145–6
Condé, Prince of, 143–4
Constantinople, 137
Cornwall, Cornish jury, 25, 85
corn export allowed, 134
corruption alleged, bribes offered, 26, 158, 166, 177
cotton wool, 138
Coxon, Laurence, 140
Council of State, Netherlands, 14, 21, 23, 26, 29, 187
credit, bills of, 184–5; *see also* exchange
creditors, frauds alleged, 72
Cranmer, Archbishop, 160
Cunningham, William, 196
Customs, English, commissioners appointed, 163–5
  credit granted, 164
  farming of, 163
  fees exacted, 209–10
  rates, Book of Rates, tariff, 10–11, 14, 18–20, 24–5, 28–9, 162–3, 177, 197
  receipts, yields, 4–5, 14, 64–5, 133, 167, 188
  registration, Port Books, 62
  Netherlands, 55, 70; *see also* 'double toll'
currants, 136
Cyprus, 137

Danzig, 124, 128, 188
Dartmouth, 141
Dawbenye, Oliver, 167–9
debts, priorities in collection, 56–7
Denmark, King of, 41, 121, 133
Despes, Don Guerau, 87–9, 91, 94–9, 101–3, 106–10, 117, 119, 128–9, 135–6, 154, 156–8, 161–2, 198, 200
Devonshire cloths, 141
Dieppe, 116
Don John of Austria, 185
Dordrecht, 189
'double toll', double tax, 10, 75–7, 186
Dover, 92, 95, 105, 109, 155, 174–5
Downs, the, 167
Duckett, Alderman Sir Lionel, 143
Dunkirk, 98, 182
Dutton, Thomas, 56

Eastland Company, 188
East Friesland, 120–2
    letter to the Earls of, 69
East Indies, 137
Edward IV, King of England, 207, 210, 216
Edward VI, King of England, 69
Egmont, Count of, 17, 21, 66
Ehrenberg, Richard, 196, 198
Elbe, 123, 127, 130, 135–6
Elector Palatine, 36, 90
Elizabeth I, Queen of England, 11–12, 14–15, 17, 19–20, 23, 26–30, 49, 52–4, 56–7, 65, 68–70, 74, 78, 80, 85, 91–4, 96–9, 102–3, 105–11, 118, 121, 123, 125, 129–30, 139, 154–5, 159–62, 174–82, 184–7, 190, 197, 199–201, 206–7, 211
Emden, 13–14, 41, 47, 56, 63, 65–9, 72, 77–8, 117, 120–3, 129, 131, 134, 142, 154, 165–6, 178, 187–8, 197, 219
    Lady of, 121
Emeren, Nikolaas van, 23, 26
emigration of artificers, 178
Emperor, German, Holy Roman Emperor; see Maximilian II
Employment, Statutes of, 7, 25, 70, 208
Ems, 121
Englefield, Sir Francis, 88
Espinosa, Cardinal, 87
exchange, bills of, 43, 52, 63, 86; see also credit, bills of

Exchange, Royal, 119; see also London, Bourse
exchequer, 14
Exeter, 141
Evil May Day, 'Ill May Day', 65

Fabricius, 40, 54
Faille, della, Jacob, 22
Faille, della, Jacques, 203
Faille, della, Jan, 100
'fairs and marts' in England, proposed, 67
Fiesco, Tommaso, 157–9
figs, 145
Finland, Gulf of, 62
fishing, fisheries, 62, 215
Fitzwilliams, John, Deputy Governor of the Merchants Adventurers, 20–1, 35, 45, 65, 76, 100
Flanders, 5, 17, 21, 66, 71, 75, 98, 102, 182, 184, 186
Fleetwood, William, Recorder of London, 168
Flemish industrial interest, 21, 74
Florence, Florentine merchants, 101, 157–8
Flushing, Flushingers, 175–6, 179–82
fly-boats, 176
forced loan, 131–2
Fowey, 93–4
France, 10, 12, 42, 47, 67, 78, 88, 129, 161, 180, 219
    King of; see Charles IX; Francis I
Francis I, King of France, 7, 11
Frankfurt-am-Main, 67, 78, 127, 134, 204
French ports, shipping, 62, 90–2, 153; see also La Rochelle; piracy
Frederick II, Holy Roman Emperor, 201
free port proposed, 67
freight charges, 134
Friesland, 121; see East Friesland; West Friesland
friction, social, between merchants and landowners, 146
fustians, 136

gall, 138
Garrard, Sir William, 22
Gascon wine, 62
Gascoyne, George, 184, 199
Gelderland, 5, 37

Geneva, 36, 46
Genoa, Genoese merchants, 78, 86, 91–2, 101, 157–8, 187
German currency laws, 86
Germany, German market, 2, 9, 47, 53–4, 72, 121–2, 130, 132, 134–5, 137, 178, 189, 195
Ghent, 54, 182
Gibraltar, Straits of, 62, 188
Gilbert, Sir Humphrey, 176
Gillis, Joachim, 20–1
Gilpin, George, 124, 126
Gloucestershire cloths, 72
Goddard, Richard, 179–80
gold dust, 139
Golden Fleece, Order of the, 15, 39
Gore End, Kent, 101
Granada, Moors of, 153–4
Granvelle, Cardinal, 13, 21–2, 24, 90, 197
Gravelines, 182
Gravesend, 106, 167
Gresham, John, 106
Gresham, Sir Richard, 79
Gresham, Sir Thomas, 22, 39, 45, 48–52, 54–6, 65–7, 71, 79, 101–2, 106–8
Guaras, Anthony, 119, 177
*Gueux*, Beggars, 36–9, 43, 45, 49
*Gueux de Mer*, Sea Beggars, 174–9, 181–3, 187
  financing of, 176
Guicciardini, Giovanni-Battista, Florentine agent, 26, 43
Guinea, West Africa, 79, 139–41

Habsburg family, 2
Hackett, Governor John, 6
Haddon, Walter, 17, 27, 206, 219
Hakluyt, Richard, the elder, 168
Hamburg, 14, 21, 67, 72, 78, 111, 120, 122–7, 129–38, 153–5, 165–6, 174–5, 178–80, 182, 185, 187–8, 196–7, 204
  agreement with merchants, 125–8
Hampton Court, 99
Hansards, Hanse merchants, 23, 65, 123, 163
Hanseatic League, Hanse Towns, 6, 121, 123, 125, 128
Hanse privileges, 122, 128, 163, 188
harbour dues, English, 7
Harvye, Alderman James, 168

Harwich, 130
Hawes, Alderman James, 168
Hawkins, John, 62, 79, 91, 101, 139
head money, 7
Heidelberg, 86
Henry IV, King of England, 207
Henry V, King of England, 207
Henry VI, King of England, 207–8
Henry VII, King of England, 2, 67, 207, 211, 216
Henry VIII, King of England, 4, 6, 8, 206
Herle, William, 199
herrings, 213–15
Heton, Governor Thomas, 179, 184–5, 187, 203
Hoddesdon, Governor Christopher, 187, 189
Holland, Hollanders, 21, 24, 27, 45, 77, 166, 175, 179, 183, 187, 189, 196, 204
Holstein, 50, 133
Hooftman, Giles, Gillis, 22–4, 39, 49–51, 66, 70, 75, 202–3
Hoorn, Count of, 17, 21, 54
Horsey, Sir Edward, 93–4, 185
Huguenots, 53–5, 86, 90, 92, 94, 109, 116, 129, 143–4, 162, 174
Hull, 67
Hundred Years' War, 2

Iceland stockfish, 122
import problems, 135
Inquisition, Spanish-style, 36
*Intercursus, Magnus Intercursus* (the Intercourse), 3, 6–7, 9, 15, 17–19, 22, 26, 30, 71–2, 74–5, 78, 177–8, 186–7, 198, 207–8, 212–13, 216–17, 218–19
interlopers, 62, 98, 189
invasion scare, 161–2
Ipswich, 140–1
Ireland, Irish, 12, 71, 157, 200
Italy, Italian merchants, 42, 52, 62–3, 67, 77–8, 86, 90, 153, 157–9, 165, 182–3, 189
ivory, 145

Jarnac, 85
John, Count of East Friesland, 120
jury, Cornish, reprimanded, 25

Kent, 10

Killigrew, Henry, 131
King's Bench, Court of, 169
Knightley, George, 73, 77

Lanherne, 94
Laredo, 95
La Rochelle, 85, 94, 144, 175
La Mothe Fénélon, Bertrand de
    Salignac de, French ambassador,
    95, 104–5, 116–17, 129, 132, 134–
    5, 160
leather trade, 214
Leicester, Earl of, 23, 55, 67, 96, 107,
    117, 155–6, 158, 177
Leipzig, 78, 127, 134
Levant, 67, 72, 137, 143, 188
Lewys, Lewis, Dr David, 219
licences, trading, 70, 129, 181
Lier, 189
lighterage, 208–9
Lille, 24
linens, 80, 122, 136
Lisbon, 137–41, 143
loans, English, to States-General, 187
Lodron, Count, 97
London
    agents nominated, 20
    Bourse, Royal Exchange, 79–80
    Blackwell Hall, 92, 128, 163
    Bridewell, 101
    Cheapside, 99, 119
    cloth trade, clothworkers at, 1, 65 ff.
    Custom House Quay, 164, 167
    fears of social unrest, 120, 129–30
    Grocers' Company, 143
    Guildhall, 119–20
    Italians at, 129
    Lollards' Tower, 160
    Lord Mayor of, 106–7, 119
    Mercers' Company, Mercers' Hall,
        65, 79
    money market, 51, 108
    municipal relations with Antwerp, 6
    Old Wool Quay, 164
    Paget House, 103
    plays forbidden, 119
    St Paul's cathedral, 35
    Steelyard, 122, 130, 145, 180
    Tower, 101–2, 107–8, 158
Louvain, 54, 98
Lübeck, Lübeckers, 124–5, 128
Lucchese merchants, 101
Lutherans, 44–5, 130, 133

Lyons, 67

Maastricht, 183
Madrid, 28, 51–2, 87, 109, 153, 161
Magnus Intercursus; see Intercursus
Malaga, 137
Man, Dr John, 28, 87, 103, 200
Mannheim, 86
Marck, Count de la, 175
Margaret of Austria, Regent of the
    Netherlands, 5–6
Margaret, Duchess of Parma; see
    Parma
Marranos, 142–3
Marseilles, 137
Marsh, John, Governor of the
    Merchants Adventurers, 20, 49,
    67, 69, 75–6, 106, 117, 123–4, 129,
    131–2, 142, 159–60, 164–5, 176,
    179
Mary I, Mary Tudor, Queen of
    England, 9–11, 28, 69, 88, 160,
    200
Mary, Queen of Hungary, Regent of
    the Netherlands, 5, 8–9
Mary, Queen of Scots, Mary Stuart, 89,
    103, 110, 156–7, 177, 197, 200
Massacre of St Bartholomew, 162, 176
Maximilian II, Holy Roman Emperor,
    86, 125, 130
Mechelen, 42
'Mede Hole', Osborne Bay, Isle of
    Wight, 144
Médicis, Catherine de, Queen Mother
    of France, 53, 95, 162
Medina Celi, Duke of, 175–6
Mendes, family of, 142–3
Mendoza, Bernardino de, Spanish
    ambassador, 200
Merchants Adventurers of England,
    Company of
    cloth fleets superseded, 56, 76–7
    deceived by Queen, 30
    Deputy Governor of, 20, 64, 68, 131,
        134, 190; see also Fitzwilliams, John
    General Court held at London, 165
    Governor of, 5, 8–9, 20, 48–9, 127;
        see also Heton, Thomas;
        Hoddesdon, Christopher; Marsh,
        John
    heresy among, 48
    cloth-shipping licences held by, 23
    numbers estimated, 19

refuse to pay loan to Queen, 131–2
metal trade, 139
Middelburg, 42, 71, 175, 189–90
Mildmay, Sir Walter, 131
Milles, Richard, 168
molasses, 144
Moncontour, 85
Montague, Viscount, 17, 27, 206
Montigny, Sieur de, 17, 24, 26–7, 30
Morlaix, 142
Morocco, 22, 62
Müller, Dr Wilhelm, *Syndicus* of
   Hamburg, 127
Münster, 46
Muscovy Company, Muscovy trade,
   62, 79, 139; *see also* Russia
Mutiny of Spanish troops, 183

Nale, Austin de, 138
Narva, 62, 139
Nassau, Louis of, 45, 54, 85, 121, 143,
   174
Navarre, Queen of, 85
Nedham, George, 68–9
Netherlands, unification of, 5
Nieuwpoort, 182
New Draperies, 179
Norfolk, Duke of, 107, 200
Norfolk, trouble in, 133
Normandy, 116
Norris, Sir John, 190
North Foreland, 167
Northumberland, Earl of, 103, 156
Nunez, Hector, 143
Nuremberg, 135, 145, 204

oil, from rape-seed, 136
Orange, Prince of, 13, 21–2, 37–8,
   42–6, 48–51, 53–4, 85, 89, 121,
   143–4, 167, 174–5, 177, 179–82,
   184, 186, 190, 200
Oriana, Queen, 104
Ortelius, 22, 79
Ostend, 182
Oudenarde, 136
outports, English, 7, 68, 73, 141

Palavicino, Horatio, 187
Palavicino, Tobia, 78
pardon, Netherlands, 48, 52
Paris, 52, 87, 116
Parma, Margaret Farnese, Duchess of,
   Regent of the Netherlands, 12–14,

17–18, 20–1, 23, 26–7, 29–30,
   35–7, 41–6, 53–4, 69–70, 73–4,
   76–7, 121, 125
Parma, Prince of, 186, 188, 195
Pembroke, Earl of, 55, 117
Perez, Marcus, 39, 51
Persia, 79, 139
Picardy, 129
pirates, freebooters, piracy, 25, 85–6,
   90, 133, 144, 175, 177, 219
Pirenne, Henri, 196
Poland, 198
   King of, 41
Pope, the, 12
Port Books; *see* customs
port charges, English, 19, 25
Portugal, 62, 67, 188
   King of, 137, 139
Portuguese trade, 138–43
Pottey, Herman, 'Harman Peter',
   100
poundage, 26, 30, 207
Philip the Good, Duke of Burgundy,
   207
Philip II, King of Spain, 2, 10–12, 14,
   18–19, 26, 28–30, 35, 47–8, 50–2,
   56, 69, 78–9, 85, 87–9, 92, 95–100,
   102–4, 106, 108–10, 116, 121, 126
   130, 137, 153–4, 157–8, 161, 165,
   175–9, 189, 195, 198–201, 203,
   211
Physicians, College of, 143
Prats, Secretary of State, 178
prices, rise in, 146
privateers, privateering, 144–5, 167
Privy Council, English, 8–9, 23, 29,
   62, 66, 70–1, 92, 100, 102, 104,
   106–7, 116, 119–20, 129, 131–2,
   141, 159, 165, 175, 179, 188
proscription of merchants, 73
Pruin, Christopher, 49

Quadra, Alonso de la, Bishop of Aquila,
   87, 89, 103, 199

Radermacher, John, 24
Ragusa, Ragusan shipping, Ragusans,
   62, 137–8
raisins, 136, 145
Rantzau, Maurice, 50
Rates, Books of; *see* customs; rates
rebellion of the northern earls, 156,
   159–60

record search, 26
re-exports, 188
refugees, Netherlands, 65
Requescens, Luis de, 181–3
Rhine, 86, 145
Richard II, King of England, 207–8, 216
Ridolfi, Roberto, 156–7, 160–1
Robinson, Francis, 124
Rochester, 105
Ross, Bishop of, 89, 103
Rome, 78
Rotterdam, 189
Rouen, 116, 129, 165
Rowe, Sir Thomas, Lord Mayor of London, 98, 100
Royal Navy, escort provided by, 129–30, 134
Russia, 22, 63, 135–6; see also Muscovy

Sahara gold dust, 141
salt trade, 136, 180
Saltash, 93–4
Saltonstall, Richard, 159
Santander, 90
Saragosa, 39
satins, trade in, 136
scavage, 7, 208–9
Schanz, Georg, 196
Scheldt, 7, 9, 41, 174–5, 180–6, 189, 195–6, 202, 204
Schetz, Jasper, 54
Scotland, 10, 12, 47
Shipping regulations, 215–16
Shrewsbury, Earl of, 117
Sierra, Lope de la, 90, 93–5
silks, trade in, 136
Silva, Don Guzman de, 14, 25, 52, 56, 69, 74, 76, 85–7, 121
silver reals, bullion, 86, 90, 96–7, 101–2, 108, 158
Sinksen mart, 186
slave trade, 139
Sluys, 182
Smythe, Customer, 166–7
Snepel, Paul, 123
Sound, The, 41
Southampton, 93–5, 144, 167
Southwick, George, 179–81
Spain, Spanish ports, 2, 11, 13, 17, 35, 39, 41, 62, 67, 69, 77–8, 85–8, 90, 92, 99, 116, 125, 130, 135–6, 143, 146, 154, 161–2, 183, 188, 195, 200

Spanish Fury, the, 184–5
spice trade, 136, 138–45
Spinola, Benedict, Benedetto, 91–2, 157–8, 187
Staplers, Merchants of the Company of the Staple, 1, 10, 18, 20, 27, 29, 71, 98, 120, 130, 179, 197, 218
Star Chamber, 25
Starkey, Randal, 73, 77
Starkey, Thomas, 100
Statutes, suspension of, 70
collected and printed, 207, 217
'stint', allowance of cloths for export, 73
Stockholm, 41
Story, Dr John, 160–1
Stralen, Antoon van, 37–8, 47, 54
Suderman, Dr Herman, Secretary of the Hanseatic League, 125
Suffolk, trouble in, 133
cloths of, 133, 138, 141
sugar trade, 136–8, 144
Surgeons, Royal College of, 143
Sussex, Earl of, 17, 55, 76
Sweden, King of, 41

Tagus, 140
tapestries, 136
taxation of foreigners in England, 75
terms of trade, 134–6, 145
Thames, 41, 132, 167, 180, 182
tonnage and poundage, 11; see also customs
Torre, Secretary de la, 155
Toulouse pastel, 136
Trier, 22
Turco-Venetian war, 137–8
Turks, Turkey, 67, 101, 154

usury laws, 145
Utenhove, Jan, 199
Utrecht, 5

Valois Dukes of Burgundy, 2–3
Venice, Venetian ships, 22, 67, 101, 136–9, 198
Viglius, President, 76, 125, 177, 202
Vitelli, Ciappino, Marquess of Cetona, 155–6, 158

Walcheren, 175, 179
Walsingham, Sir Francis, 187
Welsers of Augsburg, firm of the, 50